Christopher Smith
Sally Cox

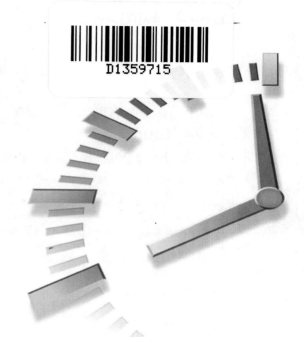

SAMS
Teach Yourself

Adobe® Acrobat® 5

in 24 Hours

SAMS

201 West 103rd St., Indianapolis, Indiana, 46290 USA

Sams Teach Yourself Adobe® Acrobat® 5 in 24 Hours

Copyright © 2002 by Sams Publishing

International Standard Book Number: 0-672-32314-1

Library of Congress Catalog Card Number: 2001088015

Printed in the United States of America

First Printing: December 2001

04   03   02   01   4   3   2   1

Trademarks

Warning and Disclaimer

ACQUISITIONS EDITOR
Jennifer Kost-Barker

DEVELOPMENT EDITOR
Jonathan Steever

MANAGING EDITOR
Charlotte Clapp

COPY EDITOR
Alice Martina Smith

INDEXER
Angie Bess

TECHNICAL EDITOR
Steve Moniz

TEAM COORDINATOR
Amy Patton

INTERIOR DESIGNER
Gary Adair

COVER DESIGNER
Aren Howell

PAGE LAYOUT
D&G Limited, LLC

Contents at a Glance

Contents

About the Authors

Christopher Smith is president of American Graphics Institute, the largest Adobe Certified Training Provider in North America. He is an Adobe Certified Expert and Adobe Certified Instructor for Adobe Acrobat versions 3, 4, and 5. He teaches classes on Acrobat and other publishing software at American Graphics Institute's Boston training center. He has been involved in teaching electronic publishing and electronic document distribution for more than 10 years. He works with many of the world's largest publishers helping them adopt new publishing software through the development and delivery of customized training programs.

Sally Cox is a software trainer for American Graphics Institute, a Certified Technical Trainer, and an Adobe Certified Expert in a variety of Adobe programs, including Acrobat. She spent 20 years in the printing/electronic prepress industry before joining AGI's team of professionals. Based out of American Graphics Institute's Philadelphia office, she teaches both Web-based and print-based classes. Her extensive background in traditional print, combined with expertise in current technology, give her a unique perspective on the industry that she is delighted to bring to the classroom.

Dedication

To the workers killed and injured in the September 11, 2001 attack on the World Trade Center.
You went to work and were met by the most senseless act imaginable, our thoughts are with you.

To the rescue workers killed and injured in the same tragedy. You are heroes.
You bravely put your lives at risk to help others.

You were sons, daughters, mothers, and fathers. You were co-workers, brothers, and sisters.
Our hearts and thoughts go out to your families and friends.

As we were putting the finishing touches on this book, the most horrendous, cruel, and senseless tragedy
occurred in New York City. And it has had a profound impact on so much of what we do.

It makes us put much of our lives in perspective. We are both very lucky.
We can return to our families, children, and friends at the end of the day.
Thousands of people who were in lower Manhattan on September 11 are not so fortunate.

We both travel to American Graphics Institute's New York City training center frequently.
We work with many clients in Manhattan. Those trips to New York will never be the same.

Acknowledgments

This book could not have been completed without the help of several very talented people:

Emma, who entertained herself countless times so that Mom could write this book.

Steve Moniz, a fabulous technical editor and fellow instructor at American Graphics Institute. He made sure that nothing erroneous slipped through the cracks.

Jennifer Kost-Barker, our acquisitions editor who can show you pictures of one of the authors and a crazy man on stilts if you ask her.

Alice Martina Smith and Jon Steever, thanks for correcting our prose and keeping our writing on track! You two are great!

Joe Smith and Mike Silverman at Adobe Systems. Your help through the past several years has made it a pleasure to teach Adobe software and to work with Adobe Systems.

Karen Richter, Tim Plumer, Ron Thornburn, Carrie Cooper, Ali Hanyaloglu, and countless others at Adobe Systems. Your generous support of our instructional efforts is appreciated.

Jennifer Smith, co-author of *Sams Teach Yourself GoLive in 24 Hours*. Thanks for the great technical and writing advice. Without your support and chocolate-chip cookies, this book would never have been completed.

Grant, who forced me to take a few breaks from writing. Thanks for keeping me focused on what's important—you!

All the instructors and support staff at AGI, who provide brilliant insight and input into everything we do. Thanks for making this book a team effort.

Tell Us What You Think!

As the reader of this book, *you* are our most important critic and commentator. We value your opinion and want to know what we're doing right, what we could do better, what areas you'd like to see us publish in, and any other words of wisdom you're willing to pass our way.

You can e-mail or write me directly to let me know what you did or didn't like about this book—as well as what we can do to make our books stronger.

Please note that I cannot help you with technical problems related to the topic of this book, and that because of the high volume of mail I receive, I might not be able to reply to every message.

When you write, please be sure to include this book's title and author as well as your name and phone or fax number. I will carefully review your comments and share them with the author and editors who worked on the book.

E-mail: graphics@samspublishing.com
Mail: Mark Taber
         Sams Publishing
         201 West 103rd Street
         Indianapolis, IN 46290 USA

Introduction

Advances in the business world in recent years have caused many companies to rethink how they handle the sharing of information. With the invention of e-mail, our lives have changed dramatically. No longer must we wait for a reply to arrive in the mail or by courier. Replies can be instantaneous: the sender clicks the Send button and off goes the message! But we still tend to print, fax, and courier documents unnecessarily. The Adobe Portable Document Format (PDF) provides a way to maintain the original intent of your document on any recipient's computer screen or printer. It enhances this with the capability to secure, electronically mark-up, and even digitally sign PDF files.

The speed and efficiency gained by adding the PDF format to the office workflow have greatly increased our ability to share information. PDF provides a common file format for transferring documents among a wide audience. It eliminates the concerns about working on different computer platforms, because the Acrobat Reader used to view and print PDF files is available on more than one dozen computer platforms. PDF also eliminates concerns of having the same software used to create a document because virtually any electronic or paper file can be converted to PDF. Advantages of PDF include smaller file size for easy e-mailing and a universal format—regardless of the application used to create the original file. In other words, your clients can view the PDF documents you created, whether you used Microsoft Word, Adobe PageMaker, or QuarkXpress to create the original file; they simply have to download the free Acrobat Reader from Adobe's Web site, and they are up and running.

Each year, more and more people are learning about the many benefits of using Adobe Acrobat and its PDF file format. PDF documents are used in every corner of the world, by all types of businesses, for every imaginable use. Contracts and legal documents are sent in PDF format as e-mail attachments where they can be marked-up and digitally signed, brochures are saved as PDF files for use on the World Wide Web where they can be secured against modifications, and documents used for high-end printing and saved in PDF format provide a single high-quality file to transfer to a commercial printer. Whether you are looking to make your electronic files more accessible, convert paper documents to digital files, or improve your workflow by allowing on-line document review across many computer platforms, Acrobat provides a solution for you.

Who Should Read This Book?

Anyone who wants to learn more about the many benefits and features of Acrobat would do well to read this book. The instructions are clear and concise, with hands-on exercises and lots of tips and tricks. The book is geared for beginners, and each chapter, or hour, will guide you through a particular feature of the program. But even if you've been using Acrobat for years, we've packed the book full of useful tips and tidbits that will save you time and improve the ways you use Acrobat.

Can this Book Really Teach Adobe Acrobat 5 in 24 Hours?

Yes! This book will have you up and running in Acrobat in no time. Each hour focuses on a particular element of Acrobat; as you progress through the book, you will gain more insight into how the elements work together as a whole. After finishing the book, you will be ready to put your newfound knowledge to use, creating the best PDFs for your particular purpose—whether for the web, commercial printing, or secured using passwords.

What This Book Assumes

This book is not, and does not claim to be, a beginner's guide to computer technology. Whatever computer platform you use, you should be familiar with the software program you want to use to create your original documents, such as Microsoft Word, Excel, QuarkXPress, or PageMaker. This book explains how to convert those documents to PDF files.

In addition, having some knowledge of what you plan to use the PDFs for would be helpful. Some people will use them strictly for e-mailing proofs; others will want to post them on the World Wide Web.

How This Book Is Organized

In **Part I, "Getting Started with Acrobat and PDF"** (Hours 1–2), we cover the reasons you might have for choosing the PDF format for your documents. You'll also find a discussion of the benefits of PDF. We explore the different components that make up the Acrobat application, and provide an overview of the features to be covered in greater depth as the hours progress.

In **Part II, "Creating PDF Files"** (Hours 3–7), we explain how PDF documents are made from almost every program imaginable. The uses of PDF files are far reaching, to every corner of the world and in every type of business. Saving PDFs for different purposes allows you to control such things as file size, color management, compression settings, and so on. We even cover how to take your paper documents and convert them to searchable PDF files. We will explore these topics and more, as we begin to delve into the creation and implementation of PDFs.

In **Part III, "Using and Adding Navigational Tools to PDF Files"** (Hours 8–10), you learn how Acrobat's many navigational features provide quick and easy access to the documents. For example, if you are searching for a particular page in a PDF file, thumbnails allow you to see miniature renditions of the pages. Links and bookmarks take you effortlessly to other parts of the page (or to other pages) with just a click. In this part, we begin to work with the different navigation tools and discuss how and when to use each to better suit your PDF needs.

In **Part IV, "Reviewing and Editing PDF Files"** (Hours 11–13), we cover how to edit a PDF file. We teach you how to extract images and text from the PDF documents, edit text and text attributes, and add comments to the files as well. Everyone in the office can add comments in a different color, using various tools. You will learn how to filter the comments so that you can read only certain ones, as well as how to export them for use later.

In **Part V, "Document Security and Digital Signatures"** (Hours 14 – 15), we talk about security as it relates to PDF files. Imagine being able to "sign" a file or to add security that requires a password for someone to read the file. It is all possible with PDF. We will take you through the use of digital signatures, creating them and applying them. We also will discuss ways to add security features and will give some examples of why this can be helpful.

In **Part VI, "Forms and Buttons"** (Hour 16), you learn how to work with form data— especially interactive forms that contain buttons, links, and actions. Yes, Acrobat can do all this, too! We'll have you creating forms in no time, adding form features such as check boxes and radio buttons (and we will explore the differences between these features). Great tips on designing your forms are also included, and we'll even cover how the data is handled when exported and submitted.

In **Part VII, "Using PDF Files for Multimedia Presentations"** (Hours 17–18), you'll learn how to set up full-screen PDFs and add movie and sound files to your PDF documents. Dazzle everyone with your professional presentations and learn tips to help make your PDFs work effortlessly every time.

Part VIII, "Advanced Topics" (Hours 19–24), covers topics and tasks you'll want to know more about after you're comfortable with the basics. Turbo charge your workplace using batch processing, a great feature of Acrobat that gives you the power to work with multiple PDF files at the same time. You will learn to edit the batch sequences, which

Acrobat uses to perform the tasks at hand, and we'll even show you how to copy these sequences to other computers so that the entire office can be as efficient as you are.

What's on the Web Site?

We have set up a companion Web site for this book at http://www.AcrobatIn24.com. There you will find exercises to use in conjunction with certain parts of this book. Additional technical information and a section on updates will keep you up-to-date with your newfound PDF knowledge. Check it out!

Conventions Used in This Book

This book provides instructions for both IBM-compatible and Macintosh computers.

You'll see these icons in the book:

This is a note. It indicates information that's related to the current discussion.

This is a tip. It indicates information that can save you time or effort as you work with Acrobat.

This is a caution. Don't skip the cautions. We've reserved them for information that can mean the difference between success and, um, Big Trouble as you work with Acrobat.

Now that we've got your curiosity about PDF, let's get moving and begin the journey into PDF. Be sure to take breaks between the hours and don't move on until you are fully comfortable with the materials presented in the current hour.

We guarantee that you are in for an exciting and informative journey. Good luck, and let's begin!

PART I

Getting Started with Acrobat and PDF

Hour

HOUR 1

What's So Great About PDF?

In 1993, Adobe Systems released the first version of Acrobat, and the world of distributing documents electronically was changed forever. But the PDF format didn't reach its full potential until the widespread use of Internet messaging several years later. As more and more people wanted to share documents, an increasing number of problems arose: Some people work on IBM-compatible systems, others on the Macintosh platform. The person designing a document might use certain software that other people do not have on their computers. And even when computer platforms and software are the same, fonts often are not. So documents could be sent by e-mail, but they would not open or they would look different when opened. The business world needed a uniform "digital paper" on which to exchange documents.

The PDF format eliminates the need for paper documents: now you can e-mail documents in a universal, cross-platform format. The recipient of a document does not have to work on the same computer platform as the person who created it. Using the free Adobe Acrobat Reader, anyone can view and print PDF documents. Regardless of whether they use a computer running a Linux, Windows, Unix, or Macintosh operating system, people can view the files exactly as they were intended to look. Because the free Reader is available on more than a dozen computer platforms and in as many languages, PDF truly is "platform independent."

In this hour, you will learn about the following:

- How PDF documents differ from other documents
- The difference between Acrobat and Reader
- How Acrobat supports WYSIWYG
- How to navigate in Acrobat
- Acrobat's tools and their uses

How Can PDF Change Your Office Environment?

As shown in Figure 1.1, you no longer have to wait at the fax machine for your documents to transmit, you don't have to stuff crucial data inside interoffice envelopes, and you can forget courier fees and days of waiting for those papers to arrive. With the ease and peace of mind the PDF workflow offers, these situations are obsolete.

FIGURE 1.1

The PDF workflow simplifies the distribution of documents from most business applications.

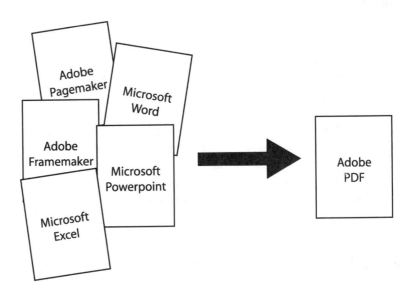

Consider this scenario: You work on an IBM-compatible PC platform and have to send documents to a Macintosh user at another office. You created the document in Adobe PageMaker, but the recipient uses only Microsoft Office applications. In the past, this would have presented a problem. But if you save the document in the PDF format, it can be viewed by the recipient—even without the original application (see Figure 1.2). Because Adobe PDF is a universal format, available for all types of computers, the documents can be viewed by anyone who has Acrobat or its scaled-down, free counterpart, Acrobat Reader. Any program that allows you to print is capable of producing PDF files.

As you can see, PDF is a time and money saver. Because of its universal acceptance, government agencies such as the Internal Revenue Service make all U.S. federal tax forms available on their Internet Web site using PDF. They are assured that the forms look and print identically on any computer. In the business world, PDF has changed the way we think about distributing documents.

> Users send e-mail messages with attached PDF documents from within Acrobat. The Send Mail command communicates with your default e-mail application and sends the current open document. Simply click the envelope icon on the Acrobat toolbar, and Acrobat creates a new mail message within your e-mail software and attaches the PDF file. This feature is available for both IBM-compatible and Macintosh platforms.

FIGURE 1.2

PDF documents can be produced from any program that has printing capabilities, regardless of platform. Because of the universal acceptance of PDF, some applications (such as Microsoft Office applications and Adobe PageMaker) include a utility for exporting directly to PDF, using Acrobat Distiller.

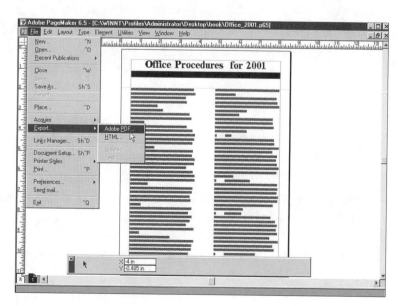

And there's more! Your PDF documents can be viewed on Palm devices, as well. And the latest technology—eBooks—are also a form of PDF. The advantages of using PDF in the business world are as varied as the industries in which it is used today.

How Do PDF Documents Differ from Other Documents?

PDF documents are designed for universal distribution. They can be viewed, marked up, and printed on many computer platforms. However, they are very different from software that you may be accustomed to using, such as Word, Excel, or PageMaker. PDF files are not intended to be edited. So the trade-off for universal acceptance of the file is that the PDF format does not provide extensive editing capabilities. If you convert a document to PDF for distribution, you will still have your original document, which you should use for any significant changes.

PDFs can be opened in Acrobat or Acrobat Reader (we'll discuss these two programs in more detail later). The PDF document typically has a smaller file size than the original document. Because of its small file size and universal acceptance, it is more appropriate for e-mailing and for posting on a Web site. PDF documents maintain the look and feel of the original document, with no line-break changes and no font surprises. PDF documents provide a clean, consistent match to your original document.

When creating a PDF file, you can also establish security settings. The security settings allow you to limit the viewer's ability to change, save, print, or even open a PDF file.

Additionally, comments can be added to PDF documents, indicating changes, additions, and so on. Acrobat provides a variety of annotation and commenting tools, and comments can be imported and exported easily for easy distribution. For example, there is no need to send the entire document back with your comments. Simply export the comments and e-mail them; the recipient can import the comments into their version of the PDF file and see the exact placement of the comments. The annotation and comment features are so great that we've devoted an entire hour to them later in the book (see Hour 13, "Adding Comments and Annotations").

The bottom line is that PDF documents look the same as the original documents but provide more possibilities for electronic distribution.

Adobe Acrobat or Reader—What's the Difference?

A free, scaled-down version of Acrobat—Adobe Acrobat Reader—is available from Adobe's Web site and can be used to view, search, and print PDF files. Anyone can download this free, scaled-down version of Acrobat by accessing http://www.adobe.com/products/acrobat. If you create and distribute PDF files, Adobe will even let you distribute the Adobe PDF Reader free of charge. The Reader does not offer the editing and interactive features of the full version of Acrobat (see Figure 1.3), but it does allow the viewer to see and print the document quickly without having to buy any additional software.

FIGURE 1.3

Although the interfaces of Acrobat and Reader resemble each other, the complete version of Acrobat allows editing and commenting capabilities that are not available in Reader.

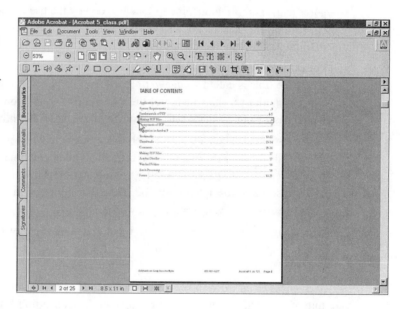

Millions of users worldwide have made Adobe Acrobat Reader an industry standard for viewing paperless documents. It is an easy-to-learn, easy-to-navigate application.

When they hear the word Acrobat, most people think of the free program, Acrobat Reader. Acrobat Reader is a viewing program, intended for simply reading PDF documents. From within Reader, you can also print or select and copy text.

Acrobat does allow the viewing of PDF documents, but possesses a plethora of extra features and tools to give you total control over the document:

- Comments can be added and distributed separately or included with the PDF file. Hour 13, "Adding Comments and Annotations," details this feature.

- Bookmarks can be created instantly out of Microsoft Office applications or created in Acrobat for easy navigation through the PDF file. See Hour 9, "Creating an Interactive TOC with Bookmarks," for details on this feature.

- Interactive forms, for use in the office or on your Web site, can be created in Acrobat, with fillable fields, radio buttons, and other features for the user to submit data. Hour 16, "Creating and Using Interactive Forms," details the creation of such forms.

- Interactive features can be added to PDF files (such as buttons, links, and bookmarks) to ease document navigation and add visual interest for presentation purposes and so on. PDF documents can also deploy the use of movies and sound clips. Hour 17, "Enhancing a PDF with Multimedia," describes how to set up your PDF files to contain these features.

  For example, you can choose a specific sound to play when someone goes to a specific page (this is called a *page action*). Movies can be added to the document, and various options for the viewing of the movie allow you to control many aspects of the process. Hour 17 demonstrates how to add sounds and movies.

- PDF files can also contain active Web links, interactive tables of contents, and thumbnails for easy document organization. You can combine PDF documents and have different-sized pages with different orientations[md[such as having portrait *and* landscape pages in the same file. *Wow!* For information on how to use thumbnails, see Hour 8, "Managing Pages with Thumbnails."

- Digital signatures are a feature of Acrobat that allow the viewer to digitally validate or "sign" the document. This is a useful part of Acrobat that we will explore in Hour 14, "Creating and Applying Digital Signatures."

- Web pages or entire Web sites can be converted to PDF using the Web Capture feature of Acrobat, which is discussed in Hour 7, "Converting HTML to PDF with Web Capture."

- Archiving PDFs is a snap with Acrobat Catalog, which creates a searchable index of PDFs you can place on a CD, use on your own computer, or access over an intranet. We explore the Acrobat Catalog feature in Hour 21, "Searching Multiple PDF Files."

- Scanned documents can be converted to Image Only PDF format (they will be graphics files). By using Acrobat Capture or Capture Online, you can convert them into searchable and editable PDF documents. Hour 3, "Where Do PDF Files Come From?," explains this process in greater detail.

The possibilities of what you can do with PDF are virtually unlimited. What's so great about PDF? Now you know!

Because of the way Acrobat saves documents, the documents remain exactly as they were originally created. This process is referred to as WYSIWYG (What You See Is What You Get). The graphics and text appear exactly as saved; line breaks remain consistent as well. Fonts can be embedded (or saved within the document) to allow editing to occur at a later stage.

Fonts can be embedded to allow text editing later. Graphics retain the quality of the original document, or they can be downsampled to produce a smaller file for posting on the Web.

Often, printed pieces are required to be posted on company Web sites. This can present a problem because HTML, the programming language used to create Web pages, differs from PostScript, the page description language most applications use to create documents.

Web sites can vary in their look and feel depending on the browser used to view them and the computer platform (among other variables).

PDF to the rescue! The obvious answer is to create a PDF file of the original document and post it on the Web site. In the PDF file, the original format is retained, and fonts and graphics remain consistent. Mission accomplished—in a fraction of the time it would take to re-create the document in HTML.

In addition, adding an Acrobat plug-in to your browser allows the browser to act as a "helper," that is, the PDF documents can be viewed from within the browser window with the addition of Acrobat Reader menus, navigation tools, and other features.

System Requirements

Before you install the full version of Acrobat on your computer, make certain that Acrobat can run on your computer. These are the system requirements for the full version of Acrobat. The free Reader has different requirements for all the platforms on which it can be installed. Be sure that your system meets the Acrobat requirements before attempting to install the application.

Adobe Acrobat Version 5 for Macintosh

Adobe Acrobat Version 5 for Macintosh has the following system requirements:

- Power PC processor or G3 or G4 processor
- Mac OS software version 8.6 or later

- 32MB RAM with virtual memory on (64MB recommended)
- 105MB available hard-disk space
- Additional 70MB hard-disk space for Asian fonts (optional)
- CD-ROM drive

Adobe Acrobat Version 5 for Windows

Adobe Acrobat Version 5 for Windows has the following system requirements:

- Pentium-class processor
- Microsoft Windows 95, Windows 98, Windows Millennium Edition, Windows NT 4.0 with Service Pack 5 or greater, Windows 2000, or Windows XP
- 32MB RAM (64MB recommended)
- 115MB available hard-disk space
- Additional 70MB hard-disk space for Asian fonts (optional)
- CD-ROM drive

What's in the Box and What's Available

When you install Acrobat on your computer, you will be installing the original application as well as many other components. Let's take a look at what you get when you buy Acrobat:

- **Acrobat Reader**. This component allows the viewer to read and print PDFs, but provides no editing capabilities. Reader can be used to fill out forms on Web sites and to select/copy text for use in another application. It can also be downloaded free of charge from Adobe's Web site.
- **Acrobat.** Similar to Reader, but it is an expanded program used to view, print, edit, and customize PDF files. In addition, interactive features such as movies, sound clips, actions, bookmarks, links, and so on may be added. Comments may be added to files and managed through various features of the program.
- **Acrobat Distiller**. This component converts PostScript files to PDF format, allowing you to choose options for how fonts and graphics will be handled. Distiller comes with sets of presaved job settings, but allows you to create your own or import settings from another source.
- **Acrobat Catalog**. This component creates a searchable index of PDF documents, perfect for archiving purposes. This system can be used on a single computer, over an intranet, or saved onto CDs for future use. Both Distiller and Catalog are now

accessible from within the Acrobat version 5 program; they were not available in previous versions.

- **PDFMaker**. This IBM-compatible component automatically adds a utility to Microsoft Office applications that permits direct export to PDF. This feature works with Word 97, Word 2000, Excel 97, Excel 2000, PowerPoint 97, and PowerPoint 2000. PDFMaker creates tagged Adobe PDF files and maintains Web-link styles and bookmarks already present in the original document.

- **Acrobat Messenger**. This component allows PC users to e-mail PDF files using the Adobe Messaging Application Program Interface. It is as simple to use as a fax machine or copy machine. Copy or scan the documents, convert them to PDF using the Open As PDF command, and e-mail them right from Acrobat.

- **Plug-ins.** Adobe Acrobat uses plug-in technology. Adobe encourages third-party software vendors to improve Acrobat by writing additional software that operates right within the Adobe Acrobat interface. Some of these tools expand the editing capabilities of Acrobat, others allow you to determine the colors used in pictures inside of a PDF file. Although Adobe maintains a list of plug-ins for Acrobat on its Web site, a great clearinghouse of plug-ins for Acrobat is ThePowerXChange (http://www.thepowerxchange.com). This site sells all sorts of software that runs from inside Acrobat and further expands the capabilities of PDF files.

The Acrobat Interface

Let's begin to look at the interface of Acrobat and learn about the tools and basic appearance of the Acrobat window.

First, we will have to launch the program and open a document in Acrobat.

If you have used other Adobe applications, you will notice a distinct similarity between Acrobat and other Adobe programs. We will explore different ways to navigate through the file in Hour 2. For now, let's just get used to the general look of the program.

The Features of Acrobat

The tools are the most important aspect of Acrobat; they allow you to perform a variety of functions.

You can drag the tools off the toolbars in small groups dragging over the beveled bar (called the Separator Bar) on each of the tool sections (see Figure 1.4). This feature allows easy access to the tools in case you are using the same tool or tools over and over. You can put them away again by dragging on the same beveled line and returning the palette to its original position. In addition, you can combine tool palettes by dragging the palettes onto each other.

All palettes are located under the Window menu, in case you need to find any unopened palettes.

FIGURE 1.4

Acrobat's many tool and navigation icons give the user unlimited control over the PDF document; you can also use basic Adobe keyboard shortcuts for added speed and simplicity.

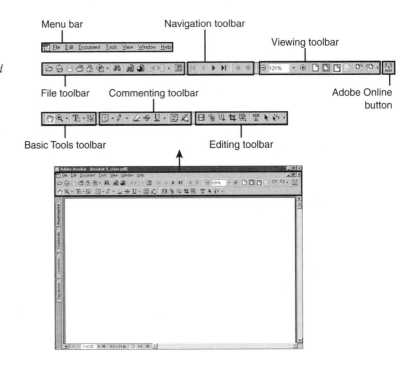

Here is a list and brief explanation of the different features you will see when you open Acrobat:

- **Menu bar**. Use the menu bar to access the pull-down menus of Acrobat such as File, Open; Edit, Copy; View, Fit In Window; and so on. To the right of each menu option is a keyboard shortcut, which you might prefer to use instead of accessing the menus.

- **File toolbar**. This toolbar contains the file tools, such as Open, Save, Open Web Page, and so on. The icons give a clue to the functionality of the tool; clicking the icon puts the action in motion for you.

- **Navigation toolbar**. This toolbar houses the navigation tools such as First Page, Last Page, and so on. This toolbar allows you to speedily access different sections of the PDF document.

- **View History toolbar**. The Previous View and Next View tools are located in this toolbar. You can easily return to the last page you were on by clicking the Previous View toolbar button.

- **Viewing toolbar**. This toolbar contains the magnification options, such as Fit In Window, Fit Width, and so on. Depending on the size of your document, you might want to choose different viewing sizes from this toolbar.

- **Adobe Online button**. This button automatically takes you to Adobe's Web site, provided that you have an active Internet connection. On the Web site, you can learn about other exciting Adobe programs and discover third-party plug-ins to add more features to your Acrobat document.

- **Basic tools**. The Hand tool and Zoom tool are just two of the tools you will find in this area. The Hand tool is the most commonly used tool; we will explore its many uses in Hour 2.

- **Commenting toolbar**. If you want to add or edit comments on a PDF document, these tools will allow you to do so. There are graphic markup tools and comments tools that provide a full range of editing and annotating capabilities.

- **Editing toolbar**. Adding interactive features, such as movies, can be done with these editing tools. We will learn more about adding interactivity with these tools in Hour 17.

Navigation Pane and Tab Palettes

The Navigation pane houses the tab palettes, such as Bookmarks, Signatures, and Thumbnails. You can choose to show or hide this pane, depending on your needs. Figure 1.5 shows the easy access Acrobat offers to these palettes.

In addition, the tab palettes have pop-up menus on the right side that give added functionality. Click the down-facing arrow on the right side of the palette title bar to access the menu.

Status Bar

The status bar shows the size of the currently displayed page and the current page number; it also offers some navigating features. Other features of the status bar include the Magnification Level, First, Last and Previous Page buttons, and the Navigation Pane button.

Scrollbars

The scrolling features allow you to scroll horizontally or vertically inside the document. As Figure 1.6 shows, you can click and hold the black arrows to scroll, and you can drag the little beveled square in the scrollbar as well.

FIGURE 1.5

The Navigation pane holds various palettes (Thumbnails, Signatures, Bookmarks, and Comments). To show or hide the pane, simply click the tab.

Navigation Pane

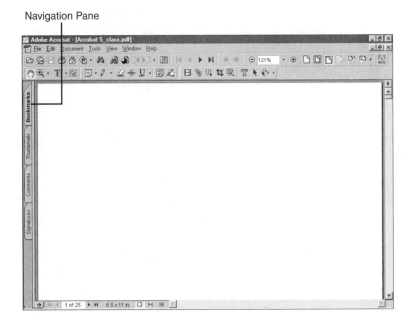

FIGURE 1.6

Acrobat features a variety of scrolling options, adding to the user-friendly approach of Adobe products.

Navigation toolbar   Scrollbars

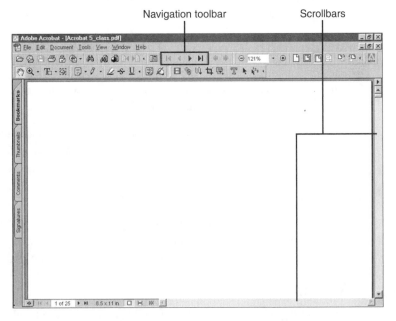

A third way to move around is to simply click in the gray areas of the scrollbars; you will move around the document more quickly this way.

Exploring the Many Acrobat Tools

Figure 1.7 depicts the tools of Acrobat, which we will use in greater detail later. For now, let's get familiar with them.

FIGURE 1.7

The Acrobat 5 tools offer a variety of interactive features, in addition to navigation and editing capabilities.

Click and drag beveled bar to separate toolset from toolbar

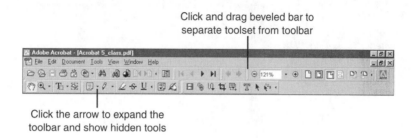

Click the arrow to expand the toolbar and show hidden tools

You will notice that some of the toolbar buttons have a little triangular arrow on their right side. If you click the arrow, a menu of additional related tools appears; click to select the desired tool in the menu. You can choose to expand the tool section by holding down and dragging over Expand This Button.

Tools and Their Keyboard Equivalents

Notice that each tool has a keyboard shortcut to the right of it. You can easily select an individual tool by pressing the appropriate keyboard shortcut, as well as by clicking the toolbar button. Each section of tools has a letter assigned to it; the Shift key will navigate you through the accompanying tools.

Suppose that you want to use the Circle tool. The letter assigned to that set of tools is N. Press N on your keyboard to go to the first tool of the set, the Notes tool. Press Shift+N to cycle through the list of tools for that set until you get to the Circle tool.

Navigating in Acrobat

You can navigate in Acrobat in a variety of ways. First, the right and left arrow keys on your keyboard will take you page-by-page through the current document (see Figure 1.8). The up and down arrow keys on your keyboard will scroll you through the document vertically.

On the toolbar, you will find the First Page, Last Page, Previous Page, and Next Page icons, all geared to ease you through the file effortlessly. (The same icons appear in miniature view at the bottom of the Acrobat window and work exactly the same way.)

To the right of these icons on the command bar are the Last View and Previous View icons. These icons will help you move forward and backward through the document.

FIGURE 1.8

Arrow keys allow you to navigate easily in Acrobat; coupled with the other navigation features, they give you complete control over the viewing of the PDF document.

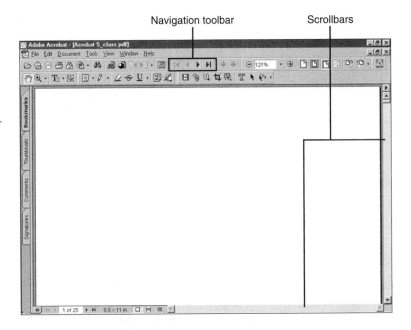

Navigation toolbar · Scrollbars

Other ways to navigate through a PDF document include using bookmarks, thumbnails, and links, all of which are covered in greater detail later in the book.

Summary

We have made it through the first hour and have learned what PDF files can offer and how they differ from other file formats.

In addition, we have explored the interface of Acrobat and have become more familiar with the tools. Using the program on a regular basis is a great way to become fully acquainted with it, and familiarity is a key to gaining speed and efficiency in Acrobat.

As you can see, PDF files provide you with great flexibility. As you progress through the hours in this book, we will explore the tools and features of Acrobat that allow this flexibility, and the ways you can incorporate them into your workflow.

In a short time, you will be up and running in Acrobat, converting your documents to PDF and using the many features Acrobat has to offer.

As we progress through the exercises in the ensuing hours, we'll be working with the tools and components of Acrobat, learning new ways to add creative and innovative features to PDF files.

Workshop

This workshop helps hone your skills in the materials covered in this hour. The Question and Answer (Q&A) section introduces some new information relating to Acrobat; the short quiz asks some questions about what's covered in this hour. The workshop finishes with a few exercises that reinforce the information presented in this hour and help you put your newfound skills to work.

Q&A

Q What are three key advantages of the PDF format?

A You can obtain smaller file size, add interactive features, and set security settings. In addition, you can also save PDFs for use on the Web or for high-end printing.

Q Can PDF documents be edited in any way?

A Yes. If the fonts were embedded properly in the PDF file, the user can perform minor text edits. The text can even be saved out in RTF (Rich Text Format) for use in another application; graphics can be edited if you have additional software such as Photoshop or Illustrator.

Quiz

1. **The Navigation pane allows you to do what?**

   a. Show/hide multiple palettes, such as Thumbnails and Bookmarks, in a vertical space.

   b. Click to go to other closed PDF documents.

   c. View Web sites while in Adobe Acrobat.

2. **The difference between Acrobat and Acrobat Reader is**

   a. Reader is for foreign language use.

   b. Reader is a free, read-only version available from Adobe.

   c. There is no such thing as Adobe Acrobat Reader.

3. **Notes you can add to the PDF document are referred to as**

   a. Comments

   b. Discussions

   c. Attachments

Quiz Answers

1. **a**   The navigation pane allows you to show or hide multiple palettes in a vertical space.

2. **b**   Reader is a free, read-only version of Acrobat.

3. **a**   Comments are notes that can be added to a PDF document.

Exercises

1. Practice showing and hiding the navigation pane. Experiment with the different ways to do this, using the icons at the top and bottom of the window. Click the triangle at the top of the palette (such as the Bookmarks and Thumbnails palettes) to display the choices.

2. Become familiar with the process of customizing your tools: drag them out as separate toolbars, close them by clicking the box at top, and show them again by choosing Window, Toolbars and finding the options that are not selected.

3. Open Acrobat Reader and notice that many of the same features apply here as they do in Acrobat. Note that the editing and interactive feature tools are not present in Reader, but Reader is an easy alternative for viewing and printing PDFs.

HOUR 2

Navigating in PDF Files

In this hour, we'll take an in-depth look at various ways to get around in Acrobat 5. Adobe has incorporated features such as keyboard shortcuts and zooming options from its other applications to ease navigation in Acrobat. If you use other Adobe programs, you will find the similar interface in Acrobat a real time-saver.

In this hour, you will learn to master the following:

- Page modes
- Page layouts
- Zoom tools
- Moving between documents
- Navigating PDF files in Web browsers
- Bookmarks and thumbnails

Page Modes

Depending on the actual size of the document you are viewing in Acrobat, you might want to change the viewing options for that page. For example, if you are viewing a 4" × 5" postcard, an 8.5" × 11" contract, or a 20" × 24" poster, you might want to view these documents at different magnifications, depending on the project at hand.

In another scenario in which you are viewing the PDF to look for typographical errors, you might have to zoom in tighter on the actual type. If you are checking the finished design of a document, on the other hand, you might want to zoom out to see an overall view. Having different viewing options gives you more control over the final document and allows you to be in the driver's seat when viewing the PDF.

You can access page modes in several ways. The first is to open the View menu at the top of the program window. From this menu, you can choose different page modes such as Fit in Window, Actual Size, Fit Width, and so on (see Figure 2.1).

FIGURE 2.1

The View pull-down menu offers different page modes to control how the page appears onscreen depending on the document size.

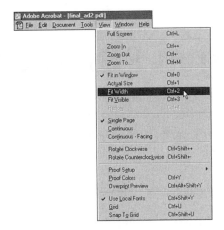

The first page mode, Fit in Window, is a *varying page mode*. In other words, the percentage of magnification varies depending on the circumstances. For example, consider the 4" ×5" postcard: To view this document in its entirety, you can choose the Fit in Window option. Acrobat makes the decision about what percentage to show the entire document onscreen, based on the document's "real" size. The 20" × 24" document, set to Fit in Window, would appear at a different percentage entirely, because it is a larger document and must be reduced onscreen accordingly.

Choose the View, Fit in Window option first and then resize the window. Acrobat resizes the document to fit into the new window size every time you resize the window.

The Actual Size page mode option is a *nonvarying page mode*. In other words, the document displays at 100%. If you select this option, the entire document may not display the onscreen because it could be too large to fit in its entirety at 100%. The Actual Size view can be useful when you want to see detail exactly as it will print because you are viewing the document at the exact finished size.

The Fit Width page mode option displays the PDF document's width but not necessarily its entire height (see Figure 2.2). In other words, Acrobat enlarges or reduces the view of the document to display the entire width of the document onscreen. You might have to scroll to show the bottom of the document. (We'll get to scrolling a little later in this hour.)

The size of the page onscreen might not exactly match the printed size because of monitor resolutions (for example, the page appears smaller at 1024 × 768 pixels than it does at 800 × 600 pixels).

FIGURE 2.2

When you choose Fit Width as your page mode, the zoom percentage varies depending on the width of the original document.

The Fit Visible page mode option shows the visible elements (text and graphics) of the page in full view in the Acrobat window. This page mode differs from Fit Width in that it does not show margins, only the actual elements of the page. As with the Fit Width option, you might have to scroll to view the entire document.

These four page modes are accessible from the toolbar, as well. Whether you use the View pull-down menu, the keyboard shortcuts, or the icons on the toolbar, these page modes offer great control and versatility over the viewing of the PDF document.

> Using keyboard shortcuts to change page modes is a great help in increasing speed and efficiency. The keyboard shortcuts are always located to the right of each option in the View pull-down menu. For example, the keyboard shortcut for the View, Fit In Window command is Ctrl+0 for IBM-compatible users and Command+0 for Macintosh users.

Page Layout

In addition to the various page modes, Acrobat allows you to control how the pages are viewed: one page at a time or as a continuous flow of facing pages. These page layout options can be found in the View menu at the top of the document window. You can also access them by clicking the icons in the status bar at the bottom of the document window or by right-clicking (Ctrl+clicking for Macintosh users) a blank area in the document window to access the context menu.

The Single Page option shows the document "one page at a time." This viewing option is useful if you find viewing multiple pages distracting or are interested in viewing the pages as separate entities.

The Continuous option allows the document to be vertically scrollable—that is, you can easily slide from one page to the next by using the up and down arrow keys on your keyboard. This option is useful for quickly surveying the document because you can scroll through it at a much faster pace.

You might also want to see how certain pages will look next to each other in the finished piece. In this case, choose the Continuous-Facing option (see Figure 2.3). This page layout gives you the "two pages at a time" viewing option, but also allows the vertical scrolling available with the Continuous option.

Facing pages are based on the page layout designated in the creating application. When facing pages are used in a program such as QuarkXPress or PageMaker, page 1 is typically a right page and therefore has no facing page.

FIGURE 2.3

If you want to see the facing pages and be able to scroll through the document quickly, choose Continuous-Facing as your page layout.

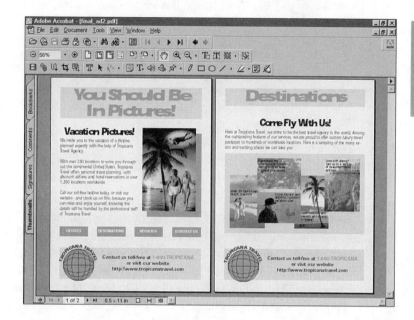

Navigation Tools and Techniques

In the following sections, we'll explore the different ways you can navigate through a PDF document. Acrobat offers a variety of options, and we will become familiar with them in the following pages.

Zoom Tools

Acrobat's zooming tools reside on the toolbar and offer easy options for changing the size of view. Like the zoom tools in other Adobe applications, Acrobat's Zoom In and Zoom Out tools can be accessed with keyboard shortcuts as well.

The Zoom In tool's icon resembles a magnifying glass with a plus (+) sign; click it to zoom in on the document at preset increments up to 1600%.

The Zoom Out tool is located on the toolbar next to the Zoom In tool (you might have to expand the toolbar by clicking the arrow to the right of the Zoom In tool and choosing

Expand This Button). The Zoom Out tool looks like a magnifying glass with a minus (–) sign on it.

You can see the current view magnification in the Zoom text box in the toolbar at the top of the program window (see Figure 2.4). You can also use the plus and minus signs on either side of the Zoom text box to further zoom in and out.

FIGURE 2.4

The current view magnification is always displayed at the top of the Acrobat window so that you don't have to access a pull-down menu to find it.

Current view magnification

As if there aren't enough ways to zoom in and out, Acrobat offers one more! As mentioned earlier, the keyboard shortcuts offer you the freedom of using one tool and being able to zoom without leaving that tool. For instance, if you are selecting text with the Text Select tool and want to zoom in to make your selection, simply press Ctrl++ (hold the Ctrl key and press the plus key on the keyboard); Mac users press Command++ (hold the Command key and press the plus key). To zoom out, press Ctrl+– (hold the Ctrl key and press the minus key on the number keypad); Mac users press Command+– (hold the Command key and press the minus key). To view the entire document, press Ctrl+0 (zero); Mac users press Command+0.

Another useful keyboard shortcut is to press Ctrl+spacebar (Macintosh users press Command+spacebar) to access the Zoom In tool. Press Ctrl+Alt+spacebar (Macintosh users press Command+Option+spacebar) to Zoom Out.

Click and drag with the Zoom In tool; the area you draw the "marquee" around will fill the entire window. This shortcut is very useful when you're working with large documents, or if you just want to proofread a line at the bottom of the file. Zoom in on that section instantly by clicking and dragging the marquee around it.

Right-click (Macintosh users can Ctrl-click) while using the zoom tools to access a context menu. This menu gives you quick viewing options such as the magnification views and page modes discussed earlier in this hour.

Working with Multiple PDF Documents

Acrobat offers some exciting features you can use to compare documents and work with multiple documents at once.

The Window, Tile menu command offers two options for placing multiple documents side by side. The Tile Vertically option displays two documents: one on the right and one on the left. Tile Horizontally displays them one on top and one on the bottom. Figure 2.5 shows how several documents look when you select the Tile Vertically option.

FIGURE 2.5

You can tile multiple documents vertically on the screen.

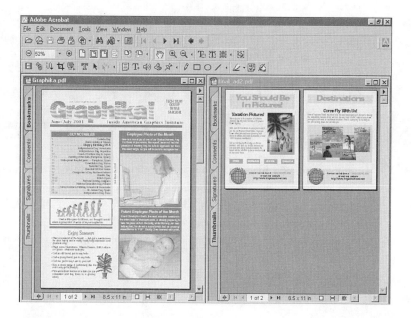

Another option for viewing multiple documents is Cascade. This arrangement of documents allows you to view the title bars of multiple PDF files in a cascading format (see Figure 2.6). The last document you opened appears in front of the other documents. The title bars of the other files are visible behind this last document. Click a title bar to bring that document to the front of the stack. Access this arrangement by choosing Window, Cascade.

FIGURE 2.6

You can stack multiple documents in a cascading arrangement with the Window, Cascade command.

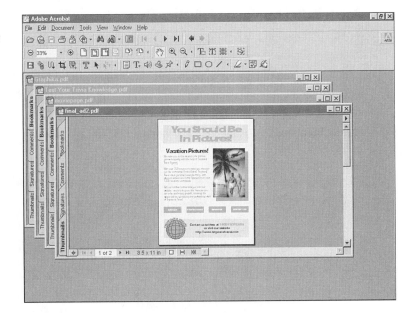

Another helpful method for working with multiple opened documents is the file list in the Window menu. Open the Window menu to see a list of the currently opened documents at the bottom of the pull-down menu (see Figure 2.7). Simply click the name of the document you want to work on, and it will be brought to the front of the stack of opened documents, in whatever viewing arrangement is currently in effect.

FIGURE 2.7

FIGURE 2.7

Switch between opened documents by selecting the document name from the Window menu.

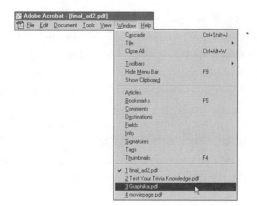

Task: Navigating Multiple PDF Documents

In this task, begin by opening two PDF documents. Then follow these steps to experiment with the different tiling options.

1. Choose Window, Tile Horizontally and examine the view of the documents.

2. Expand the two documents by clicking the expand button in the upper-right corner; tile them vertically by choosing Window, Tile Vertically.

3. Use the Window pull-down menu to toggle between the documents when they are expanded on your screen. (Open the Window pull-down menu and select the name of the document you want to bring to the front of the screen from the list of open documents at the bottom of the menu.)

4. Expand the open documents and choose Window, Cascade. Notice that the documents are placed on top of each other, but staggered vertically so that you can click the title bar of the one you want to bring to the front.

Other Viewing Options

Another navigation feature in Acrobat is the way you can change views by using the toolbar or the pull-down menus. On the toolbar, you will find four triangular arrows (see Figure 2.9): First Page, Last Page, Previous View, and Next View. These arrows offer additional ways to work your way through a file.

- Click the First Page arrow to automatically go to the first page of the document, regardless of where you are currently in the document.

- Click the Last Page arrow to go to the last page in the document, regardless of what page you are on currently.

- Click the Previous View arrow to go to the page you were on before the current page. For example, if you started on page 4 and switched to page 7, clicking Previous View puts you back on page 4.
- The Next View arrow works just like Previous View, but takes you in the opposite direction. These two arrows are useful when you're using links to work your way through a file and are retracing your steps.

Not surprisingly, there are also keyboard shortcuts you can use to access the different views:

- First Page: Ctrl+Shift+PageUp, Ctrl+Shift+Home, or Alt+D+F (Macintosh users press Home)
- Last Page: Ctrl+Shift+PageDown or Ctrl+Shift+End (Macintosh users press End)
- Previous Page: Ctrl+PageUp, Ctrl+UpArrow, or Alt+D+R (Macintosh users press PageUp or UpArrow)
- Next Page: Ctrl+PageDown or Ctrl+DownArrow (Macintosh users press PageDown or DownArrow)
- Go To Page: Ctrl+N or Alt+D+P, and type the page number (Macintosh users press Command+N, and type the page number)
- Go Back: Alt+LeftArrow or Alt+D+B (Macintosh users press Command+LeftArrow)
- Go Back to Document: Alt+Shift+LeftArrow or Alt+D+K (Macintosh users press Command+Shift+LeftArrow)
- Go Forward: Alt+RightArrow or Alt+D+O (Macintosh users press Command+RightArrow)
- Go Forward to Document: Alt+Shift+RightArrow or Alt+D+W (Macintosh users press Command+Shift+RightArrow)

Using Bookmarks

Bookmarks are linked section headings you can add to a PDF document to provide a quick access to specific areas of the file. You can set up bookmarks to ease your readers' navigation through the file, and you can choose to have the Bookmarks palette open automatically each time the file opens.

Here are some quick facts about bookmarks; you can find details about this helpful feature in Hour 9, "Creating an Interactive TOC with Bookmarks":

- Bookmarks reside in a palette. The user can click a specific bookmark to jump to a specific area and percentage of view in the file.

- Bookmarks allow you to jump to another section of the same PDF document, to another document (whether or not that document is a PDF), or to a Web page.

- The File, Document Properties, Open Options menu option allows you to specify that the Navigation pane and Bookmarks palette should open when the file opens.

- Click the Bookmarks tab on the left side of the screen to display the Bookmarks palette (see Figure 2.8).

FIGURE 2.8

The Bookmarks palette gives readers a quick way to jump around a document.

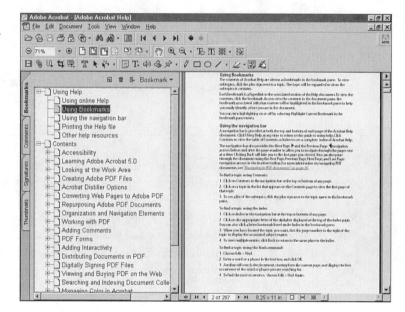

Using Thumbnails

Thumbnails are mini-versions of a document page; they are most helpful in rearranging pages and for viewing a quick rendition of what is on a particular page. For a sample of what thumbnails look like, refer to Figure 2.9.

Additionally, you can easily copy and paste pages between documents by dragging and dropping thumbnails from one document to another. Drag the Navigation pane all the way to the right so that you can view the Thumbnails palette at the width of your application window. You can view the icons in the Thumbnails palette at larger sizes if you open the Navigation pane to full view. Small thumbnails are displayed at approximately 38×48 pixels; large thumbnails are displayed at approximately 76×98 pixels.

FIGURE 2.9

Thumbnails in Acrobat are a useful tool for moving and reorganizing pages. They can be embedded (saved with the PDF file) or unembedded as necessary.

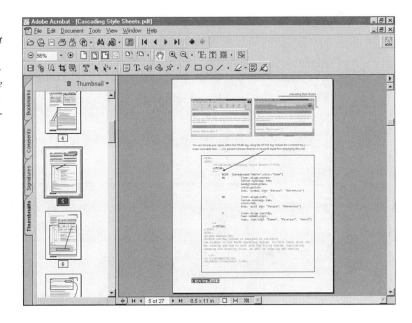

Acrobat 5 creates temporary thumbnails when you open the document; unless you specifically embed these thumbnails, they are not saved with the file. By not embedding the thumbnails before you save and close the PDF, you keep the file size small—crucial for PDFs being displayed on the Web. Each thumbnail can add approximately 3K to the file size, which increases download time and hinders performance. Although 3K might not seem like a lot, when you are preparing images and files for the Web, a group of PDF pages, each with a 3K thumbnail, can significantly affect the file size.

You can specify whether you want to create thumbnails when you create your PDFs in Distiller. This option is covered in Hour 4, "Creating PDF Files from Your Electronic Documents."

For more information on thumbnails, see Hour 8, "Managing Pages with Thumbnails."

Super Slide Sorter

Documents with many pages can be viewed more easily by choosing the Small Thumbnails or Large Thumbnails option from the Thumbnail palette menu. You can hide the menu bar and toolbar by pressing the F9 and F8 keys (or choosing these options from the Window pull-down menu). If you then open the Navigation pane across the screen, you can view all the pages in the PDF file at once (see Figure 2.10). This arrangement of elements is called the Super Slide Sorter; you can use it to easily reorder the pages or simply to find a specific page.

FIGURE 2.10

The Super Slide Sorter is an optimized arrangement of thumbnail icons that can help you quickly navigate and manage the pages in the document.

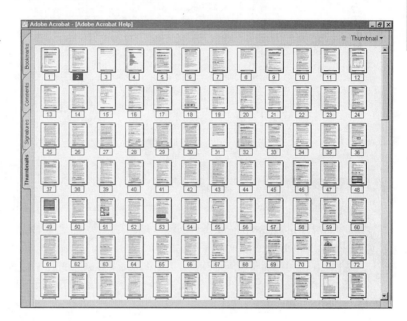

Navigating PDF Files Within Web Browsers

When a PDF file is displayed in a Web browser, all the Acrobat Reader tools are available, including all zooming and navigating tools (see Figure 2.11).

FIGURE 2.11

PDFs displayed in a Web browser retain many of the features provided by the Acrobat Reader.

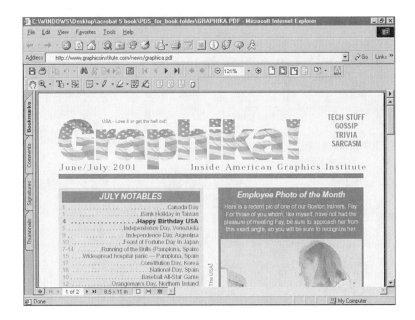

Summary

As you have learned in this hour, navigating in Acrobat is easy and intuitive; the program includes many tools and features for just that purpose. The zooming tools offer an easy way to enlarge or reduce the page view, even while you are using another tool.

We discovered that bookmarks and thumbnails are a useful addition, giving the user easy access to different parts or pages of the PDF document. Thumbnails are miniature representations of the pages that allow you to find a certain page quickly and to rearrange them easily.

With the skills gained in this hour, you will be able to navigate through PDF documents easily and work with multiple PDF files as well. Using the cascade and tiling options, you'll be able to toggle between documents effortlessly.

Workshop

This workshop reviews what you have learned about navigating in Acrobat. We'll start with some questions and answers on related issues. Then you can take a short multiple-choice quiz to review some important topics. Finally, some quick hands-on exercises will help you practice some of your new navigation skills in a PDF document.

Q&A

Q What are the different page modes in Acrobat, and how do I access them?

A Page modes include Fit in Window, Fit Width, Actual Size, and Fit Visible. Page modes are accessed from the View pull-down menu or by clicking the icons in the toolbar.

Q What are the minimum and maximum amounts I can zoom in a PDF document?

A You can zoom from 8.33 to 1,600 percent in 1-percent increments. Use the View, Zoom To command (or press Ctrl+M; Macintosh users press Command+M) and enter a percent.

Q I want my document to open in Continuous Facing Page mode. How do I control that within Acrobat?

A Choose File, Document Properties, Open Options. Click the Page Layout tab and choose Continuous Facing Pages. The document will open in that mode unless you change it again with this command.

Q How can you view all thumbnails at the same time for large documents?

A You can choose the View All Thumbnails command, but remember that you can actually see only as many as will fit on the screen. You can scroll the Thumbnails palette to see the additional thumbnails.

Quiz

1. **What is the difference between First Page and Previous View?**

   a. They are the same. Both views show the page before you made changes, in its original saved format.

   b. They are the same. Both views show the first page that was created in the PDF file.

   c. First Page takes you to the first page of the PDF file. Previous View allows you to go to the last page you were on, before the current one.

2. **Where can I find my toolbars if I accidentally put them away?**

   a. Choose Window, Toolbars and select the toolbars that do not have a check mark next to them. The toolbars with a check mark are already displayed.

   b. Choose View, Show All Toolbars.

   c. Close the document and reopen it. The toolbars will be displayed again.

3. **How to you reorganize pages?**

    a. You cannot reorganize pages in a document after they are in PDF format.

    b. Use the Thumbnails palette to move them around.

    c. Choose Document, Reorder Pages.

Quiz Answers

1. **c**   First Page view takes you to the first page of the PDF file. Previous View allows you to go to the last page you were on, before the current one.

2. **a**   Choose Window, Toolbars, and select the toolbars you want to display.

3. **b**   Use the Thumbnails palette to move pages around.

Exercises

1. Create a PDF document that contains numerous pages. Practice moving the pages around in the Thumbnails palette and watch carefully where the insertion line appears between the icons in the palette. As you drag a page thumbnail, a line appears at the spot where the page will be placed when you release the mouse button. Become familiar with accurately moving thumbnails to where you want them.

2. Get comfortable with the zooming options in Acrobat. There will be times when you want to zoom to a particular spot on the page; the Zoom In tool is perfect for that—if you click and drag a marquee around the area you want to see closer. Try the keyboard shortcuts for zooming—and the page modes as well—so that you can effortlessly choose the one you need.

3. Think of ways you can use bookmarks efficiently. For example, an online newspaper can use bookmarks for each of the stories within the document. An employee directory can have a bookmark for each person's name, nested within bookmarks for each department.

4. Examine how the Zoom In and Zoom Out tools, located on the toolbar, allow easy enlargement and reduction of the page view. Practice using the keyboard shortcuts without interrupting your use of another tool. Practice using the keyboard shortcuts you think you will use most often, and add a few new ones each time you use Acrobat. Before long, you will be a keyboard-shortcut expert!

PART II

Creating PDF Files

Hour

Hour 3

Where Do PDF Files Come From?

In this hour, we will learn how PDF files always start out as something else. Maybe it is as a word processing document, or as a desktop publishing layout. Sometimes it is as a printed piece or as a fax for which no electronic original is available. All of these types of documents—whether digital or analog—can be converted to PDF files. Turning documents into PDF files makes them easier to share—and easier to archive.

Let's say that you want to distribute an employee manual electronically to all the employees in your company. You might not want to give everyone in your company access to the employee handbook in Microsoft Word format, where they can edit and delete text as they want. Converting the document to a PDF file allows you to restrict access so that the file cannot be edited. But the PDF file you want to post on your company's intranet site or e-mail to co-workers around the world is probably not the same PDF file you would send to your commercial printer who is creating the hard-copy versions of your employee manual. The differences between these types of PDF files are explained in this hour.

This hour is designed to give you an overview of all the tools you have available for creating PDF files. Each of these tools is then discussed in further detail later in the book.

In this hour, you'll learn the following:

- What utilities are available for making PDF files
- Why all PDF files are not the same
- How to choose the best option for making your PDF files

Not All PDF Files Are the Same Quality

When making PDF files, it is important to consider how they will be used. Are they going to be sent as e-mail attachments or posted on a Web site? Are they going to be given to a commercial printer for high-quality offset duplication? Maybe they are just going to be used around the office and printed on laser printers.

Knowing how a PDF file will be used allows you to select the best way to create a PDF that will meet the needs of the recipient. If you post a PDF online that was designed to be sent to a commercial printer, the file will be much larger than necessary and take a long time to download. If you send a printer a PDF that was designed for posting to a Web site, the colors in the file might not print accurately and will not look as expected. The settings used to create the PDF file can change the appearance of the PDF file, as you can see in Figure 3.1.

FIGURE 3.1

Graphics in PDF files look different based on how the PDF file is created and which settings are used when making the PDF file.

Posting PDF Files on Web Sites

PDF files posted on Web sites should be designed to download as quickly as possible and to look good on the recipient's computer screen. To make these PDF files look good on-screen, save them in RGB (Red Green Blue) color mode—the same color mode used on all computer displays. This mode provides for more vibrant colors, but these colors cannot always be reproduced when printing. Also, the RGB color mode takes up less space in the file than the mode used to build PDF files for printing.

To allow your PDF files to download more quickly, the resolution of graphics in PDF files that are posted to Web sites should be set to the same resolution as most computer monitors: 72 pixels per inch (sometimes referred to as dots per inch, or dpi). This resolution makes graphics look fine on a computer screen, but they will not be of a very high quality if you have to print the file. The resolution of graphics is separate from the resolution of text; creating a PDF with low-resolution graphics helps reduce the size of the file, but the quality of the text is not affected.

To further reduce the file size of PDF files that are posted on the Web, it is a good idea to remove the fonts from the file. You don't have to worry that your document will look different after you have removed the fonts because all versions of Acrobat—including the free Reader—include font substitution technology. This technology allows you to remove the fonts from the PDF file while being assured that the person who receives the file will still see a document that matches the intent of what you created. Your line breaks will not change and no pages will be added or deleted because of text reflow. PDF files always look the same on all recipients' computers—regardless of the platform they are using and regardless of the fonts installed.

Use the Web settings for PDF files that will be sent as e-mail attachments. This keeps the file size small and makes the files easier to send and receive.

High-Quality PDF Files for Printing

Most commercial printers love to receive PDF files from their clients. They know what you want your file to look like, and they have no concerns that what they print will not match what you intended. They can take your PDF file and output it on their specialized, high-resolution equipment. However, there is one warning: You must create your PDF files for printing differently than those you create for posting to a Web site or for use around your office.

Your printer will want a PDF file that includes all the fonts you used when the piece was designed. Including the fonts in the PDF ensures that the file the printer receives is an exact match to what you created—not just a very close resemblance. Although PDF files created without including the fonts can look pretty similar to the original (it may take a magnifying glass to see the difference), printers are much more particular. The graphic arts industry wants an exact match, so your printer will require a PDF file with all the fonts included. Including the fonts in the PDF file makes the file size larger; this is the trade-off for creating an exact match of the original. You can see how including the fonts in the PDF makes the file less desirable for online posting, and why you want to create different types of PDF files for different purposes.

The colors used on a printing press are different than those used onscreen. Printers use CMYK (Cyan, Magenta, Yellow, and Black) for printing. The colors used in a PDF that is sent to a printer should reflect this fact instead of using the colors used for on-screen viewing. Using CMYK colors for your PDF file will make the colors appear more muted, and not as attractive on-screen. This also increases the file size slightly.

PDF Files for General Office Use

PDF files that will be used around your office, printed on laser printers, and posted to a company intranet site (which is typically faster than an Internet site) should be of a higher quality than those posted to an Internet Web site, but they do not have to be as high-quality as those being sent to a commercial printer. The primary difference between PDF files that are sent to a commercial printer and those created for general office use is the resolution of the graphic files. Both office-quality PDF files and print-quality PDF files are converted to CMYK color because office printers also use these colors for printing. PDF files for both these purposes include fonts to ensure consistency and accuracy when printing and viewing. But the graphic resolution for office-quality PDF files is about half of that used for commercial printing purposes.

PDF Files as eBooks

PDF files that will be distributed as eBooks are files that can be launched in an electronic software program. They should be of a slightly higher quality than PDF files that are used for onscreen viewing only. eBook PDF files also embed all the fonts used in the original file, ensuring that the eBook readers get an exact representation of the original file. The higher resolution and the inclusion of fonts creates a slightly larger file size.

Tools for Creating PDF Files

To make PDF files, you must first purchase software. The free Reader lets you only view PDF files, not make them. Whether you purchase Adobe Acrobat, which includes multiple ways to make PDF files, or use the Web services available on Adobe's Web site, you can't make PDF files without first purchasing the software or buying the online service. The most common ways for building PDF files are listed in Table 3.1.

TABLE 3.1 Methods for Creating PDF Files

Component	Included with Acrobat?	Provides Control of Security & Quality?	Converts Paper to PDF?
Acrobat Distiller	Yes	Yes	No
PDF Writer	Version 4 and earlier only	No	No
Acrobat Capture	Yes	No	Yes
Acrobat Capture Server	No	No	Yes
Create PDF Online	No	Quality control only	No

Acrobat Distiller

Adobe Acrobat Distiller is the most common utility used to create PDF files (see Figure 3.2). It is a separate software program that is included when you purchase Adobe Acrobat. It provides the widest assortment of options for creating various types of PDF files. Distiller works only with print-to-disk files created using a special print driver or with Encapsulated Post Script (EPS) files. For this reason, it is a bit more complicated to use, but the control you have over the quality and security of the files makes it worth the effort. You'll learn all about using Acrobat Distiller in Hour 4, "Creating PDF Files from Your Electronic Documents."

PDF Writer

Up through version 4, Adobe Acrobat also included PDF Writer as a separate utility for creating PDF files. This print driver allowed you to easily create PDF files without having to create print-to-disk files. Although PDF Writer is very easy to use, it lacks many important features found in Distiller. PDF Writer is still a good option for creating PDF files that do not contain any graphics or images, only text. Because many users still have

PDF Writer installed on their computers, we cover the features of PDF Writer along with Distiller in Hour 4. Many of the Adobe Distiller features discussed in Hour 4 can be used with PDF Writer, giving you both control and ease-of-use, without giving up quality.

FIGURE 3.2

Acrobat Distiller lets you choose the quality of the PDF files you create.

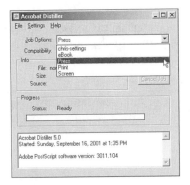

Converting Hard-Copy Documents to PDF

If you own a scanner and Adobe Acrobat, you can easily convert any paper document to a PDF file. You can then send these files to co-workers instead of faxes or you can archive them instead of putting the paper copies into a filing cabinet. PDF files take up less space than their paper counterparts: An entire filing cabinet worth of data can be placed on a CD-ROM using the PDF file format. And PDF files are typically less expensive to send than a fax because you do not have to worry about telephone charges.

If you expect to do a great deal of paper-to-digital conversion using Acrobat, you can even use a scanner with an automatic document feeder to easily convert a large number of pages to PDF files. The files you convert to PDF can also be made searchable. These capabilities are included with Adobe Acrobat. If you plan to convert hundreds (or thousands) of pages to PDF files, you will want to consider the Adobe Acrobat Capture Server software, which is designed for high-volume conversion from paper documents to PDF files. This software is not included with Adobe Acrobat, but has some enhanced capabilities beyond those found in Adobe Acrobat. All the options associated with scanning and converting paper documents are covered in Hour 6, "Converting Paper Documents to PDF."

Making PDF Files from Web Sites

If you've ever wanted to send an entire Web site to a co-worker or to capture a Web site for viewing later, you'll appreciate this option. Adobe Acrobat includes Web Capture, which provides extensive control for creating PDF files from Web sites. This option is covered in Hour 7, "Converting HTML to PDF with Web Capture."

Online Service

If you don't want to buy Acrobat but need to make PDF files, this option may be for you: You can upload a variety of file formats to the Adobe Web site, and the site will send you back a PDF file, as shown in Figure 3.3! There is an annual subscription fee for this service, but it might be worth it if your computer doesn't fit the minimum system requirements for Acrobat and you still want to create PDF files. Access this option at www.createpdf.adobe.com.

FIGURE 3.3

Adobe's online service makes it possible to build PDF files even if you do not own Acrobat. You can try it free and then register to use it on a month-by-month basis or for an entire year.

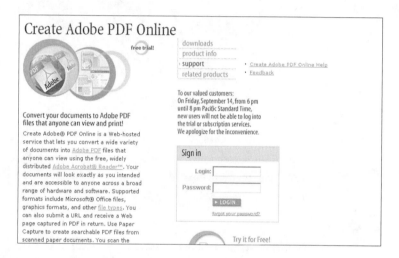

Making PDF Directly

Because of the broad acceptance of PDF files, some software companies have included the ability to convert directly to the PDF file format, as shown in Figure 3.4. Programs such as WordPerfect from Corel and Macromedia FreeHand include these capabilities. Of course, most Adobe software allows you to save directly to a PDF file format without going through any extra steps. Adobe PageMaker, Adobe InDesign, Adobe Illustrator, and Adobe Photoshop all can save files directly to the PDF format.

Although it would be nice if all software saved directly to the PDF format, it is up to each software manufacturer to decide which formats they will support. If your favorite software package does not save directly to the PDF format, contact the manufacturer and request this feature. Adobe does make some utilities to help Microsoft Office users more easily convert their files, even though Microsoft programs do not directly convert to the PDF format. These tools are covered in Hour 5, "Easy PDF Creation for Microsoft Office Users."

FIGURE 3.4

Many popular programs, such as Adobe PageMaker, allow you to export or save files directly as PDF files while still providing controls over quality and security.

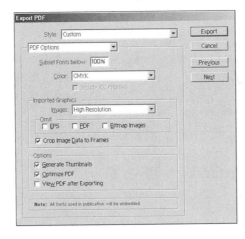

Summary

You should now understand how PDF files designed for online viewing are different from those used for high-quality printing. You have seen how PDF files can be created from a variety of sources, using different software and online services.

Workshop

We've seen that there are a number of sources for PDF files. But with all these ways to make them, there are some questions we should answer, and some exercises that will help complete your understanding of these different types of PDF files.

Q&A

Q Must all the pages in a PDF document be created in the same way?

A No. PDF files allow you to mix and match pages, regardless of how they were created.

Q Is one method for creating PDF files better than the others?

A The answer to this question depends on how the original file was created. If you only have a paper document, scanning is your only option. But for most electronic documents, it is best to use Acrobat Distiller unless the originating software supports the ability to save directly to PDF, as do Adobe PageMaker and Corel WordPerfect.

Q Doesn't Microsoft Word convert directly to PDF? My copy of this program has a small Acrobat button that makes my document into a PDF file when I click it.

A No. Microsoft Word does not convert directly to the PDF format. The Acrobat icon you might see in your copy of Word is essentially a macro that was installed into Word at the time you installed Acrobat. The macro automates the creation of print-to-disk files and automatically launches Acrobat Distiller. You will have this option available only if you installed Adobe Acrobat after installing Microsoft Word (or Microsoft Office) on your computer.

Quiz

1. **To what color format (color space) should you convert PDF files that are being posted on a Web site?**

   a. CMYK

   b. RGB

   c. LAB

   d. Any color is fine

2. **What happens to a PDF file if you do not include the font in the file when it is created?**

   a. Acrobat displays symbols where the font would appear.

   b. All versions of Acrobat include font-substitution technology, so a document still looks like the original even without the fonts.

   c. The text will reflow, but it still can be viewed.

3. **What program gives you the most control over the security and quality of PDF files when making them?**

   a. PDF Writer

   b. Acrobat Capture

   c. Acrobat Distiller

   d. All of the above provide these controls

Quiz Answers

1. **b** The RGB color space makes the files somewhat smaller and looks better on screen. RGB colors do not always accurately reflect how they will print.

2. **b** One of the many great features of Acrobat is that documents look the same on any computer, even if the viewer does not have the same fonts as the person who

made the file. Font-substitution software included with Acrobat (even the free Reader) keeps your PDF files looking consistent across platforms.

3. **c** Acrobat Distiller provides the greatest control over quality, color, and security when creating PDF files.

Exercises

Learn more about making PDF files by trying the following exercises.

1. Visit Adobe's Create PDF Online site at `http://createpdf.adobe.com`. Try the free sample to see how you can make PDF files even if you don't have Adobe Acrobat.

2. Locate a PDF file that includes color images. Print it on a color printer and compare the differences in the hues of the colors. Look at the quality of the graphics on the printed piece and compare them to what is onscreen. Can you guess whether the file was made for printing or onscreen viewing?

Hour **4**

Creating PDF Files from Your Electronic Documents

Adobe Acrobat lets you create PDF files from either paper documents using a scanner or electronic documents using various conversion utilities. If you have both an electronic version of a document and a printed version, it is always better to convert the electronic document to PDF rather than scanning the printed document. You will have more control over the file quality and size, and the resulting PDF file will be searchable without any extra effort on your part. In this hour, we look at the methods for taking electronic documents—whether they are word processing files, spreadsheets, or desktop publishing files—and converting them to PDF files. As we discussed in Hour 3, "Where Do PDF Files Come From?," several methods exist for creating PDF files. Our focus in this hour is on Acrobat Distiller.

Acrobat Distiller is a separate program that ships with Adobe Acrobat. It is used to create PDF files from print-to-disk (.prn) files that have been made using the PostScript print driver. These files will sometimes have the .ps file extension, or they may use the .prn extension. The extension does not matter—as long as the files have been created with the PostScript print driver. Distiller provides an array of settings that allow you to customize the type of PDF file you will create to best meet your needs. For example, you can optimize PDF files for Internet viewing or for high-resolution printing, or you can apply security settings to them. All these settings can be applied when making a PDF file using Acrobat Distiller.

After you create settings that are to your liking, you may never have to open Acrobat Distiller again. Although Distiller version 5 provides control over how PDF files are created, it also includes a great deal of automation that makes it possible to apply Distiller settings while you're still in the original program for the file you want to convert to PDF.

In this hour, you'll learn the following:

- How to control the quality and file size of PDF files made using Acrobat Distiller
- How to efficiently create multiple PDF files using predefined settings
- How to create security settings while building a PDF file

A Short History of WYSIWYG

The way PDF files are created is a bit odd. You might expect to simply select the Save As command from within your favorite program and then choose PDF as the file format. However, Adobe cannot mandate that all software companies allow their files to be saved as PDF files. Although Adobe encourages companies to adopt the PDF standard, very few actually allow you to save directly to a PDF file. Word Perfect, InDesign, Illustrator, FrameMaker, PageMaker (version 7 only), FreeHand, and Photoshop are the only programs that currently save directly to the PDF file format. All other files require conversion—usually using Acrobat Distiller.

Even popular programs such as Microsoft Word, PowerPoint, and Excel do not save directly to the PDF file format, but these programs have some special utilities that Acrobat installs to make it easier to create PDF files from within these applications. These utilities are covered in Hour 5, "Easy PDF Creation for Microsoft Office Users."

To help better understand the way PDF files are created, you need to understand a bit about the history of Adobe Systems, the company that makes Acrobat. Most people see Adobe as the developer of desktop publishing software. After all, the company also makes Photoshop, PageMaker, Illustrator, and a host of other software packages.

But Adobe traces its origins back to the development of a printing technology known as PostScript. PostScript essentially created the desktop publishing revolution by allowing you to create on paper an exact replica of what was on your computer screen. PostScript is a device-independent page description language. It tells a printer—any printer that understands PostScript—how to precisely print what is on your computer screen. This is the meaning of WYSIWYG (What You See is What You Get). PostScript is still used today in printers used by graphic design professionals and commercial printers.

The ability to print an identical page on any printer is the foundation for PDF. Rather than printing an identical image on any printer, you are instead printing an identical "image" of a document on any computer. PDF files are like a digital-paper version of your documents. And like their paper cousins, PDF files are easily distributed, but not easily edited or modified.

To create a PDF file, you will be "printing" to a PDF file. A special print driver supplied with Acrobat creates a print-to-disk file and starts Acrobat Distiller to convert the document to a PDF. With this process, Adobe has created a method for all programs to create PDF files, even if the software doesn't have a specific Save As PDF option.

The Best Choice for Making PDF Files: Acrobat Distiller

Acrobat Distiller has only one function: to convert PostScript print-to-disk files and EPS (Encapsulated PostScript Files) to PDF.

Acrobat Distiller allows you to create PDF files from any software program that is capable of printing. In earlier versions of Acrobat, it was sometimes necessary to create print-to-disk files and then process them through Distiller if you wanted to change the settings being used by Distiller. With Acrobat version 5, it is now very easy to create customized settings for building your PDF files. You can now access these settings right within the software program you use to build the documents that will be converted to PDF. Acrobat version 5 enhances the Print dialog box interface to provide these controls so that the process of creating PostScript files and accessing Distiller remains automated.

Although you can access all these settings right within most programs while printing, it is still important to understand which controls are available when you're building a PDF file. These controls allow you to minimize your file size or maximize the quality of a PDF file. We'll look at each of these controls in detail.

The Acrobat Distiller Main Window

You can access Acrobat Distiller using one of two methods. The first option is to select Distiller from the Tools menu while working in Adobe Acrobat. This command is new in

Acrobat version 5. This command launches the separate Acrobat Distiller program. You can also go to the folder containing Acrobat, locate the Distiller folder, and then launch the Distiller program (AcroDist.exe). When you start Distiller using either of these methods, the main program window shown in Figure 4.1 opens.

FIGURE 4.1

The Acrobat Distiller window tells the status of any file being processed and what settings are being used to make the PDF file.

In the top part of the Acrobat Distiller window, you will find a Job Options pull-down menu. This menu includes four preset choices (Screen, Print, Press, and eBook) along with any custom settings you have saved. These settings determine what type of PDF file will be created. The option you select from this menu determines the quality and size of the PDF file you will create. We'll cover the four preset choices in the following sections; later in this hour, we will discuss how to create customized settings. Understanding these settings is critical if you want to control the size, quality, and compatibility of the PDF files you create.

The Screen Setting

The Screen setting is used to create PDF files that will be distributed online. Quality is downgraded to create the smallest possible PDF file. PDF files created using this setting convert any graphics in the file to a low resolution (72 pixels per inch). All colors are converted to Red, Green, and Blue so that they look good onscreen but may not print accurately. Fonts used within the original file are not built into the PDF file; Adobe Acrobat will use a font-substitution technology to create a close resemblance of the original font. Don't be too concerned about the fonts; in almost every case, the substituted fonts will look fine. A more detailed discussion of the font-substitution technology takes place later in this hour.

Files created with this setting can be viewed by the broadest audience: anyone with any version of the free Acrobat Reader from version 3 and later can view files created with the Screen setting. This is useful to note if you are distributing files over the Internet and are concerned that your audience might have older versions of the Acrobat Reader software installed.

The Print Setting

The Print setting is used to create PDF files that will be viewed onscreen and also be printed. Colors are optimized for an office color printer, graphic resolution is increased, and fonts are built into the PDF file. The Print setting creates PDF files that are somewhat larger than those created using the Screen setting because it assumes that you will be sharing the files across a local network (not the Internet) where file size is not a major concern. Files created with the Print setting can only be viewed with the free Acrobat Reader version 4 or 5.

The Press Setting

The Press Setting is the highest quality setting and should be used by graphic designers or others who are creating PDF files that will be sent to a commercial printer for reproduction. Commercial printers have film and computer-to-plate printers that image at a much higher resolution than those in a standard office environment. This Acrobat Distiller setting keeps high-resolution graphics at their intended resolution and embeds fonts into the PDF file.

PDF files created with the Press Setting are the largest PDF files in terms of file size. Although you can open them with Acrobat version 4 or later—including the free Reader—these files can become very large and slow on computers not equipped to work with large files. Commercial printers typically have faster computers with large amounts of memory to deal with these types of files. Also, because of their size, they are inefficient to e-mail.

The eBook Setting

The eBook setting is an update on the Screen setting. It is intended for PDF files that will be viewed primarily onscreen using the latest versions of Acrobat (versions 4 or 5). Images are brought to a lower resolution than what might be used for high-quality printing, but they are not as low a resolution as the Screen setting delivers. Fonts are also built into PDF files created using the eBook setting. The eBook setting creates a slightly larger file than PDF files made using the Screen setting.

The settings used when creating PDF files will affect the files' compatibility, size, and the quality of images, as you can see in Table 4.1.

4

TABLE 4.1   Acrobat Distiller Settings

	Screen	Print	Press	eBook
Compatibility	Acrobat 3.0 and later	Acrobat 4.0 and later	Acrobat 4.0 and later	Acrobat 4.0 and later
Fonts	Not embedded	Embedded as subsets	Embedded as subsets	Embedded as subsets
Image Resolution	72 pixels per inch (ppi)	300 ppi	300 ppi	150 ppi
Color Images	Converted to RGB	Colors are unchanged but are tagged for color management	Colors are unchanged	Converted to RGB
Used For	PDF files placed on the Web or e-mailed	General office use; may be too large to e-mail over the Internet	PDF files sent to commercial printers	General office use; looks good onscreen or printed

Making a PDF File Using Distiller

As mentioned earlier, it is possible to allow Acrobat Distiller to operate in the background and automatically create PDF files for you. However, there are a few reasons why you might want to know how to operate Distiller manually rather than automatically converting your files:

- If you are unhappy with the four preset choices in the Job Options drop-down list and want to customize them, you will have to do this within Distiller.
- If someone wants to provide you with a file but you do not have the software they used (and they do not have Acrobat), you can have them provide you with a PostScript print-to-disk file. You can then use Distiller to convert the file to a PDF.
- If you have a large number of files to convert to PDF, it is often more efficient to create multiple print-to-disk files and then use Distiller's batch processing capabilities to convert the files to PDF when you are not at your computer.

Using Acrobat Distiller is very straightforward. First, select the type of PDF file you want to create from the Job Options menu on the main Distiller window. Then select a file you want to convert to a PDF. Remember that the file you select must be either a print-to-disk (.prn) file created using a PostScript print driver or an EPS file. To select the file to be converted to PDF, simply locate it on your computer and drag the file into the main Acrobat Distiller window—just as if you were moving it from one folder to another. Acrobat Distiller will then convert the file to a PDF and place the PDF file in the same folder as the original file. By default, Acrobat Distiller does not delete the original file; you will have both the original and the PDF when you are done.

> Do not drag your original document (such as a Word document with a .doc extension) into the Distiller window. Distiller cannot convert files unless they have been printed to disk or saved as an EPS file.

If you don't want to drag and drop files into the Distiller window, you can use the program's menus. The Distiller File menu allows you to open files in the EPS or print-to-disk format. Files opened in Distiller are immediately converted to PDF using the Job Options settings that were selected before the file was opened.

That's all there is to it! If you can drag and drop, you have the skills necessary to create PDF files.

4

> If you work on a Macintosh platform, you should increase the memory allocation provided to Adobe Acrobat Distiller. Doing so will significantly increase the performance of the application. To do this, select the Distiller program within the Finder by clicking it once, then choose the Get Info command from the File menu. Increase the preferred memory size to 36,000 (if your computer has enough RAM installed, you can choose a higher value). This step is not necessary on the PC platform.

Customizing Distiller Settings

Now let's take a look at the more detailed settings surrounding the creation of a PDF file. By customizing the four preset Job Options, you can more precisely control the file size and quality of the PDF file you create. The four preset options are quite good for most PDF files. It is only when you want to create an extra-small PDF file or an exceptionally high-quality PDF file that you will have to modify the default settings.

To modify the default Job Options settings and create your own customized Job Options, first select the option from the Job Options drop-down list in the main Distiller window that most closely matches your needs. Then select Job Options from the Settings menu to display the Job Options dialog box for the selected setting (see Figure 4.2). There are five tabs across the top of the Job Options dialog box: General, Compression, Fonts, Color, and Advanced. Each of these tabs contains settings we can customize.

FIGURE 4.2

The Job Options dialog box allows for extensive customization of how PDF files will be produced using Distiller.

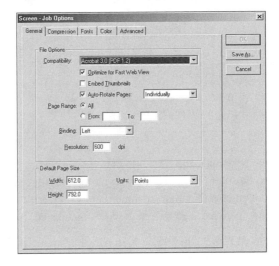

The General Tab

The General tab contains a variety of options, as shown in Figure 4.2. The most important are Compatibility, Embed Thumbnails, and Resolution.

Compatibility

The Compatibility option lets you determine what version of Acrobat Reader will be necessary to view the PDF files you create. If you select a lower version, such as 3.0, then all versions of the software since that version will be able to view the PDF file. The file created using the settings in Figure 4.2 can be viewed with Acrobat Reader versions 3, 4, and 5. However, if you select a higher version, only that version and higher can view the files you create. For example, if you select Acrobat 5 from the Compatibility drop-down list, people with version 4 software cannot read your files.

Although it might appear to be a good idea to select the lowest version to allow the most people to access your file, this is not always the best idea. For example, if you have to send a PDF file to a commercial printer, you will want to use at least version 4 because of several enhancements in the file format that are useful for commercial printers. Similarly, if you require 128-bit high security on your PDF file, you must choose version 5 to incorporate this option in your files. Earlier versions support encryption, but not at this heightened level.

The Optimize for Fast Web View option should always be enabled if you are posting your PDF files to a Web site from which they will be downloaded. This option ensures that the files will display in the viewer's Web browser more quickly.

Embed Thumbnails

Enabling the Embed Thumbnails option increases the size of the file. We will see how thumbnails can easily be created on demand without your having to embed them in the file. It is a good idea to keep this check box disabled unless necessary. We cover thumbnails in detail in Hour 8, "Managing Pages with Thumbnails."

Resolution

When creating a PDF, Acrobat Distiller pretends to be a laser printer. As such, it needs to set a resolution for the file it is creating. The higher the resolution, the higher the quality of the file when printing and the smoother the gradients on your page will look. Setting a higher resolution increases the time it takes for Distiller to process a file.

You should set the value in the Resolution field to match the output resolution of your printer. For most office laser printers, this is 600dpi; commercial printers have imaging equipment that can output pages at resolutions up to 4,000dpi. The Resolution setting on the General tab is not for scanned images in the file; the resolution of scanned images is controlled on the Compression tab.

The Compression Tab

Acrobat Distiller can lower the resolution of the graphics contained in files that are converted to PDF. It does this to help reduce the file size if the graphics are above a certain threshold. For example, if you are posting a PDF file to a Web site and you want the file to download quickly, you might choose to lower the resolution of the graphics to help reduce the file size. If you also want to send the file to a commercial printer for reproduction, you'll have to create another version of the same PDF.

Acrobat Distiller cannot improve the quality or resolution of images. If you have a low-resolution image in a document that you convert to PDF, the image will remain at that same resolution; the resolution will not improve regardless of what values you place in the resolution fields.

The Compression tab in the Job Options dialog box allows you to set compression settings separately for Color Images, Grayscale Images, and Monochrome Images, as shown in Figure 4.3.

4

FIGURE 4.3

*You can customize the
resolution settings for
color or black-and-
white images; you
can also determine
whether graphics will
be compressed.*

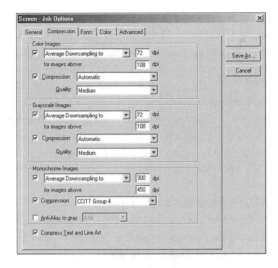

Color Images and Grayscale Images

There is little reason to create separate settings for Color Images and for Grayscale
Images; what you define for one should be mirrored for the other. Your settings on this
tab should reflect the quality and file size you need. If you want a small file size and are
willing to accept lower-quality images, set the downsampling to 72dpi. At this resolution,
images will look good onscreen but not when printed. If you want an even smaller file
size, set this option to a value less than 72dpi, which will cause the images to look poor
both onscreen and in print, but will enable the file to download quickly.

Lowering the image resolution throws data away (which is what makes the file smaller).
After image data is discarded, it can never be recovered. Because of this, it is sometimes
necessary to create multiple PDF files: one for online distribution and another for printing. These resolution changes affect only the images embedded in the PDF file. The original files used when designing the document are not modified by these settings.

If you are creating a PDF for the Web, set the resolution field to 72dpi. When creating a
file that includes graphics to be printed on an office or home printer, set the downsampling resolution to 150dpi. If you are creating a PDF file to be sent to a commercial
printer for reproduction, set the resolution value to 300dpi (unless your printer tells you
otherwise). These are the default graphic resolution settings you will find with the preset
Screen, Print, and Press Job Options.

The first field in each of the three sections on the Compression tab is a drop-down menu
that provides you with additional downsampling and subsampling options. The downsampling method of reducing the resolution of an image is faster and less accurate than

subsampling. Use the Downsampling option to quickly reduce the resolution of images in PDF files intended for the Web. The subsampling method of reducing the resolution of an image creates a more accurate representation of the original image. Subsampling takes longer than downsampling, and the slightly higher quality is not worth the extra time if images are to be viewed onscreen only. Subsampling is a good choice when you are creating PDF files that will be printed more than viewed onscreen.

Acrobat Distiller does not lower the resolution of all images. It lowers the resolution of only those images that are above a certain resolution that you specify in the For Images Above fields. With these settings, you can have Acrobat Distiller ignore images that are only marginally beyond your desired resolution. Distiller can then operate faster while still lowering the resolution of images beyond the limit you specify.

You should always enable the Compression option and set it to Automatic. Select the desired quality of the final images. If you select Medium, Low, or Minimum quality, expect that your images will not look as good as the original. One of the methods used for compression can cause the graphic quality to degrade if you select a lower quality setting. This is not a concern if you select High or Maximum quality. With these quality options, Acrobat Distiller can reduce the file size for the image while keeping imperceptible the changes from the original image file, even when you need the image at a very high resolution.

Monochrome Images

Monochrome images are black-and-white (not grayscale) scanned images. Monochrome images are typically logos or line art. The term "monochrome image" refers only to scanned images, not to artwork created using a drawing program such as Illustrator or FreeHand. Distiller provides a separate section to control the resolution of monochrome images because they must maintain a higher resolution than most photographic images. The solid edges of monochrome images will appear saw-toothed or jagged if they are reduced to a very low resolution. Typically, you should not reduce the resolution setting in the Monochrome Images section to less than 300dpi, even if the image is intended for the Web. For files that will be printed, select 1,200dpi. Specify a threshold at which the downsampling should occur; I use 25 percent as the threshold. So for a 300dpi downsampling target, I set the For Images Above field to 375.

The Fonts Tab

To make PDF files appear identically on all computer platforms, you might think that fonts must be built into each PDF file. This is not exactly the case. PDF files can have fonts built into them, but it is not necessary. It is possible to create a PDF file that has no fonts built into it, or one that has only certain fonts built into it. It is even possible to include only certain characters from a font family into a PDF file.

But if you don't include the fonts in a PDF file, how can the recipient's computer display it accurately?

When you send a PDF file to someone, the Acrobat Reader first tries to use the fonts included in the PDF file. If there are no fonts in the PDF file, it then tries to use the fonts located on the recipient's computer (these "resident" fonts are usually in the operating system). If none of these fonts match the fonts called for in the PDF document, Acrobat uses a font-substitution technology, in which it inserts replicas of the original fonts in place of the actual fonts. In most cases, it would take a great deal of examination to distinguish the substituted font from the original.

This font substitution does not cause any reflowing of the text. If your document was exactly two full pages, it will remain two full pages. Words that ended a line in the original document will still end the line in the PDF file, regardless of what fonts were substituted. The font-substitution technology used by Acrobat maintains all line breaks along with the width and size of each character. The font-substitution technology is based on two foundation fonts: serif fonts (those with "feet" on the bottom such as Times and Bookman) and sans serif fonts (those that are more plain, such as Helvetica and Arial). Acrobat can accurately reproduce serif and sans serif fonts even if they are not embedded into the PDF file. Additionally, all copies of Acrobat—including the free Reader—ship with a group of commonly used fonts that are installed in the Acrobat folder. Acrobat also uses these fonts if it needs them.

By not including the fonts in a PDF file, you help make the file smaller. You are accepting that the document will *almost exactly* match the original in exchange for keeping the file size small. But some fonts cannot be accurately reproduced using font substitution, such as ornate scripted fonts that might be used in a wedding invitation. In these cases, you might not want font substitution to occur, even if it does create a close resemblance of the original. Let's say that you are a graphic designer who has spent a great deal of time identifying the exact fonts and styles you want to use in a job. In this case, you will want Acrobat to embed the fonts into the PDF file to make certain that you get an exact match in the PDF when compared to what you designed.

The Fonts tab of the Job Options dialog box provides an Embed All Fonts option (see Figure 4.4). Enable this check box to include in the PDF file all the fonts used when the document was created. If you select this option, you are assured that whatever you designed will always *identically* match what the recipient views and prints. Note that selecting this option does increase your file size.

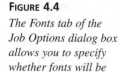

FIGURE 4.4

The Fonts tab of the Job Options dialog box allows you to specify whether fonts will be built into PDF files.

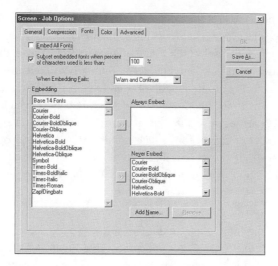

The Subset Embedded Fonts option causes Acrobat to embed in the PDF only those characters from a font that were used in the document rather than embedding the entire font. For example, if you used only 10 characters of a font in a headline, Acrobat would embed only these 10 characters of the font in the PDF file and skip the unused characters. This option provides you with a guarantee that your PDF file will look exactly as it was designed while keeping the file smaller than if you had embedded the entire font.

The Subset Embedded Fonts When Percent of Characters Used Is Less Than option lets you enter a percentage value at which Acrobat will subset the fonts. If the percentage used is at or above the percentage specified, Acrobat embeds the entire font family rather than subsetting only those characters used. This option provides a sliding scale for determining, based on the percent of fonts used, when Acrobat will subset fonts rather than embed them.

The When Embedding Fails drop-down list gives you the ability to choose what type of warning you will receive if Acrobat Distiller is unable to embed a certain font into a PDF file. If it is critical to you that fonts be embedded (for example, you are a graphic designer creating PDF files to send to a printer), you will want to select Cancel Job. In most cases, Distiller's inability to embed a certain font is not a big deal because of Acrobat's font-substitution capabilities. The Warn and Continue option is sufficient for most users.

4

In the Embedding section of the Fonts tab, you can select exactly which fonts to embed (if you prefer to select individual fonts rather than embedding them all). To embed or not embed only certain fonts, select the font you want to embed from the list on the left and drag it to the Always Embed list on the right. Similarly, if there are fonts you do not want to embed, select the font you do not want to embed and drag it to the Never Embed list on the right. The Embedding section also lets you choose which fonts you are viewing. The Base 14 category lists the fonts included with Acrobat. Click the drop-down menu to select other groups of fonts, such as those stored in your operating system. Acrobat lets you specify other font locations to add to this drop-down list by using the Settings, Font Locations command in the main Acrobat Distiller window.

The Color Tab

The Color tab of the Job Options dialog box allows you to specify whether you want Acrobat to convert the colors in your document (see Figure 4.5). This control is useful if you expect your PDF to be viewed only onscreen. You can convert the colors in your document to the Red, Green, and Blue (RGB) colorspace used by monitors and displays. If you are a graphic designer and have used specific colors in a file, select the Leave Color Unchanged option from the Color Management Policies drop-down list.

The Color Management Policies section of the Color tab applies to advanced graphic design and prepress users who are using color management workflows.

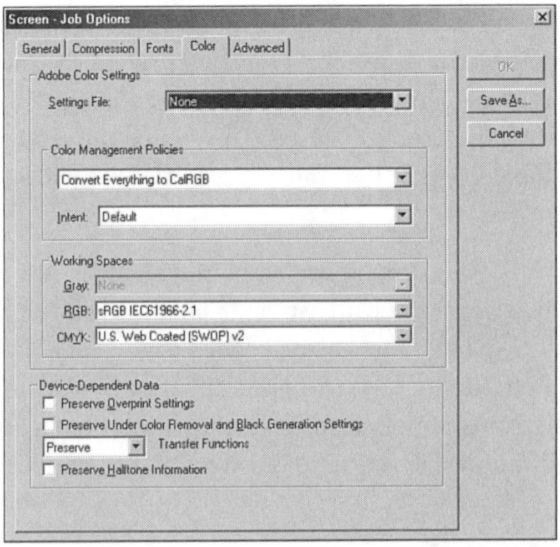

FIGURE 4.5

Use the Color tab to determine whether all graphics in a document (and any other colors specified in the pages of the document) should be converted to a certain color range.

The Advanced Tab

The Advanced tab of the Job Options dialog box is very specialized and is used for high-end electronic prepress work. Even most commercial printers will not have to adjust the settings on the Advanced tab.

Creating Personalized Settings for Distiller

After customizing any of the settings on the tabs in the Job Options dialog box, you'll want to save them for future use. Click the Save As button on the right side of the dialog box. This customized set of Job Options saves all the settings you have customized, including compression and font settings. These Job Options will be available any time you create PDF files.

Share your Job Options with others! Acrobat Distiller saves your customized Job Options in a Settings folder inside the Acrobat Distiller folder. You can share your customized Job Options files in this folder with co-workers and friends. These other people simply have to place your Job Options files in the same location on their machines—the Job Options Folder inside the Acrobat Distiller folder.

4

Security

Whenever you build a PDF file using Acrobat Distiller, you can limit those who can access the file. You can password-protect the entire file or limit access to certain functions such as editing or printing. To create security settings for files you want to run through Distiller, select Security from the Settings menu. The Security dialog box opens as shown in Figure 4.6.

Setting Passwords

In the Security dialog box, enable the Password Required to Open Document check box if you want to require that all viewers have a password before they can see the PDF files you create. Then enter a password.

If you require a password to open the document or limit any permissions (such as printing), you should always require a separate, unique password in the Password Required to Change Permissions and Passwords field. If a

separate password is not specified, anyone who can access the document
can also access the security settings and disable or change any passwords to
eliminate any restrictions you have placed on the document.

FIGURE 4.6

Use the Security set-
tings to password-pro-
tect your PDF files;
users without the pass-
word cannot open the
PDF file.

Permissions

Permission settings allow you to limit very specific functions within a PDF file. If you
want people to view your PDF file but not be able to print the document, enable the No
Printing option. To restrict people from editing the text or graphics within PDF files you
make, enable the No Changing the Document option. To keep others from copying text
and graphics from your PDF file into other programs, enable the No Content Copying
option. You can also disable others from adding or changing comments by selecting the
No Adding or Changing Comments option.

Any settings you make in the Security dialog box remain active until you return to this
dialog box and disable them.

Automating Distiller: Creating Watched Folders

Acrobat Distiller can look through the folders on your computer and convert any print-
to-disk PostScript or EPS files in these folders to PDF. Distiller can monitor multiple
folders simultaneously and can apply different settings to each of the different folders it
is monitoring. This batch processing feature can save you a great deal of time.

Task: Creating a Watched Folder

Watched Folders are any folders on your computer or network that Acrobat Distiller monitors to determine whether new files have been placed in them that should be converted to PDF. In this task, you learn how to create a watched folder.

1. Create two new folders on your computer named Make PDF for Print and Make PDF for Web.

2. Launch Acrobat Distiller.

3. Select Watched Folders from the Settings menu. The Watched Folders dialog box opens.

4. Click the Add button and navigate to the Make PDF for Print folder. Repeat this step to select the Make PDF for Web folder.

5. In the Watched Folders dialog box, select the Make PDF for Print folder by clicking it once and then click the Load Options button. Choose the Print Optimized Job Options.

6. Now select the Make PDF for Web folder by clicking it once and then click the Load Options button. Choose the Screen Optimized Job Options.

7. Change the Check Watched Folders Every option to 10 seconds. This setting tells Acrobat Distiller to look at each folder every 10 seconds to see whether there are any files to Distill.

8. In the Post Processing section of the Watched Folders dialog box, tell Acrobat Distiller to move the completed PostScript files to the Out folder when it's done processing. Figure 4.7 shows all these settings.

4

FIGURE 4.7

Use the Watched Folders dialog box to create a group of folders that Acrobat Distiller constantly reviews for files to be converted to PDF. Each folder can may have unique settings for converting files to PDF, including font, graphic compression, and security settings.

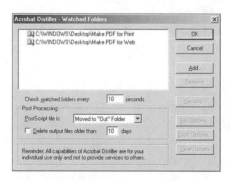

As you can see in Figure 4.7, the Watched Folders dialog box includes an advisory: You should not use the Watched Folders option to create one Watched Folder to share with all of your co-workers and friends who may not have Acrobat. This feature is designed to help you automate your personal use of Acrobat. If you have to create a single Watched Folder to share across your entire organization, Adobe has a separate product called Acrobat Distiller Server that is optimized to run on a file server. Acrobat Distiller Server allows everyone in your workgroup or company to offload the processing of PDF files to one centralized machine so that individual worker's computers are never tied up waiting for files to distill.

Download the PostScript print driver from Adobe's Web site to create PostScript print-to-disk files. The print driver allows you to print files to disk that can be processed using Distiller at a later time. The driver also allows you to create files on one computer but process them on another.

Creating PDF Files Without Launching Distiller

You now know how to convert individual files to PDF after they have been printed to disk. But it is not necessary to print files to disk and then launch Distiller every time you want to create a PDF file. In many cases, it is more convenient to select Acrobat Distiller as your printer so that the file will print to disk and convert to PDF all in one simple step.

To do this, open a document you want to convert to PDF. Select the Print command as you normally would when printing, and then select Acrobat Distiller as your printer. Distiller launches in the background when you print and creates a PDF file for you in one step. You can select which Job Options you want to use by selecting Page Setup before printing.

Depending on the size of the file you are "printing" to Distiller to create your PDF, this process may slow your computer considerably. If you have many files to process, you may want to consider printing the files to disk in the usual way and then use a Watched Folder to process them at some time when you do not need to use your computer. Although there is no way to schedule Distiller to work at a certain time, you can simply place all the files you want to process in a single folder and use the Watched Folders feature to process the files when you plan not to use your computer for some time.

Task: Creating PDF Files Without Launching Distiller

We can also automate Distiller to process PDF files, as we see in this task.

1. In its native application, open a document that you want to convert to a PDF file. For example, in Excel, open a publication.

2. Select the Print command and choose Acrobat Distiller as your printer. (You must have installed Acrobat on your computer to have this choice available.) Acrobat Distiller will be used to create the PDF file, but it will run in the background (you will not see it start).

3. Click the Properties button in the Print dialog box and then choose the Job Options you want to apply to the PDF file you are about to create (see Figure 4.8).

▲ 4. Click the Print button; your PDF file will be ready momentarily.

FIGURE 4.8

The Page Setup dialog box in most software packages allows you to access your default or customized Job Options settings. Get to this dialog box by clicking the Properties button in the Print dialog box after you choose Acrobat Distiller as your printer.

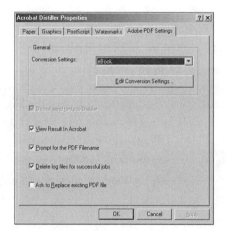

Summary

You should now understand how Acrobat Distiller is used to convert print-to-disk files and EPS files to PDF. You should also understand that Acrobat Distiller can be automated to efficiently convert a large number of files to PDF without your intervention. You know how to customize Distiller's settings for how fonts and graphics are handled and whether the files will have security settings applied. Finally, you should know how to save custom Job Options settings, share them with others, and apply them to files you are converting to PDF.

Workshop

In this hour, we have seen that Acrobat Distiller provides options for controlling the quality and size of PDF files. You may still have a few questions, so we've tried to answer some of the most common ones and have set up some exercises to wrap up this hour.

Q&A

Q Can Acrobat Distiller directly convert Word and other Microsoft Office documents to PDF?

A No. Acrobat Distiller works only with PostScript print-to-disk files and Encapsulated PostScript (EPS) files. To convert a Microsoft Office document to PDF, you must first create a print-to-disk file. You can streamline this process by selecting Acrobat Distiller as your printer when you print your original document. Or use the Convert to Adobe PDF button, discussed in Chapter 5.

Q When should fonts be embedded in PDF files?

A Fonts should be embedded only when you are creating high-quality PDF files for printing or if you are using very unique fonts—such as cursive and scripted fonts. In most other instances, you can dramatically reduce the file size of your PDF and still create high-quality PDF files with accurate-looking text without embedding the fonts thanks to Acrobat's font-substitution capabilities.

Q Do I have to create my own customized Job Options files?

A Not at all. In fact, the four preset Job Options files work well for the vast majority of Acrobat users.

Quiz

1. **When creating a PDF file that will be posted on a Web site, where quick downloading is more important than high-quality graphics, which Job Option should you select in Distiller?**

    a. Screen

    b. Print

    c. Press

    d. eBook

2. **Which are reasons that Acrobat Distiller might fail to convert a file to PDF?**

    a. The file is not a PostScript or EPS file.

    b. Colors in the graphics would not convert to RGB.

    c. Fonts in the file could not be embedded in the PDF file.

3. If you have a large number of documents to convert to PDF, which is the most efficient method to process them?

    a. Drag the folder containing the original documents into the Acrobat Distiller window so that the contents of the entire folder are converted to PDF files.

    b. Process all the files using the Screen Job Options setting because it is the fastest.

    c. Create multiple print-to-disk files and then process them all at once using a Watched Folder.

Quiz Answers

1. **a**   The Screen Job Options setting creates the smallest PDF files that are compatible with the most versions of Acrobat Reader. It is the best choice for PDF files that will be posted to a Web site.

2. **a and c**   Acrobat Distiller converts only PostScript and EPS files. All others will not convert directly to PDF. Acrobat Distiller will also fail to create PDF files if it cannot embed fonts (if you are using the Press Job Options) or if you have created a customized Job Options file that calls for Acrobat to halt the processing of a job if it cannot embed fonts into the PDF.

3. **c**   Acrobat Distiller's Watched Folders option makes it possible to process hundreds of files and to dictate exactly what settings will be used on the files as they are converted to PDF.

Exercises

Learn more about making PDF files with Acrobat Distiller by trying the following exercises.

1. Download the sample PostScript print-to-disk file DistillerTest.ps from the AcrobatIn24.com Web site and process it using each of the four preset Job Options. Why does it process on some Job Options settings but not others? Compare the quality of the PDF file created using the Screen settings with the PDF file created using the Print settings after you process the file using both settings.

2. Create several Watched Folders using a different Job Options setting for each. Customize the security settings for each Watched Folder to disable printing or to require a password to open the documents created.

HOUR 5

Easy PDF Creation for Microsoft Office Users

If you are a Microsoft Office user on the PC and need to create PDF files, you are in luck. Adobe includes a utility with Acrobat that automates the entire process of making PDF files. The utility is called PDFMaker, and it will automatically link MS Office applications and Acrobat Distiller so that you can create PDF files with one click of the mouse. This utility is available only on the PC and only for MS Office applications. It requires the full version of Acrobat because it simply streamlines the process of working with Distiller.

PDFMaker makes it easier to create PDF files, but still provides access to any customized Job Options you might have built using Acrobat Distiller. PDFMaker also provides the ability to automatically generate bookmarks and hyperlinks on the fly. These features make your PDF files much more usable without any extra work. For example, if you had an MS Word file and used the features in Word to create a table of contents (TOC), PDFMaker can automatically create hyperlinks from the TOC entries to the appropriate pages when it builds the PDF file. This automation can save you hours of time creating manual links with the linking tool Acrobat provides. In this hour, you'll learn about this and other great features that make Acrobat a great companion to MS Office.

In this hour, you'll learn the following:

- How to quickly create PDF files from MS Office applications
- How to automatically convert headings and titles into PDF bookmarks
- How to create security settings while building a PDF file
- How to use PDFMaker's default settings
- How to customize PDFMaker
- How to convert Microsoft Word styles to PDF bookmarks
- How to convert Microsoft Word hyperlinks to PDF links

PDFMaker—Creating PDF Files Easily

When you install Adobe Acrobat 5, the program looks to see whether MS Office or any of its component applications are installed on your computer. If it finds them, the setup program automatically installs PDFMaker. PDFMaker appears as a toolbar icon right within your office applications. The PDFMaker icon looks like a single PDF page, as shown in Figure 5.1. Adjacent to this icon is the Convert to PDF and Email icon, which is discussed later in this chapter. Open a document and click this icon to convert the document to a PDF file in one easy step. Clicking the icon creates the print-to-disk file, launches Distiller, and saves a PDF file for you—all in the background. You simply have to name the file and tell PDFMaker where to save the file.

FIGURE 5.1

The PDFMaker icon appears on the toolbar within MS Office applications such as MS Word.

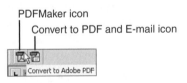

PDFMaker icon

Convert to PDF and E-mail icon

It is possible that PDFMaker is not installed in your Microsoft Office applications (Word, Excel, and PowerPoint). This occurs most frequently when you install a copy of Office (or any of its component programs) after you have already installed Acrobat. To access PDFMaker, you must have Office installed on your computer *before* you install Acrobat. If you upgrade to a new version of Office, you should reinstall Acrobat: Choose the Custom Install option and then select to only install PDFMaker.

Customizing Settings for PDFMaker

After PDFMaker is installed, you will also notice a new menu that appears within your Word and Excel programs—the Acrobat menu, which can also be seen in Figure 5.1. (Note that Word and Excel benefit from a new Acrobat menu option; PowerPoint also gets the PDFMaker icon. The Outlook and FrontPage components of the Office suite of applications don't benefit at all from Acrobat because they are not used to create documents.) This menu appears to the right of the Help menu at the top of your application window.

To modify the settings that will be applied when you use PDFMaker to create your PDF files, open the Acrobat menu and select the Change Conversion Settings command. A dialog box opens with five tabs, as shown in Figure 5.2. PDFMaker also provides options not found in Distiller, such as the capability to automatically create bookmarks and hyperlinks.

FIGURE 5.2

The PDFMaker dialog box allows for extensive customization of the settings used when creating PDF files from MS Office applications.

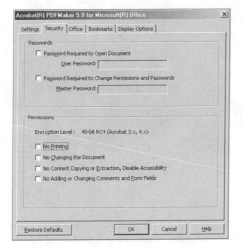

The Settings Tab

The Conversion Settings are identical to the Job Options discussed in Hour 4, "Creating PDF Files from Your Electronic Documents." You can choose the Job Options files to be used to create the PDF file from the drop-down menu. The Screen, Press, Print, and eBook settings, as well as any custom settings, are all available. For some reason, the Job Options are called Conversion Settings in this dialog box, but the two terms refer to the same thing. If you want to customize these settings, click the Edit Conversion Settings button, which is shown in Figure 5.2. You can then customize all the settings for font embedding and graphics without leaving the PDFMaker window. When you are done customizing these settings, they are saved as Job Options and can be used from both Acrobat Distiller and PDFMaker.

The Security Tab

The Security settings are identical to those discussed in Hour 4 (see Figure 5.3). You can require a password to open a document and can also restrict access to editing or printing a PDF file.

FIGURE 5.3

The Security tab of the PDFMaker dialog box.

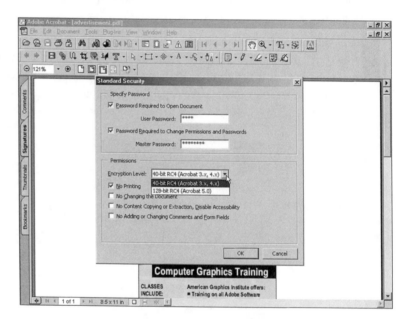

 Remember that if you restrict access to a certain feature, such as printing, you should always apply a Password to Change Permissions and Passwords. Otherwise, anyone can disable your restriction. Details regarding security are discussed in Hour 14, "Creating and Applying Digital Signatures."

The Office Tab

The Office tab in the PDFMaker dialog box is where PDFMaker begins to show some of the seamless integration between Office files and PDF files. The Office tab provides capabilities not normally found in other applications, such as the automatic conversion of links and comments.

Settings available on the Office tab include the following:

- **Convert Document Info** will take any information stored about the author and convert it into similar meta data that is stored within the PDF file. This information can be useful if you are conducting a search for PDF files authored by a certain person or created within a certain date range. *Meta data* is data stored within the PDF file that is useful when archiving or searching for a PDF file based on its author or creator. This data is not visible within the file itself.

- **Convert Cross-Document Links** will take any hyperlinks to other documents and convert them into hyperlinks in the PDF file.

- **Convert Internet Links** will create hyperlinks to Web sites within the PDF file using any hyperlinks that existed in the Word document.

- **Save Files Automatically** is a helpful option that automatically saves your MS Office documents before converting them to PDF files. PDFMaker requires that the Office files it is converting be saved before it will conduct the conversion. Enabling this option keeps you from seeing a warning dialog box requesting that you save the document each time you are converting to PDF.

- **Comments to Notes** will take any comments used in your Office files and convert them to PDF annotations. PDF annotations are covered in great detail in Hour 13, "Adding Comments and Annotations to PDF Files."

- **Text Boxes to Article Threads** converts MS Word text boxes to article threads. Article threads are a PDF feature used to create links between text that is broken into columns or across pages.

- **Page Labels** transfers any unique page numbering used in your Microsoft Word document over to the PDF file.

- **Cross-References & TOC Links** will create automatic hyperlinks within your PDF file from any cross-references or tables of contents built using these features within Word. As you will discover in Hour 10, "Using Links to Add Interactivity to PDF Files," creating links manually can be time consuming. The Cross-References & TOC Links option makes your Word documents much easier to read and use when they are distributed for onscreen viewing as PDF files.

- **Footnote & Endnote Links** creates links from footnote and endnote markers to the actual notes within the document.

The Bookmarks Tab

The Bookmarks tab allows you to build PDF bookmarks. Bookmarks are covered in Hour 2, "Navigating in PDF Files," and Hour 9, "Creating an Interactive TOC with

5

Bookmarks." Bookmarks make it easy to navigate to specific locations with a PDF file. The options on the Bookmarks tab allow you to automatically convert the styles and headings used in Word documents to PDF bookmarks (see Figure 5.4). For example, if you have applied a certain style to all your chapter titles throughout a book, you can have PDFMaker automatically build links to these titles as bookmarks.

FIGURE 5.4

The Bookmarks tab of the PDFMaker dialog box.

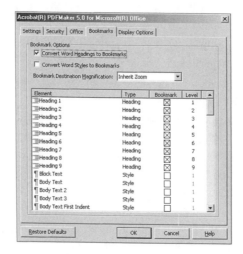

The Display Options Tab

When the PDF file is opened by a viewer, the settings made on the Display Options tab determine what a viewer will see. For example, you can specify what pages will display first and at what magnification. You can also specify whether hyperlinks will be visible and whether comments made in Word and Excel files will appear in the PDF file. These options vary between Word, PowerPoint, and Excel.

For example, if you created bookmarks, it makes sense to have the document open using the Bookmarks and Page option so that both the bookmarks and the page appear together. If you did not create bookmarks, select the Page Only option to display the document with only the page.

To force the PDF file to open on a specific page, use the Page Number option to input the page on which you want the document to open.

The Open Magnification option allows you to set the zoom percentage to use when the document first opens. Use this option to force the document to fit in the window or to open at its actual size.

The Link Appearance options allow you to control how links within the PDF file will be displayed. Will they be visible or invisible? Think about your reader's familiarity with links when making these selections. If your readers are not very familiar with the concept of onscreen hyperlinks, you may want to make them visible and an intuitive color such as blue. If you want the appearance of the document to not be altered by links, keep them invisible.

The Highlight portion of the Link Appearance section allows you to determine the appearance of a link at the time someone clicks it. These options do not affect the link itself, they only change the way the link looks when it is being clicked with the mouse.

The Comments area allows you to convert comments made by reviewers or editors into PDF annotations. If you have to distribute a document that is not yet complete to someone who does not normally work within Word, you can use a PDF file. Each reviewer's comments will be carried over into the PDF file. In Figure 5.5, you can see the highlighting and comments in the Word document. Figure 5.6 shows how these comments appear if you use the Comments area to carry them over into the PDF file.

FIGURE 5.5

Microsoft Word allows various editorial comments to be inserted along with text highlighting. These comments can be maintained or discarded when converting to a PDF file.

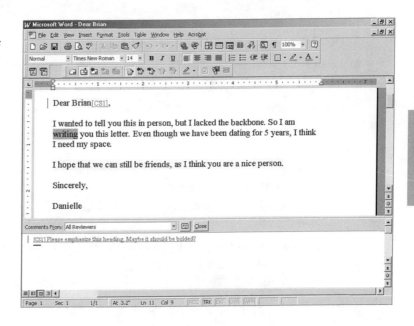

The Change Conversion Settings options are identical in Word and Excel. Excel also provides a Security tab, but none of the other features (such as conversion of styles to bookmarks or setting opening view percentages) are available in Excel.

FIGURE 5.6

The Word file shown in Figure 5.7 has been converted to a PDF file here. The highlighting remains visible, and the comments have been converted into PDF notes that appear next to the text to which they have been applied. The note color was selected in PDFMaker at the time of the conversion.

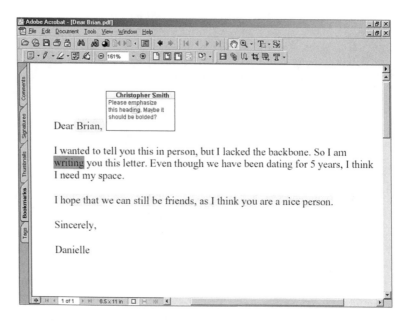

Task: Creating a PDF Using PDFMaker

In this task, we will use PDFMaker to convert a Word or Excel file to PDF in just a few quick steps.

1. Open an existing MS Word or Excel file.

2. From the Acrobat menu, select Change Conversion Settings. The PDFMaker dialog box opens to the Settings tab.

3. Select Screen from the Conversion Settings drop-down list and click OK. You will return to your Office document.

4. Select View Result in Acrobat from the Acrobat menu. This option causes the PDF file to launch in Acrobat after you have converted it.

5. Click the Convert to Adobe PDF button or select Convert to Adobe PDF from the Acrobat menu.

6. Name the file and specify the location where it should be saved.

Your files should open in Acrobat where you can view the results.

If you cannot find the Create Adobe PDF icon, either PDFMaker was not installed or you must change your preferences to tell it to appear. You can easily tell whether PDFMaker is installed by confirming that there is an

Acrobat menu to the right of the Help menu in the menu bar of the Office application. If there is indeed an Acrobat menu, but you do not see a Create Adobe PDF button, do the following: From the Tools menu, select Customize. Under the Toolbars tab, select PDFMaker 5.0 and click the Close button. The Create Adobe PDF icon will now appear in the toolbars of your Office applications.

Using the Convert to Adobe PDF and Email Option

All the settings used by PDFMaker also apply to PDF files that you intend to e-mail. Click the Convert to PDF Email icon (next to the Create Adobe PDF icon in the Office toolbar) to convert the current file to a PDF file. PDFMaker then tries to launch your e-mail software, create a new message, and attach the PDF file to the message. The e-mail option works well with Outlook and most major e-mail clients. However, I have encountered some e-mail clients with which this option does not work reliably. If the Convert to PDF Email icon does not work for you, simply create the PDF file as described earlier in this hour and attach it to an e-mail message like you would any other file.

Summary

You should now understand how PDFMaker can help ease the process of creating functional PDF files from MS Office applications—especially Word and Excel. You should understand how to automatically create PDF bookmarks from MS Word styles and headings and how to retain hyperlinks contained in your Word documents when they are converted to PDF files.

Workshop

Microsoft Office applications are some of the most commonly used applications on both the Macintosh and Windows platforms. It's no surprise that you will want to convert these files to PDF to preserve the formatting while making them available to a wider audience. We wrap up this hour by addressing some common questions about conversion of Office applications to PDF, and then we suggest some exercises to build your skills.

5

Q&A

Q Can PDFMaker automatically convert a large number of Word files to PDF?

A Not on its own. If you print multiple files to disk using the PostScript print driver, you can use Acrobat Distiller's Watched Folders feature to achieve this goal (see Hour 4 for more information on Acrobat Distiller). If you are still looking for something more automated, you can create a macro or script within Word to do this.

Q How can I be sure that the number of pages Word or Excel is telling me are in the document is the same as the number of pages I will get in my PDF file?

A Create Adobe PDF does not provide an option for determining the number of pages before converting. If you want an exact view of the page layout before printing, specify Acrobat Distiller as your printer. After selecting Acrobat Distiller as your printer, try the Print Preview option within Word or Excel (this option is available in the File menu). If there is still a discrepancy, install the Adobe PostScript print driver and set it to print to file. Check the print preview and then create a Print to Disk file and use Distiller to create the PDF file. This procedure will always give you the exact number of pages you see in your Print Preview window.

Q Why are some of the PDF files I create using PDFMaker larger than others?

A Remember to select your Conversion Settings (found by selecting the Change Conversion Settings command on the Acrobat menu). Settings for Screen and eBook produce smaller files than those made using the Print or Press settings.

Quiz

1. **PDFMaker works within which programs?**
   a. MS Office applications for Windows.
   b. MS Word using Macintosh and Windows.
   c. All MS Office applications regardless of platform.
   d. MS Word and WordPerfect.

2. **How do you set the first page that will be displayed when someone opens a PDF file that came from MS Word?**
   a. After converting the file to PDF, change the Display Options.
   b. Modify the Display Options within MS Word by selecting Change Conversion Settings from the Acrobat menu.
   c. It is not possible to set the opening page of a PDF file.
   d. Whatever page is on your screen when you convert your document to PDF will automatically become your default page.

Quiz Answers

1. **a** Only MS Office for Windows users benefit from PDFMaker. Even if you have only one of the components of Microsoft Office (such as Word), PDFMaker will still work for you.

2. **b** Although this could be modified after the fact inside Adobe Acrobat, it is much easier to set the default opening page within the Display Options of PDFMaker.

Exercises

Learn more about making PDF files with PDFMaker by trying the following exercises.

1. Download the sample MS Word file `WordTest.doc` from the `AcrobatIn24.com` Web site and convert it to PDF using PDFMaker. Try turning off and on the visibility of the hyperlinks. Also try creating bookmarks and setting PDFMaker to automatically open the PDF file showing both the bookmarks and the PDF page.

2. Create your own MS Word file and add comments, highlighting, and styles. Try various conversion options to see how these items will be converted when making a PDF using PDFMaker.

3. Take an MS Word document and click the Convert to PDF and Email icon. See how it creates a PDF file and automatically attaches it to a blank e-mail message using your default e-mail client software.

5

HOUR 6

Converting Paper Documents to PDF

In the past few hours, we've focused on converting digital documents to PDF files. Although this is a very useful process if you have electronic documents, it doesn't help if you have only a hard-copy version of the document. To remedy this situation, Adobe includes two features as components of Acrobat: Scan and Paper Capture. These features will let you convert paper documents into PDF files.

Paper documents can be converted easily to PDF files if you own a scanner. These converted documents are more than just a picture of the original document; you can convert them to fully searchable and editable files. With these features, Acrobat allows you to take the contents of a filing cabinet and digitally archive the papers as PDF files. Everyone in your organization can then search for specific documents right from their desktops—even if they have only the free Acrobat Reader software. Similarly, old product manuals and data sheets that previously had to be faxed to customers or co-workers can now be converted to PDF so that they can be viewed and searched online.

People viewing the file can print copies if necessary, or you can restrict access to the file to maintain security.

In this hour, you'll learn the following:

- How to quickly convert paper documents to PDF files
- How to make converted paper documents searchable
- Conversion settings for optimizing scanned PDF files
- How to work with Acrobat's Optical Character Recognition (OCR)
- How to correct OCR mistakes

About Acrobat Capture

The Paper Capture feature has been included with Acrobat for the past several versions. But for some reason, when Adobe first introduced Acrobat 5, they left out Paper Capture. If you purchased an early copy of Acrobat 5, you might not have Paper Capture. After hearing from many disgruntled customers, Adobe quietly started shipping Acrobat with this feature included again. If you have a version of Acrobat 5 without these features, Adobe has not left you hanging. The Acrobat plug-in that provides the Paper Capture features is available for download from Adobe's Web site for the Windows versions of Acrobat. Macintosh users have been shortchanged, but the feature exists in versions 3 and 4 of Acrobat for Macintosh or you can use the online service discussed later in this hour.

Scanning Documents into Acrobat

If you have a scanner attached to your computer, you can scan your paper documents directly into Acrobat. In most cases, your scanner will automatically work with Acrobat. But in case you are having trouble getting your scanner set up, we'll first cover the details of making Acrobat work with your scanner: Your scanner must use a TWAIN scanner driver (an industry-standard scanner driver used by almost every scanner). If your scanner does not have a TWAIN driver, you can use a Photoshop scanner plug-in if one is available for your scanner—simply place the plug-in for the scanner in the Acrobat Scan folder.

▼TASK

Task: Scanning Paper Documents into Acrobat

This task looks at how Acrobat makes it possible to scan a paper document directly into a PDF file if you have a scanner hooked up to your computer.

1. Start your scanner and place the first page in it.
2. In Acrobat, choose File, Import, Scan.

▼

3. Choose the scanner and a page format from the pop-up menus. The Device pop-up menu lists all TWAIN drivers and Photoshop Acquire plug-ins installed on your system. If you have more than one scanner, be certain to select the correct one.

4. Set the scan resolution to 300 dpi. This resolution makes certain that the scanned text will be clearly readable.

5. Click the Scan button.

6. For each additional page you want to scan, place the page in the scanner and click Next in the Acrobat dialog box.

7. When you're finished scanning pages, click Done. The scanned pages open in Acrobat.

▲

If you do not have a scanner hooked up to your computer, but want to try this feature, go to the Web site that was set up for this book: www.AcrobatIn24.com. Download the file samplefax.pdf from the Exercises folder. This file is a sample of text that has been scanned and converted into a PDF file.

All paper documents that have been scanned are considered graphics because they are pictures of the text. Use the Acrobat Zoom In tool to increase the magnification of the text that has been scanned. It should be clear that the text is merely a picture of the type. It is not actually text and cannot be edited.

To convert a large number of paper documents into PDF files, you will want to use a scanner with an automatic document feeder. The feeder allows you to stack a large number of documents into it so that each page is automatically scanned. Without an auto document feeder, you will have to manually place each page in the scanner and click the Scan button for each individual page.

Adobe also makes Acrobat products designed to scan hundreds or thousands of pages. If your project load includes that many paper documents to convert, you should consider either Acrobat Capture Server or Acrobat Messenger. These products focus on efficiently converting paper documents to PDF. These separate products do not ship with Adobe Acrobat, but they are discussed in Hour 1, "What's So Great About PDF?"

6

Converting Previously Scanned Files to PDF

Files you have scanned and saved on your computer as graphic files (such as TIFF images) can also be converted to PDF files. Acrobat 5 has simplified this process. Choose Open As PDF from the File menu and select the graphic file you want to convert to PDF. Acrobat will then handle the conversion for you. This process works for most popular scanned graphic file formats, whether they are photographs or images of text.

Making Scanned Files Searchable: OCR in Acrobat

After scanning a file into Acrobat, you can make the file searchable so that viewers can find specific passages of text within the file. You can make the file searchable without altering the original image—important if you are scanning a contract or legal document that should not be changed.

You can also convert the scanned bitmap text into electronic (vector) text that looks cleaner both onscreen and when printed. This process *does* alter the original image and is not a good idea for sensitive documents, such as contracts, that should not be changed. Whether you have altered the text or not, this process uses Optical Character Recognition (OCR) technology. It looks at the shapes of the characters in the scanned file, determines what characters and words they look like, and then converts them into searchable text. After text has been made searchable, it can be copied and pasted into other documents.

To make the scanned text file searchable, you will use the Paper Capture feature of Acrobat. Access this feature by selecting Paper Capture from the Tools menu. Use the Paper Capture dialog box (shown in Figure 6.1) to determine whether you want Paper Capture to work on only a certain page or on all pages within the document. If the PDF file contains pages that do not have to be searchable or edited, you can save time by selecting only certain pages.

Figure 6.1

The Paper Capture dialog box lets you specify which pages will be processed. Click the Preferences button to access the settings used in the process.

Setting Paper Capture Preferences

Click the Preferences button at the bottom of the Paper Capture dialog box to specify the language you want the OCR software to use. It is important to accurately set this option because Acrobat has to recognize characters and words within the scanned file if it is to process it successfully.

Within the Preferences dialog box, shown in Figure 6.2, you also can set the PDF Output Style. This setting determines whether Acrobat will alter the original scan. You have three choices:

- **Formatted Text & Graphics**: This option allows Acrobat to convert text to electronic vector-based text that is both searchable and editable. It will dramatically improve the quality of the scanned text, but be aware that mistakes could be made in the OCR process or that the PDF file could be manually edited. For these reasons, select this option only if it is acceptable for the PDF version of the file to vary slightly from the original scanned file. This option usually produces the smallest PDF file size.

- **Searchable Image (Exact)**: With this option, Acrobat creates an invisible, searchable layer of text that resides behind the original scanned file. The original image is not altered, but the file becomes searchable. This option typically creates the largest file size because it contains both a bitmap layer and a searchable text layer.

- **Searchable Image (Compact)**: This option applies compression to the original scanned image without altering the text. If you must keep the original file intact but still make it searchable, this is the best option because it helps reduce the file size of the PDF. It applies JPEG compression to color images and compresses one-bit images (that is, black and white images) using ZIP compression.

FIGURE 6.2

The Paper Capture Preferences dialog box is available if you have installed the Paper Capture plug-in. It allows you to configure how pages will be processed and what they will look like.

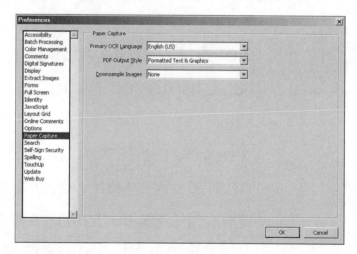

The Downsample Images option in the Preferences dialog box can be used to reduce the file size of a PDF file by lowering the resolution of any graphics it contains. Select a resolution from the drop-down menu. The lower the resolution, the lower the quality of the graphics—but the greater the reduction in file size.

The Paper Capture feature has a 50-page limit. If you need to scan more pages than this, you must process them in separate groups or purchase the Acrobat Capture software (formerly called Acrobat Capture Server).

Cleaning Up OCR Mistakes

If the Paper Capture feature isn't certain how to substitute words, it marks the words as Capture Suspects. You can leave suspects as they are, or use the Touch Up Text tool to correct them. Suspects are shown in the PDF file as the original bitmap of the word, as you can see in Figure 6.3. The suspect text is included on an invisible layer behind the bitmap of the word. This arrangement makes the word searchable even though it is displayed as a bitmap and even if you do not correct it. You will find Capture Suspects only if you use the Formatted Text & Graphics option as the PDF Output Style.

Task: Correcting Suspect Words on Captured Pages

▼ TASK

Acrobat is not always perfect in recognizing the words in a scanned document, so you will want to correct any problems manually, as we do in this task:

1. Select the Touch Up Text tool from the Tools palette.
2. Choose Tools, Touch Up Text, Show Capture Suspects from the menu bar. Suspect words will appear with a red border around them, as shown in Figure 6.3.

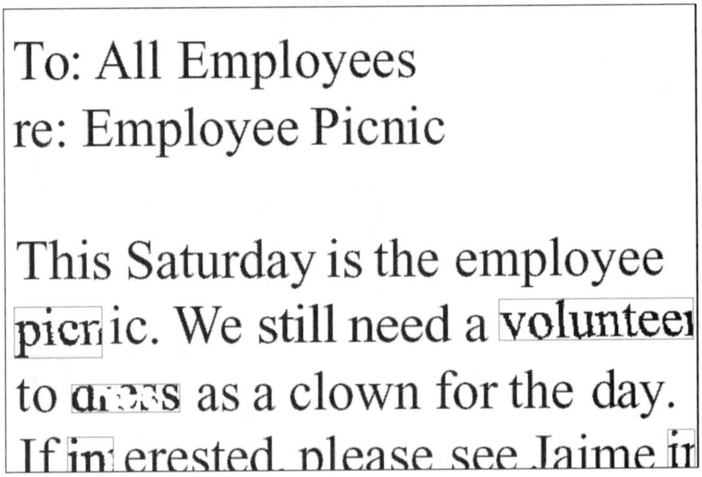

FIGURE 6.3
Capture Suspects appear with a red box around them and look bitmapped while the surrounding text appears clean.

To: All Employees
re: Employee Picnic

This Saturday is the employee picnic. We still need a volunteer to dress as a clown for the day. If interested, please see Jaime in

▼

▼   3. Choose Tools, Touch Up Text, Find First Suspect. Alternatively, you can press
     Ctrl+H (hold the Ctrl key and press the letter H) as a Windows keyboard shortcut
     to save yourself from navigating through those menu options. Macintosh users
     press Command+H. The first suspect word is highlighted and the original bitmap
     image will appear in the Capture Suspect window, as shown in Figure 6.4.

FIGURE 6.4

The Capture Suspects window magnifies the view of any selected word that Paper Capture was uncertain of how to process.

4. Compare the word on the page and the suspect word in the Capture Suspect window. Click Accept if the word is correct. The bitmap image is replaced by normal
   text. If you want to edit the already highlighted word onscreen, simply type the
   correction and click Accept. The next suspect word then appears within the
   Capture Suspect window. If you do not want to edit the word, click Next to leave
   the word as a suspect and move to the next suspect.

5. Repeat step 4 until all suspect words are corrected.

▲   6. Close the Capture Suspect window when you're finished reviewing suspect words.

After an image has been scanned, converted to a PDF file, and then captured, it can be
fully manipulated in Acrobat using all its editing tools. These tools are discussed in detail
in Hours 11, "Extracting Text and Graphics," and 12, "Editing a PDF File."

Paper Capture Online

If you are a Macintosh user or haven't downloaded the Paper Capture plug-in but still
want to use the Paper Capture utility, you must use Adobe's online service. To access this
feature, open the document you want to convert in Acrobat and then choose Paper
Capture Online from the Tools menu. Your Web browser will launch, and you will be
taken to the Paper Capture Online site, shown in Figure 6.5. After registering on your
first visit, your Web browser launches and takes you to a Web page to start the conversion process. Specify whether you want the file to reopen in Acrobat, to be e-mailed to
you, or to be sent to you as a URL (Web) link that you can download later.

6

FIGURE 6.5

Paper Capture Online is available from within Adobe Acrobat.

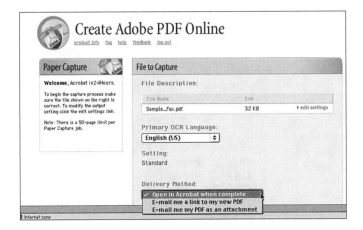

You must register for this service the first time you use it. Select the Try It for Free option and enter the required information. Be sure to select the Remember my Login option so that you don't have to enter this information again in the future. Adobe will e-mail you log-in instructions. When converting future documents by selecting the Paper Capture Online feature, Adobe's online services site will recognize you as a registered Acrobat user and allow you to easily upload files for conversion.

After registering, you can convert as many documents as you want from within Acrobat—but each document has a maximum length of 50 pages. If you have to change the conversion settings, as shown in Figure 6.6, click the Change Conversion Settings option in the initial window. If you use your login name and password to upload files from within your Web browser, you are limited to five file conversions. Files uploaded from within Acrobat are not subject to this limit.

FIGURE 6.6

You can change your conversion settings for Paper Capture Online to determine what type of PDF file will be provided.

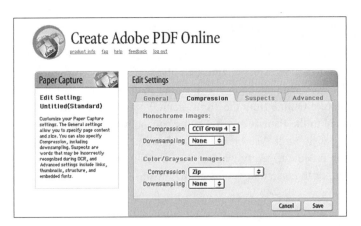

Paper documents you want to convert can also include files you have received electronically such as faxes (if you are using fax software). In this case, you can skip the instructions for scanning in the text but still perform the Paper Capture on the fax file.

Summary

In this hour, you've seen how to take paper documents and make them usable for the digital age. You can then e-mail these documents and store them electronically. You can also search through and edit them after using Acrobat's OCR features. All this goes to show that any document—whether it is digital or paper—can easily be converted to PDF for universal acceptance.

Workshop

Acrobat Capture has been through some changes and provides even more benefits than it did in its original incarnation. In this workshop, we'll address some of the questions associated with using Capture and then look at some projects that will help strengthen your understanding of these features.

Q&A

Q I had Paper Capture in my earlier version of Acrobat but I can't find it after upgrading to version 5.

A You must download the plug-in for this feature from Adobe's Web site. The Web site for this book (www.AcrobatIn24.com) provides a link to the plug-in or you can download it by going to Adobe's Web site at http://www.adobe.com/products/acrobat/papercaptureplugin.html.

Q Do I have to use Paper Capture on all files that I scan into Acrobat?

A No. Use Paper Capture only if you want to copy text from a PDF file that was scanned, or if you want to edit the file or make it searchable. If you simply want a picture of a paper document stored as a PDF file, you can save time bypassing the Paper Capture process.

Q After using Paper Capture, all the words still look jagged and bitmapped. How can I fix this?

A The Paper Capture Preferences dialog box lets you determine how Paper Capture will process a file. For example, it will clean up a file only if the Output Style is

6

set to Formatted Text & Graphics. Access the Preferences dialog box from the Edit menu or from the Paper Capture window.

Quiz

1. **Paper Capture requires that images are scanned directly into Acrobat.**
   a. True
   b. False

2. **Individual words appear jagged and bitmapped after using Paper Capture whereas the remainder of the document looks much better than the original file. What happened?**
   a. Paper Capture isn't always able to process some words, so it ignores them.
   b. Individual words that are not in its dictionary are not processed.
   c. Words that Paper Capture is not certain how to convert are marked as suspects. You can then confirm whether it processed them correctly or not.
   d. Paper Capture marks words as suspect that it does not recognize. These words are ignored when searching or copying and pasting text.

3. **How many times can you use the online version of Paper Capture?**
   a. Once
   b. Three times
   c. Five times
   d. An unlimited number of times

Quiz Answers

1. **b (False)**   Images can be scanned directly into Acrobat or they can be saved TIFF or other bitmap graphic files and then opened in Acrobat.

2. **c**   Paper Capture marks words as suspects if it is uncertain of how they should be processed. You can then use the Find First Suspect command to correct or confirm Paper Capture's choices.

3. **d**   You can use Paper Capture Online an unlimited number of times after you have registered as a user and as long as you are working from within Adobe Acrobat. If you try to access the feature directly from your Web browser, you can process only five files before you have to register and pay for the service.

Exercises

Learn more about converting scanned images to PDF files and making them searchable by trying the following exercises.

1. Download the `samplefax.pdf` file from the `www.AcrobatIn24.com` Web site or import your own scanned text file into a PDF. Process the file using Paper Capture. Try different preferences for converting the document, including Original Image and Formatted Text. Notice the improvement in clarity on the Formatted Text option compared to the Original Image option. Save the file and notice the file size, then repeat these steps with the Original Image option and notice the file size.

2. Register for Paper Capture Online at `http://papercapture.adobe.com` and try to process scanned text files online.

3. After converting a scanned text file to PDF, use the Show Capture Suspects command. Try using the Touch Up Type tool rather than using the Find First Suspect command. Both methods work when you want to correct text for which Paper Capture needs confirmation.

6

Hour 7

Converting HTML to PDF with Web Capture

Electronic and paper documents are not the only types of files you can convert to PDF. Adobe Acrobat also makes it easy to convert any HTML document or form into a PDF equivalent.

In this hour, you'll learn the following:

- How to quickly convert Web pages to PDF files
- Practical uses for converting HTML to PDF
- How to control the number of pages converted
- Conversion settings for images, text, and hyperlinks

HTML Versus PDF—What's the Difference?

Although HTML files are universally accepted, they are missing one important feature of Acrobat: the ability to look identical on every viewer's machine. Web pages look different on every computer based on the browser being used, the width of the window in which they are opened, and the preferences set by the viewer. For example, I can set my Web browser so that it doesn't show images if I want pages to load faster. I can also specify different fonts for my browser. These settings will change the way things look when I view a Web page. If I then move from my Windows computer to my Macintosh, things will look different again—even if I use the same browser on both platforms. And because my display on my Macintosh is much wider than my PC display, the lines of text do not end in the same location. Compare the Windows view of a Web page shown in Figure 7.1 to the Macintosh view of the same page in Figure 7.2.

FIGURE 7.1

A Web page viewed in a Windows browser typically has larger text and looks different than when it is displayed on other computers.

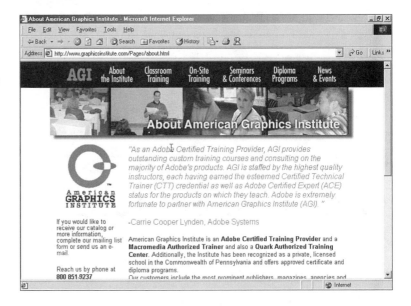

Unlike the HTML files that make up a Web page, PDF files do not differ from platform to platform or from browser to browser. Although you can make some display modifications to assist visually impaired readers, there are few modifications that can be made to a PDF file to affect its display. Fonts used in the design of a document are the same ones used to display the PDF file. Page sizes remain constant, even at different resolutions. And because PDF files can be viewed within a Web browser, they are a good alternative to HTML when you want to precisely control how a document will look on each viewer's screen and printer.

FIGURE 7.2

The same Web page shown in Figure 7.1 is shown here on a Macintosh browser where the display preferences have been modified.

FIGURE 7.2

The same Web page shown in Figure 7.1 is shown here on a Macintosh browser where the display preferences have been modified.

Why Use Web Capture?

Why bother converting HTML files to PDF files? It seems an unnecessary exercise, considering that HTML files are universally accepted and can be viewed by anyone who has a Web browser. Converting HTML to PDF might even seem counterproductive when you consider that Web browsers are more ubiquitous than the Acrobat Reader. But because viewing Web pages typically requires you to maintain a connection to the Internet, Acrobat Web Capture provides several enhancements that are not available within Web browsers:

- **Capturing a Complete Site:** To review all the pages on a site in a well-organized format, convert them to PDF. Use Web Capture to download an entire site—or as much of the site as you want to review. You can then review the site even when you are not connected to the Internet. I use this feature when traveling. If there are sites from which I need information, I use Acrobat to capture them so that I can read them when I'm on a plane or stuck in an airport.

- **Presentations**: Presentations involving Web sites can be problematic if your Web connection fails. You might not want to rely on your Internet connection to view the pages in front of an important audience. Acrobat Web Capture allows you to gather Web pages for a presentation so that you don't have to rely on an Internet connection while showing them. If you conduct presentations, be certain to read Hour 18, "Using Acrobat for Presentations: The Full-Screen Mode," which

7

describes some great features that will help you improve your presentations by using Acrobat.

- **Confirming What Is Contained on a Site**: Acrobat's role in the legal process continues to expand. If your organization is required to disclose certain information, this can often be accomplished by posting data to the Web. To confirm that this data has been posted, you can submit a PDF of the Web page to the regulatory authority. Similarly, if you want to show what was contained on a site at a specific point in time for legal purposes, you can convert the Web page to a PDF.

- **Sending a Site**: When you want to show someone what is contained on a Web page, you can e-mail them a URL. But because Web pages change so often, it is difficult to guarantee that what the other person sees is the same as what you viewed. To be certain that someone is seeing exactly what you intended to show them, convert the HTML page to a PDF file and e-mail it as an attachment. The file will be small, and you can be certain of the content.

- **Creating a Sample Site**: If you want to create a proof of a site but do not want to post it on the Web, you can design the pages in HTML and capture them as PDF pages. Use your Web design software, such as Adobe GoLive, FrontPage, or Dreamweaver. Build your pages and then use the Browse button in the Open Web Page window to locate the main page on your hard drive. Acrobat will convert the HTML file to PDF. You can then send the PDF file to others for review and comment. Remember that your reviewers can use Acrobat's annotation and comment tools to provide input on how the site should look.

> Before you use Web Capture, you must configure your Internet settings so that Acrobat knows how you access the Internet. To configure your Internet or proxy settings, choose Edit, Preferences, Internet Settings. In Windows, click the Connection tab in the Internet Properties dialog box, and provide the necessary information for your setup. If you are using a Macintosh, select the Use an HTTP Proxy Server option if you are using a proxy server to connect to the Internet. If you are not using a proxy server, leave this option deselected.

Converting HTML to PDF: Capturing a Page or Site

Like scanning a document into Acrobat, the process of converting an HTML page to a PDF file is pretty straightforward: You simply identify the site you want to capture, and Acrobat converts it to a PDF file.

Task: Converting a Web Page to PDF

In this task, you see how easy it is to convert an Internet Web page to a PDF file.

1. In Acrobat, choose File, Open Web Page. The Open Web Page dialog box opens.
2. Type the complete Web address (the URL) of the page you want to convert to PDF. If necessary, include the `http://` portion of the Web address.
3. Set the Levels option to 1, which causes only the exact page you are specifying to download, not any linked pages.
4. Leave all other buttons and checkboxes deselected or unchecked.
5. Click the Download button.
6. Wait while Acrobat downloads the Web page and converts it to PDF.
7. Save the file on your computer.

> You *must* enter the entire URL for the Web site you want to download, including the `http://`.

The time it takes Acrobat to complete the conversion processes varies greatly depending on the speed of your Internet connection and the complexity of the pages being downloaded.

When you display the Open Web Page dialog box as shown in Figure 7.3, you can see that there are a number of options available.

FIGURE 7.3

The Open Web Page dialog box provides options for converting HTML files and Web pages to PDF.

The Open Web Page options are described in the following list:

- **Browse**: This button allows you to select HTML files that are on your computer's hard drive rather than on the Internet. Use this button to locate HTML pages you have designed and convert them to PDF so that you can share them without having to post them to the Internet.

7

- **Levels**: This option determines how many connected pages Acrobat will convert. If this is set to 1, Acrobat captures only the page at the address you specify; it does not capture any linked pages. If you set this option to 2, Acrobat captures the page you specify and any pages to which there are links from the first page. If you set this option to 3, Acrobat captures the main address, any pages linked to the main page, and any pages linked to those pages. This concept is illustrated in Figure 7.4. The more levels you specify in the Open Web Page dialog box, the longer it takes to convert the site to PDF.

FIGURE 7.4

The first level of a site is the main page, the second level of a site contains any pages linked from the main site, and so on.

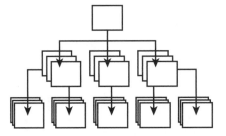

- **Only Get Pages Under Same Path**: This option downloads only Web pages that are below the URL you provide. For example, if you select http://www.adobe.com Acrobat will only download other pages at www.adobe.com; it will not download pages from other sites.
- **Stay on Same Server**: Pages that are linked from the main page may not be on the same server as the main page. Selecting this option forces Acrobat to download only those Web pages that are stored on the same server as the pages for the URL you select to download.
- **Get Entire Site**: This option causes Acrobat to download all pages on the Web site, rather than a specified number of levels.

Downloading an entire site can take a significant amount of time and use up a large amount of hard disk storage space; this option might even cause your computer to crash. Some Web sites consist of thousands of pages. Use the Get Entire Site option only when you are certain that the number of pages involved in the site is reasonable.

Conversion Settings

Click the Conversion Settings button in the Open Web Page dialog box to specify your preferences for converting a Web page to a PDF document. The Conversion Settings dialog box that opens has two tabs: Page Layout and General.

The Page Layout Tab

The Page Layout of the Conversion Settings dialog box is where you set the dimensions of the PDF file, along with margins, orientation, and scaling of the Web pages being converted to PDF documents. Figure 7.5 shows this tab. Although the default page size is a U.S. Letter page (8-1/2 by 11), you may want to adjust this page size based on the design of the HTML pages you are converting. Many Web pages are designed to look good on your monitor, and not on paper. To do this, designers often create pages that are short and wide rather than tall and thin. Many other pages are not built by professional designers and might include long flowing text all on one page.

FIGURE 7.5

The Page Layout tab in the Conversion Settings dialog box allows you to specify the size of the PDF page after it has been converted from HTML.

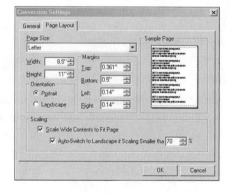

To better convert the varying types of pages you might encounter on the Web, use the following options on the Page Layout tab of the Conversion Settings dialog box:

- **Page Size**: You have the option of selecting many standard page sizes from the drop-down menu, or you can type your own page size in the Width and Height fields.

- **Orientation**: You might want to make changes to the orientation of the page. When you are converting short and wide pages that do not have a great deal of content, select Landscape rather than Portrait for best results.

- **Scaling**: Scaling makes it possible to reduce wide pages to better fit onto traditional printed pages. Enable this feature by selecting the Scale Wide Contents to

7

Fit Page option. As an alternative to manually switching between the Portrait and Landscape orientation options, enable the Auto-Switch to Landscape if Scaling Smaller Than option, and type a value in the blank (the default is 70%). If Acrobat encounters a page that requires scaling the width below the percentage you've specified, Acrobat will automatically create that page in landscape mode. If this option is not selected and the contents of the page being converted exceed the paper size, Acrobat ignores the preferred paper size and resizes the width and height to fit the page.

- **Margins**: The fields in this section of the dialog box specify the margins for the top, bottom, left, and right borders of the page. These values should correspond to the margins you will need if you are printing this PDF. Even if you are not printing the PDF, the file will be easier to read if you have margins of at least 1/4 inch on all sides.

Task: Defining a Page Layout

Acrobat lets you define the look and appearance of PDF pages converted from HTML. In this task, we'll look at the options.

1. Open Acrobat and select File, Open Web Page. The Open Web Page dialog box opens.
2. Click the Conversion Settings button. The Conversion Settings dialog box opens.
3. Click the Page Layout tab. A sample page with the current settings applied appears on the right side of the dialog box. If you are using a Macintosh, this sample page does not appear.
4. Select a page size from the Page Size drop-down menu.
5. Select either Portrait or Landscape orientation.
6. Type margin values for all the edges of the page.
7. Click OK to close the Page Layout dialog box.
8. Click Download in the Open Web Page dialog box and watch Acrobat create PDF files based on the page settings you've specified.

You can convert Web pages to Adobe PDF files by dragging a link into the Acrobat window or by dragging an HTML file located on your system onto the Acrobat icon.

The General Tab

You can use the General tab of the Conversion Settings dialog box to specify how certain elements will be converted to PDF. Figure 7.6 shows the General tab of the Conversion Settings dialog box.

FIGURE 7.6

The General tab of the Conversion Settings dialog box allows you to determine how the PDF file will look after it's converted.

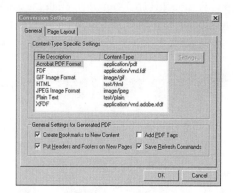

The Conversion Settings options allow you to control how your PDF file will be built when it's converted from HTML. Here are some of the options in the Conversion Settings dialog box:

- **Create Bookmarks to New Content**: This option creates an Acrobat bookmark for each downloaded Web page using the page's title as the bookmark name. If the page has no title, Acrobat uses the URL as the bookmark name. Bookmarks are covered in detail in Hours 2, "Navigating in PDF Files," and 9, "Creating an Interactive TOC with Bookmarks."

- **Add PDF Tags**: This option tells Acrobat to store a structure in the PDF file that corresponds to that of the original Web pages. This option should be selected if you are creating a PDF that will be read using screen-reading software that assists the visually impaired. The structure informs the screen-reading software of the sequence in which the elements on the page should be read.

- **Put Headers and Footers on New Pages**: This option adds a text header and footer on every page of the PDF file. The header shows the title of the Web page, and the footer shows the URL, the page sequence in the downloaded set, and the date and time of the download.

- **Save Refresh Commands**: This option tells Acrobat to save a list of all the URLs that were downloaded. Acrobat will use this list to refresh these pages if the online versions change. This option must be selected if you plan for Acrobat to update PDF pages whenever the Web site on which they were based changes.

7

Content–Type Specific Settings

The Content–Type Specific Settings list box at the top of the general tab of the Conversion Settings dialog box allow you to specify how text will look when it is converted, what fonts are used, and what colors will be used for text and links.

In the list of File Descriptions, select HTML and then click the Settings button. The HTML Conversion Settings dialog box that opens allows you to specify layout and font details by selecting options in the Layout and Fonts tabs (see Figure 7.7).

FIGURE 7.7

Use the HTML Conversion Settings dialog box to specify how text, links, and background colors will appear when converted to PDF.

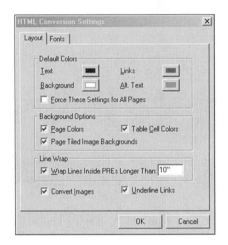

The Layout Tab

Following are the options you can specify in the Layout tab when converting Web pages to PDF:

- **Text, Background, Links, and Alt. Text**: Click the color swatch to the right of any of these options to set the default colors for text, page backgrounds, Web links, and text that is used when the image is unavailable.

- **Force These Settings for All Pages**: This option uses the colors you selected on all Web pages. If you do not select this option, the colors you specified are used only when colors have not been defined inside the Web page being converted to PDF.

- **Background Options**: Web pages can include background colors and background (tiled) images. Deselect these three options to disable the conversion of colored backgrounds on pages or colors within table cells. Disabling these options will make your PDF file easier to read when it is printed; note that deselecting any of these options will change the appearance of the page so that the PDF file is no longer an exact match of the Web page.

- **Wrap Lines Inside PREs Longer Than**: This option wraps preformatted text that is longer than the length you specify. Use this option if the Web page you are converting has long lines of preformatted text.

- **Convert Images**: This option tells Acrobat to include any images on the page when it converts the page to PDF. If you do not select this option, images in the Web page are replaced by a colored border around a blank box when converted to PDF.

- **Underline Links**: This option tells Acrobat to underline Web links in the text on the page that is being converted.

The Fonts Tab

The Fonts tab of the HTML Conversion Settings dialog box is used to specify fonts for body text, headings, and preformatted text when it is converted from a Web page to PDF. Figure 7.8 shows this tab of the dialog box. Select fonts for body text, headings, and preformatted text by clicking the Choose Font button to the right of each of these categories of text.

The Embed Platform Fonts option tells Acrobat to take the fonts used on the pages being converted and build them into the PDF file. This option assures you that the text will always appear using the fonts you specify.

FIGURE 7.8

Use the Fonts tab of the HTML Conversion Settings dialog box to specify what fonts will be used on Web pages converted to PDFs.

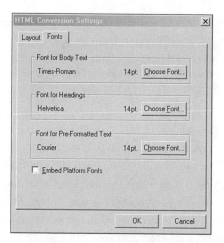

Setting Web Capture Preferences

7

Preferences allow you to customize the process of converting Web pages to PDF files. You set your Web Capture preferences in a separate dialog box; they are not a part of the general preferences for the application. Open the Web Capture Preferences dialog box by selecting Edit, Preferences, Web Capture (see Figure 7.9).

FIGURE 7.9

The Web Capture Preferences dialog box controls how frequently Acrobat will check for modified images and in which program Web links will open when they are clicked in a PDF page.

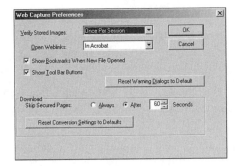

- **Verify Stored Images**: Acrobat can check whether images have changed on a Web site and redownload them if they have changed. Choose an option from the drop-down list box to specify how frequently Acrobat should check whether images on a Web page have been modified.

- **Open Web Links**: When you click on an Internet hyperlink in a PDF page, you can choose whether the linked page opens in Acrobat or in your Web browser. Select the appropriate option from the drop-down list box.

The Web links open based on the setting in the Web Capture Preferences dialog box. You can Shift+click a Web link to open the link using the opposite of what was selected in the Web Capture Preferences dialog box. If your Web Capture preferences are set to open Web links in Acrobat, a plus sign appears next to the hand tool when you move the cursor over a Web link. If your preferences are set to open Web links in a Web browser, a *W* appears with the hand tool.

- **Show Bookmarks When New File Opened**: Enable this option to automatically open the bookmarks pane when you open a new document that was created from a Web page. Bookmarks are always created if you selected them in the Conversion Settings dialog box, but they are displayed only if you select this option. You can also open the bookmarks manually from the Window menu.

- **Show ToolBar Buttons**: This option displays a button along the top of the Acrobat window that is a shortcut to the Open Web Page dialog box (see Figure 7.10).

- **Reset Warning Dialogs to Default**: This button turns on any Web Capture warning dialog boxes that may have been disabled. The dialog boxes would have been disabled by enabling the Don't Show Again option when the warnings were initially displayed.

- **Skip Secured Pages**: This option causes Acrobat to skip pages that are password protected rather than having them sit on your computer indefinitely awaiting a password. You can choose Always if you never want Acrobat to bother converting them to PDF files or choose After and specify a time period to have Acrobat skip them after a specified time period when downloading multiple levels of a Web site. If you select the After option, Acrobat displays a password dialog box that times out and skips the secured pages after the specified number of seconds.

- **Reset Conversion Settings to Default**: Click this button to change all the conversion options back to their original settings.

Figure 7.10

The Open Web Page button is displayed in the toolbar.

Locating Web Links Within a Document

Even if your PDF was not created from a Web page, Acrobat can still automatically convert URLs to Internet hyperlinks. To do this, select Tools, Locate Web Addresses, Create Web Links from URLs in Text. Acrobat will scan the text of the open PDF file; any Web addresses it finds will become Web links you can click in Acrobat to go to their destination. You can also clear all Web links by selecting Tools, Locate Web Addresses, Remove Web Links from Document. This option removes any Web hyperlinks from the document, whether they were added with the linking tool or automatically when the file was converted from HTML to PDF.

Adding PDF Pages from Web Links

You can convert Web links within a PDF file into PDF pages. You can add these pages to your current document by selecting Tools, Web Capture, View Web Links. This menu option opens the Select Page Links to Download dialog box which provides a list of all the Web links within the current document (see Figure 7.11). Select an individual link from the list and click Download to download that page and append the page to the current PDF document. If you want to download all the links, click Select All and then click

7

Download. You can also download the all links within a PDF file by selecting Tools, Web Capture, Append All Links on Page.

FIGURE 7.11
The Select Page Links to Download dialog box lists all the Web links in the current PDF document.

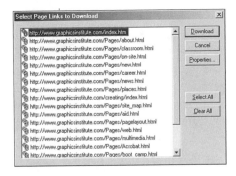

The Append Web Page command, found on the Tools, Web Capture, Append Web Page menu, allows you to select any Web page—even if it is not linked to the current page—and convert it to a PDF page in your current document. Enter the URL and click download.

Summary

After working through this hour, you should understand how to convert individual Web pages and complete Web sites into PDF pages. If you download individual Web pages, you should be able to convert additional Web pages to PDF—either individually or as a group. You should know how to control the appearance of Web links and text within a PDF document that has been converted from a Web page.

Workshop

Web Capture is a robust feature of Acrobat that lets you use HTML pages in a variety of settings. In this workshop, we will review the controls and options available for these converted pages; then we'll do a few exercises to improve your understanding of the conversion process.

Q&A

Q Does Web Capture work only with pages located on the Internet?

A You can use Web Capture to convert any type of HTML page to PDF—whether the page is on the Internet, on a company intranet, or on your hard drive. Use the Browse button in the dialog box to select the HTML file if it is on your computer or a local area network. Internet and intranet pages can be accessed the same way.

Q **Can I control the color of links, text, and the page background, even if they were already specified in the Web page I am converting?**

A Yes. These settings are accessed in the Conversion Settings dialog box by selecting HTML from the Content-Type Specific Settings list and then clicking the Settings button.

Q **How many levels of a Web site should I capture if I do not know how large it is and I am concerned about the size of the file and the time it might take to download?**

A Start by selecting one or two levels. From there, open the PDF version of the Web site and manually click links you want to follow. These links will open as new PDF pages as long as your Web Capture preferences are set to have them do so. If you select more than two levels, you should choose the Stay on Same Server and Only Get Pages Under Same Path options in the Open Web page dialog box. These options will keep your PDF file from following any links that go to other Web sites.

Quiz

1. **How does Acrobat determine the page size of Web pages that are converted to PDF?**

   a. Acrobat forces all pages to U.S. Letter size when converting.

   b. Acrobat will shrink all Web pages to whatever size is selected as your paper in your printer.

   c. Acrobat uses the Page Layout specifications from the Conversion Settings dialog box.

   d. Acrobat used the options you specify in the Page Size dialog box, which appears each time you convert a Web page to a PDF.

2. **Can I disable the text on the top and bottom of converted pages that lists the URL, date downloaded, and title of the page?**

   a. No. This text always prints on converted pages.

   b. Yes. Turn off Headers and Footers in the Conversion Settings dialog box.

   c. Yes. Disable this option when printing in the Print dialog box by disabling the Comments option.

   d. Yes. Turn off the Show Bookmarks option to disable these textual additions.

7

3. **When I input a URL for Web Capture, why doesn't it download any pages—even if the same URL opens without problems in my Web browser?**

   a. Your Web Capture settings probably do not specify how to connect to the Internet.

   b. Your Internet settings within Acrobat are probably not set correctly.

   c. Acrobat cannot download Web pages at the same time your Web browser is running.

   d. Your Conversion Settings are not set to handle HTML files correctly.

Quiz Answers

1. **c**   Acrobat uses the Page Layout specifications from the Conversion Settings dialog box to determine the size of the Web page when it is converted to PDF.

2. **b**   Yes, turning off Headers and Footers in the Conversion Settings dialog box will stop Acrobat from adding them to Web pages that are converted to PDF.

3. **b**   If your Internet settings within Acrobat are not set correctly, Acrobat will not be able to download pages. These settings usually do not have to be configured if you already had an Internet connection established before you installed Acrobat. If you set up your computer to access the Internet *after* installing Acrobat, you may have to set up Acrobat's Internet settings. To do so, choose Edit, Preferences, Internet Settings.

Exercises

Practice downloading Web sites and converting them to PDF files to improve your understanding of the Web Capture features.

1. If you have a high-speed Internet connection (DSL, cable modem, or T-1 line), try downloading several layers of Web sites from www.MSNBC.com.

2. If you are a Web designer, take a local copy of a Web site from your computer and convert it to PDF by selecting Open Web Page and clicking the Browse button to locate the index page on your hard drive. Notice how all the linked items are built into one easy-to-send package! Compare the file size of the PDF to the original HTML file and all the linked images.

3. Open and convert an HTML page to PDF using Acrobat. Open the View Web Links dialog box (from the Tools, Web Capture menu). Try opening various links both within Acrobat and within the PDF file.

PART III

Using and Adding Navigational Tools to PDF Files

Hour

Hour 8

Managing Pages with Thumbnails

Thumbnails are miniature images of the document pages within a PDF file. They can be used to rearrange pages, combine pages from different documents, and navigate within a PDF file. This hour will help you better manage your PDF files using thumbnails.

In this hour, you'll learn the following:

- How to embed thumbnails into a document
- How to rearrange the page order in a PDF file
- How to create security settings while building a PDF file

What Are Thumbnails?

Thumbnails provide miniature versions of the pages in a PDF document. They are like having your document pages reduced to the size of a postage stamp. They can be used to see which portion of a page you are viewing.

You can use thumbnails to change the magnification on a page, switch to different pages, rearrange page order, delete pages, add pages, and even merge pages from different PDF documents.

Open a view of the thumbnails in a document by clicking the Thumbnails tab on the left side of the screen. This part of the screen is referred to as the Navigation pane; the tabs in the pane are referred to as *palettes* (see Figure 8.1).

FIGURE 8.1

Thumbnails are part of the Navigation pane and are located along the far left side of a document page.

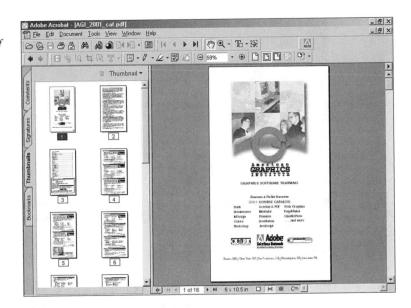

There is more than one way to access the Thumbnails palette. In addition to clicking the Thumbnails tab in the Navigation pane, you can also click the Show/Hide Navigation Pane button in the toolbar at the top of the screen (see Figure 8.2) and then select the Thumbnails palette, or you can select Window, Thumbnails.

FIGURE 8.2

The Show/Hide Navigation Pane button in the toolbar provides another way to access the Thumbnails and other navigational palettes.

Embedding Thumbnails in a PDF File

Acrobat version 5 automatically displays thumbnails for PDF files—even if the thumbnails are not built, or embedded, into the PDF file. This was not always the case with Acrobat. In earlier versions, you had to create the thumbnails in a document if they had not been embedded. When sending PDFs to readers who only use Acrobat version 5, there is no reason to embed thumbnails—they may take a few seconds to display, but Acrobat 5 generates thumbnails whenever the palette is opened. But if you are sharing files with people who use version 4 or earlier, you may want to include thumbnails in the PDF file by embedding them. When considering using thumbnails, realize that they will add upwards of 3K per page to the size of a PDF file. If your goal is to create the smallest possible PDF file, you do not want to embed thumbnails.

Task: Embedding Thumbnails in a PDF File

In this task, we'll look at how you actually embed thumbnails in a PDF file.

1. Open a PDF file that contains multiple pages.

2. Open the Thumbnails palette by clicking the tab of the same name in the Navigation pane.

3. Click the down-arrow icon in the upper-right corner of the Thumbnails palette to access the Thumbnails menu and select Embed All Thumbnails (see Figure 8.3).

4. Save the PDF document.

FIGURE 8.3

Palettes in the Navigation pane have menus you can access by clicking the down-arrow icon.

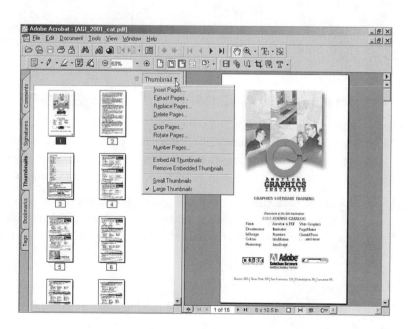

The Thumbnails palette is not stuck in place! If you want to move it to another location on your screen, click and hold the Thumbnails tab on the far left of the Acrobat window. Drag the tab to a new location on your screen and drop it; the Thumbnails palette becomes a floating window you can position anywhere on your screen. Be careful if you close it after making it a floating window because you will no longer find it in the Navigation pane. You will have to open it by going to the Window menu and choosing Thumbnails.

As an added bonus, you can take any other tab from the Navigation pane and merge it with other tabs that have been dragged out as floating windows. An example of this trick is shown in Figure 8.4. To move the floating windows back into the Navigation pane, drag the tab from the floating window and drop it back onto the Navigation pane.

FIGURE 8.4

Any of the tabs from the Navigation pane can be dragged into its own window; here, the Thumbnails and Bookmarks palettes have been joined into a new floating window.

Using Thumbnails for Navigation

You can use thumbnails to move quickly to a specific page in a PDF document. Click once on a thumbnail icon in the Thumbnails palette to move to that page. The thumbnail for the page you are viewing has a red box around the portion of the page that is visible on your screen, and the page number beneath the page's thumbnail is highlighted.

When you have displayed a specific page using the thumbnails, you can then use the thumbnails to change the magnification. The red navigation box outlining the visible area of the page also controls the zoom level for the page. Macintosh users will see a black box instead of a red box. In the lower-right corner of the box is a small, square handle. Click and drag this handle towards the upper left to increase the zoom on the page. Drag to the lower right of the thumbnail to decrease the magnification. You can also click anywhere on the thumbnail on the page, and Acrobat will change the navigation to focus on the portion of the page you clicked.

If only a portion of a page is visible because you are at an increased magnification, clicking on another potion of the same thumbnail page causes the new portion of the page to become visible in your window.

> When working with large files, you might find yourself doing quite a bit of scrolling—even with the thumbnails. To make it easier to work with larger documents, Acrobat allows you to vary the size of your thumbnails. From the Thumbnails menu in the upper-right corner of the Thumbnails palette, select Small Thumbnails. This command displays more thumbnail pages in the same area and can eliminate a great deal of scrolling.

Rearranging Page Sequence

It is possible to change the reading order of the pages in a PDF file by dragging the thumbnails of the pages.

Task: Rearranging Page Order Using Thumbnails

Thumbnails make it simple to set the sequence of your pages. In this task, we'll see how to do that.

1. Open a PDF file that contains multiple pages.

2. Click a thumbnail page that you want to relocate to a different position. Hold the mouse button down.

3. Drag the page to a new location within the Thumbnails palette. The mouse pointer changes to show a solid arrow with a page icon attached to it.

4. When the thin vertical line appears adjacent to the thumbnail page where you want to locate the page, release the mouse button (see Figure 8.5). Acrobat moves the page to the new location. If the pages are viewed one on top of the other (or "stacked"), the line that appears between the pages is horizontal.

FIGURE 8.5

Dragging a thumbnail to a new location in the palette is an easy way to rearrange pages in a PDF file.

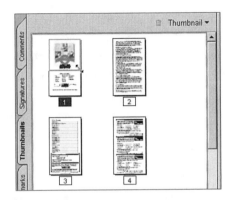

Deleting Pages

To delete pages using thumbnails, click once on the page you want to delete and then click the trash-can icon at the top of the Thumbnails palette. Acrobat asks you to confirm that you want to delete the selected page.

> To select a group of consecutive thumbnail pages, hold down the Shift key and click once on the first and last pages in the range you want to select. For nonconsecutive pages, hold down the Ctrl key while clicking the individual pages. Macintosh users should hold down the Cmd key instead of the Ctrl key. You can use these keyboard shortcuts to select multiple pages whether you want to rearrange the page order or delete multiple pages from a document.

You can also delete the selected pages by pressing the Delete key on your keyboard instead of dragging the thumbnails to the trash-can icon.

Task: Deleting Pages Using Thumbnails

In this task, we'll take a look at how easy it is to delete pages using thumbnails.

1. Open a PDF file that contains multiple pages.

2. Click the Thumbnails tab in the Navigation pane to make the Thumbnails palette visible.

3. Click once to select the thumbnail of a page you want to delete. Alternatively, select multiple thumbnail pages to delete using the Shift, Ctrl, or Cmd key.

4. Click the trash-can icon in the Thumbnails palette and respond to the confirmation dialog box to deleted the selected page or pages.

After you delete a page, you cannot recover it. The Undo command does not work when deleting pages, so be careful when using this command!

Merging Pages Between Documents

Acrobat allows you to combine several PDF files into one document. You can combine files by dragging and dropping the thumbnails between documents. Open two PDF documents and select Window, Tile, Vertically to display both documents onscreen simultaneously. Make certain that the Thumbnails palette is visible in both document windows. Then drag the thumbnails of the pages you want to merge from one window to the other. Acrobat copies the pages from the original document (leaving them in place) and places duplicates of those pages in the combined document.

Windows users can drag thumbnails between files only when the Thumbnails palette is located in the Navigation pane. You cannot merge documents by dragging thumbnail pages if you have pulled the Thumbnails palette out from the Navigation pane into its own floating window.

Using Menu Commands and Context Menus

Acrobat also makes it possible to delete pages and merge PDF files together using the pull-down menus rather than the thumbnails.

Inserting Pages

The Insert Pages command is found in the Document menu. You can use this command to merge pages between PDF files as an alternative to dragging thumbnail pages between documents. After opening the document that will contain all the combined pages, choose Document, Insert Pages from the menu bar. In the Insert Pages dialog box shown in Figure 8.6, select which pages from the new document will be inserted and select the option that corresponds to where you want the pages located.

Deleting Pages

The Delete Pages command is also found under the Document menu. Use the Delete Pages dialog box that opens to permanently remove specific pages from a PDF file. Enter the page or pages to be removed, and Acrobat will delete them. In the example shown in Figure 8.7, a single page is targeted for deletion.

FIGURE 8.6

The Insert Pages dialog box allows you to select a PDF file that can be merged with another PDF that is already open.

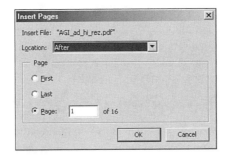

FIGURE 8.7

Use the Delete Pages dialog box to choose pages to be removed from a PDF.

Context Menus

Windows users are familiar with using the right mouse button to display context-sensitive menus. Macintosh users know to press the Ctrl key as they click to obtain the same context-sensitive options. In Acrobat, right-clicking (or Ctrl+clicking) provides a wide range of options when working with document thumbnails. With the Thumbnails palette open, right-click a thumbnail page that you would like to edit. A pop-up menu appears on the page as shown in Figure 8.8. All the options discussed in the preceding sections are also available from the context menus: inserting pages, deleting pages, and several other options. The following commands are discussed in Hour 12, "Editing a PDF File," and are available from the thumbnail context menus:

- Insert Pages
- Extract Pages
- Replace Pages
- Delete Pages
- Crop Pages
- Rotate Pages
- Number Pages—Use this command to establish sections (such as an appendix) in a document that might use a different numbering scheme.
- Print Pages—Use this option to select multiple pages (even nonconsecutive pages) and print them.

- Embed All Thumbnails—This option increases the size of the PDF file but makes it possible for users of older versions of Acrobat to see thumbnails.

- Remove Embedded Thumbnails—This option helps reduce the file size by eliminating thumbnails, but readers using older versions of Acrobat cannot see thumbnails unless they have the full version of Acrobat and know how to create thumbnails manually.

- Small Thumbnails—Use this option to change the size of the thumbnails so that you can minimize scrolling in a long document when using thumbnails for navigation.

- Large Thumbnails—If you are using thumbnails to select portions of a page to view, this option makes it easier to identify page elements in the thumbnails.

The final four options in this list are identical to the commands from the Thumbnails palette menu.

FIGURE 8.8

Context menus provide a range of page-editing options for thumbnails.

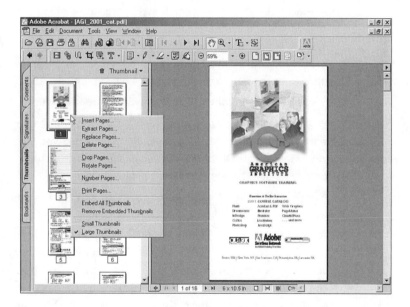

Summary

After completing this hour, you should be able to use thumbnails to affect the order of pages in your PDF document, including adding or deleting pages. You should be able to use thumbnails to navigate through your PDF documents and to merge pages between PDF files. You should also understand how to drag the Thumbnails palette from the

Navigation pane and make it a separate floating window. In addition, you should understand when you might want to embed thumbnails into a document or not embed them.

Workshop

Thumbnails provide assistance with navigation and document management. But their implementation has changed with this most recent version of Acrobat, and we have to consider some of the reasons to use them—and reasons *not* to use them. This workshop rounds off the hour with a few exercises that should clarify your understanding of thumbnails.

Q&A

Q Earlier versions of Acrobat had a Create All Thumbnails command. I can't find this in version 5. Why?

A Acrobat 5 does not have a command to create thumbnails. They are created automatically whenever the Thumbnails palette is opened. If you are sending a PDF file to someone with an earlier version of Acrobat and you expect them to use thumbnails, you should embed them in the file you send. Otherwise, the recipient of your file will have to create the thumbnails when they open the file.

Q Shouldn't I just embed thumbnails in all my PDF files?

A Probably not. If you are posting files to the Web or e-mailing them, you may not want to embed thumbnails because thumbnails increase the file size. Similarly, if you are sending PDF files to recipients who all use Acrobat version 5, you do not have to embed the thumbnails.

Q Aren't all the thumbnails options available in the Document menu? Doesn't this make the Thumbnail palette redundant?

A Although some of the Thumbnail palette's options are also available in the Document menu, many of the commands can only be accomplished using thumbnails. For example, rearranging pages and printing nonconsecutive pages can only be accomplished using thumbnails. Also, merging selective pages from one file to another (as opposed to the entire document) requires the use of thumbnails.

Quiz

1. **Small document thumbnails create a smaller file size than large document thumbnails?**

    a. True

    b. False

2. How can document thumbnails be used to merge selective pages from one document to another?

   a. Hold down the Shift key and click each of the pages you want to combine with another document. Then drag the selected thumbnails into the document with which you want to merge them.

   b. Hold down the Shift or Ctrl key and click each of the pages you want to combine with another document. Then drag the selected thumbnails into the into the Thumbnails palette in the document with which they are being merged.

   c. It is not possible to merge selective pages between documents.

   d. Shift+click the pages you want to merge and then select Insert Pages from either the Document menu or the thumbnail's context menu.

Quiz Answers

1. **b** Thumbnails add a nominal amount to the file size, regardless of whether they are large thumbnails or small thumbnails.

2. **b** Use the Ctrl key to select nonconsecutive thumbnails and the Shift key to select consecutive thumbnails. The selected pages can then be merged with another document, or you can delete or print them by using the context menu.

Exercises

Learn more about working with thumbnails in PDF files by trying the following exercises.

1. Create a multiple-page PDF file and do not embed thumbnails. Save the document. Reopen the document, embed the thumbnails, and save the second version of the document with a different filename. Compare the file size of the first document to the file size of the second.

2. Open a large PDF file and practice using thumbnails to navigate both between pages and within one page. Use the navigation box on the visible thumbnail to zoom in and out of a page.

Hour 9

Creating an Interactive TOC with Bookmarks

Bookmarks are linked section headings you add to a PDF document to provide quick access to particular areas within the file. Like thumbnails, bookmarks are located in the Navigation pane. They operate like hyperlinks. You can click a bookmark and be taken to a specific page, portion of a page, or even to a Web site.

In this hour, you'll learn the following:

- How to use bookmarks to effectively navigate a PDF file
- How to create bookmarks
- How to apply actions and links to bookmarks
- How to set your documents to open with bookmarks visible

Navigating and Using Bookmarks

Bookmarks make it easy to find content within a PDF file and navigate directly to specific pages or sections. You can also use bookmarks to link to a related item, such as a URL. Bookmarks are frequently used to link to book chapters or section headings within a document. If you create long documents, you should use bookmarks to help make your content easy to navigate. Figure 9.1 shows the Bookmarks palette in the Navigation pane and the lengthy document it helps the viewer to navigate.

FIGURE 9.1

The Bookmarks palette shows a list of available bookmarks; click a bookmark to be taken to that location in the document.

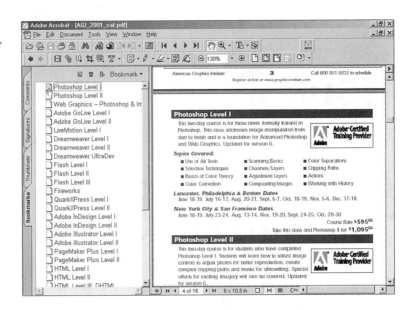

To use bookmarks, you must first access the Bookmarks palette. By default, it is tucked in the Navigation pane on the left side of the screen. If you cannot find it in the Navigation pane, select the Bookmarks command from the Window menu.

▼TASK

Task: Navigating Using Bookmarks

In this task, we'll take a look at how to use bookmarks to navigate PDF files:

1. Open a PDF file that contains bookmarks. At the `AcrobatIn24.com` site, you will find a document titled `catalog.pdf`. You can use this file for this task. Alternatively, choose Help, Acrobat Help to open the Acrobat Help file. The Help file itself is a PDF file that can be used for this exercise.

2. Click on the Bookmarks tab in the Navigation pane or select Window, Bookmarks to open the Bookmarks palette.

3. Click any of the bookmarks listed in the palette. Acrobat moves to the page associated with the bookmark.

▲

Creating and Customizing Bookmarks

There are several ways to create bookmarks; some approaches are automated, others are manual. You can create bookmarks using key commands, working with the Bookmarks palette, or using the structure built into the document (if it is an HTML Web page that was converted to PDF).

> Before creating a bookmark, you will want to navigate to the page that will be the destination of the bookmark. When you create a bookmark, Acrobat uses the current visible page and the current zoom magnification as the default destination of that bookmark. Although you can change the destination, it is much easier if you build the bookmark with the correct destination.

9

The Bookmark Palette Menu

In the upper-right corner of the Bookmarks palette is the Bookmark pull-down menu, as shown in Figure 9.2. When you have located a page that should be the destination of a bookmark, open the Bookmark palette menu and select New Bookmark. A new bookmark is added to the list in the Bookmarks palette. The bookmark's name should be highlighted, allowing you to type a new name. Type a name for the new bookmark that describes the section of text or the section of the page in only a few words. To test the bookmark, navigate to a different page in the document and then click the bookmark. It should return you to the destination page that was visible when you created the bookmark.

FIGURE 9.2

The Bookmark palette menu provides options for creating and editing bookmarks.

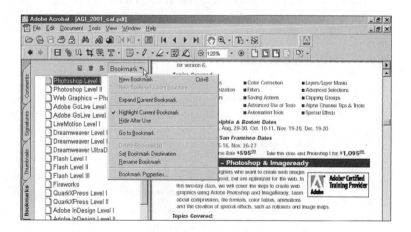

The Context Menus

Using the right mouse button to click inside the Bookmarks palette gives you all the same options available from the Bookmark palette menu. When right-clicking, be certain that your mouse is not on top of an existing bookmark; make sure that it is over the empty space in the palette (see Figure 9.3). If you are a Macintosh user, hold down the Ctrl key while clicking to access the context menus.

FIGURE 9.3

Context menus let you create new bookmarks by using the right mouse button.

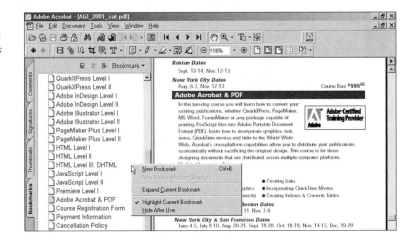

Keyboard Commands

Keyboard commands make it easy to create bookmarks without having to access any menus. After locating the destination for a bookmark, hold down the Ctrl key on your keyboard and press the B key. This action creates a new bookmark. Type a name for the bookmark as described earlier in this hour. Macintosh users should press Command+B rather than the Ctrl+B.

When creating bookmarks, you can have Acrobat use the text from the PDF file to name the bookmark. Doing so eliminates your having to type a name for a new bookmark. To do this, start by selecting the Text Selection tool and selecting the text you want to be the name of the bookmark. When you then build a new bookmark, any selected text becomes the default name for the bookmark.

Remember to adjust the zoom level on the page before creating a bookmark so that you are showing exactly what you want viewers to see.

Automatic Bookmark Creation

If you are creating PDF files from programs that can automatically create bookmarks, it is always easier to let your software create them for you.

PDF files created from Microsoft Word for Windows can have bookmarks automatically built from styles using PDFMaker. Creating bookmarks in Word saves you the step of building them manually in Acrobat. The process for this is discussed in Hour 5, "Easy PDF Creation for Microsoft Office Users."

Similar bookmarking features are available in other products. Adobe PageMaker 6 and later, InDesign 2 and later, and Adobe FrameMaker 5 and later can also build automatic bookmarks when creating PDF files. QuarkXPress can also create bookmarks, but it requires an extension: PDF Design Pro, available from The Power Xchange (at www. thepowerxchange.com).

Modifying Bookmarks

By default, bookmarks link you to whatever page you were on and use whatever magnification was set when they were created. But you might want to change the destination or magnification of the bookmark so that it links to a new location.

Task: Creating a New Bookmark Destination

In this task, we'll look at how you can modify the destination of a bookmark. Start by locating a bookmark whose destination (the location to which it links) you want to change.

1. Navigate to the new destination for the bookmark.

2. Using the right mouse button, click the bookmark that you want to change. Macintosh users must hold the Control key while clicking. A context menu for bookmarks opens.

3. Choose the Set Destination command, as shown in Figure 9.4.

4. Acrobat asks you to confirm that you are changing the destination to the new location. Click Yes.

5. Test the bookmark by moving to a new location in the file and then clicking the bookmark in the Bookmarks palette. You should return to the new destination for the bookmark.

FIGURE 9.4

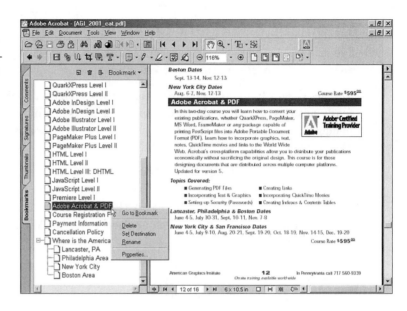

Right-click an existing bookmark to see a context menu that lets you modify the destination of the bookmark.

Other options available to edit an existing bookmark that are available from the bookmark menu, but not the context menu, include:

- **Highlight Current Bookmark**   This option causes the current bookmark to become highlighted, making it easy for you to identify which bookmark is currently being viewed.

- **Hide After Use**   When this option is selected, Acrobat hides the Bookmarks palette each time a bookmark is clicked. Select Window, Bookmarks to redisplay the palette.

- **New Bookmark from Structure**   This option is only available for PDF files that have been created from Web pages or that otherwise contain structured elements. It creates bookmarks based on the headline tags built into the HTML code before it was converted to a PDF file.

Applying Actions to Bookmarks

Although using bookmarks to navigate to certain destinations within a PDF file certainly is useful, the functionality of bookmarks does not stop there. You can add a variety of actions to a bookmark. Use the right-mouse button to click an existing bookmark. Macintosh users should hold down the Ctrl key while clicking the bookmark. From the context menu that opens, select the Properties command. The Bookmark Properties dialog box opens as shown in Figure 9.5. Select the action type you want to assign to the bookmark from the Type pull-down menu. The various action types are described in the following sections.

FIGURE 9.5

The Bookmark Properties dialog box provides options for changing the type of action associated with a bookmark.

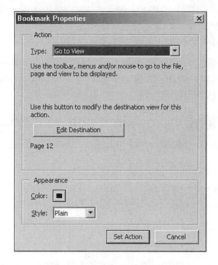

Go to View

This is the default action. It is used to take you to a specific view on a specified page. When you create a new bookmark, by default, this action is applied to it.

Task: Setting the Bookmark to Link to a New Page

In this task, we'll change the destination to which a bookmark links.

1. Right-click an existing bookmark (Macintosh users should Ctrl+click) and select Bookmark Properties from the context menu. The Bookmark Properties dialog box opens.

2. Select Go to View from the Action Type drop-down menu.

3. If the destination for this bookmark is in the same document, click the Edit Destination button, navigate to the new destination page, and click the Set Destination button. You are done!

   If the destination for this bookmark is in a different PDF, click the Edit Destination button and continue with step 4.

4. Select File, Open from the acrobat menu bar. Open the document to which you want the bookmark to link and locate the destination page you want to set.

5. When you have located the desired destination, click the Set Destination button in the Bookmark Properties dialog box. You have just created a bookmark that links from one PDF file to another.

▲

Execute Menu Item

The Execute Menu Item command is found above the Go to View command in the Type drop-down list in the Bookmark Properties dialog box, so it is easy to miss. It is the most versatile of any of the bookmark properties because it allows your bookmark to perform any menu command with one simple click. Whether it involves printing, closing the PDF file, or changing the page magnification, you can make your bookmark perform these chores using the Execute Menu Item action. Anything you can accomplish from the menus you can assign to a bookmark.

Task: Assigning a Menu Item Command to a Bookmark

▼ TASK

In this task, we'll see how to create a bookmark that causes a command from any menu to be accessed.

1. Right-click the existing bookmark (Macintosh users should Ctrl+click) and select Bookmark Properties from the context menu. The Bookmark Properties dialog box opens.

2. Choose Execute Menu Item from the Action Type drop-down menu.

3. Click the Edit Menu Item button in the Bookmark Properties dialog box. A Menu Item Selection dialog box appears, as shown in Figure 9.6. Macintosh users do not see a dialog box; instead, they should select the menu items directly from the menus within Acrobat; Acrobat records these actions.

FIGURE 9.6

The Menu Item Selection dialog box allows Windows users to apply any menu command to a bookmark.

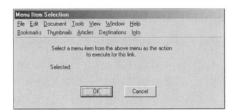

4. Using the menus reproduced in the dialog box, choose a menu command from the drop-down menus.

5. Confirm your selection by looking at the Selected: Portion of the dialog box. If the command is not correct, choose another from within the dialog box. When you are sure that the command is correct, click OK.

6. Back in the Bookmark Properties dialog box, click the Set Action button. Macintosh users click OK instead.

▲ 7. Test the newly defined action by clicking the bookmark.

Import Form Data

Use the Import Form Data action to import form data from other PDF files or form data that has been exported to .fdf files. Form data is described in more detail in Hour 16, "Creating and Using Interactive Forms."

JavaScript

Acrobat supports JavaScript actions. The JavaScript can be written right into the PDF file. Select JavaScript as the Action Type in the Bookmark Properties dialog box and click the Edit button. Type your JavaScript. If you usually write your JavaScript using a text editor, you can copy and paste it from the text editor into this window.

Movie

Select the Movie option as the action to have a bookmark start playing a movie that has been placed on a PDF page. You must import a movie onto the page before this command can be used. Movies are not embedded into the PDF file, so you must include the movie along with the PDF file if you are sending this file to someone and you want the link to work. Hour 17, "Enhancing a PDF with Multimedia," discusses how to add multimedia components such as movies to your PDF files.

Open File

Bookmarks can link to files that are not PDFs. Use the Open File action to create a link to some other file type. Whether the file you want to link to is a Microsoft Word document, a spreadsheet, or a movie, Acrobat can link to it. When you use the Open File option to create a link to the file, you are not embedding the file into the PDF document. For readers to use this type of link successfully, you must provide access to the linked item along with the PDF file. Also remember that people will need whatever software was used to create the linked file. If you are linking to a PageMaker file, for example, readers will need PageMaker on their computers for the link to work successfully.

Read Article

Use the Read articles action to create a link that takes the reader to an article. An *article* is a structured way of presenting data on a page. Articles make it easier for readers to view data that links between columns and pages. Use of articles is covered in Hour 10, "Using Links to Add Interactivity to PDF Files."

Reset Form

After a form has been filled out, the Reset Form bookmark action provides an easy way to clear out all the data in the form's fields. Hour 16, "Creating and Using Interactive Forms," is devoted to PDF forms.

Show/Hide Field

Another bookmark option relates to how fields in a form can be made visible and invisible. The Show/Hide Field action allows a bookmark to change the appearance of the fields on the form. See Hour 16 for more details on this option.

Sound

To add your favorite sound to a PDF file, use the Sound action. When the user clicks a bookmark with this action, you can have the sound play. As is true for movies, sound files are not embedded in PDF files and must be sent along with the PDF file if the link is to be successful.

Submit Form

After a form is filled with data, you use the Submit Form action to submit the data to a specified recipient, just as you would with a "submit" button. Details on this option are discussed in Hour 16.

World Wide Web Link

You can use a bookmark to create a link to the Web. Select the World Wide Web Link action from the Type drop-down list and click the Edit URL button. Type the entire URL—including the http:// component, if that's required—and click OK. Back in the Bookmark Properties dialog box, click Set Action. The bookmark will then link you to the Web page you have specified.

> If you're familiar with writing HTML code, you can use some basic HTML codes to expand on the World Wide Web Link option. For example, you can type MAILTO:"address@domain.com" in the URL field to create a link that takes you to an e-mail address rather than to a Web site.

None

Although the None option might appear to be an odd action that does not need any explanation, it is actually a very useful action type. Use the None option when creating headings or headlines within the bookmarks. These will be the top-level bookmarks that do not link to anything themselves. You can then nest bookmarks below them, as described in the next section.

Renaming Bookmarks

The name you apply to a bookmark can be modified at any time by right-clicking the bookmark and selecting Rename Bookmark from the context menu. Macintosh users Ctrl+click the bookmark to access this menu. After selecting the Rename Bookmark option, type a new name and press the Return or Enter key.

Arranging Bookmarks

Bookmarks are great—but they can become overwhelming if you get too many of them. Fortunately, you can structure them so that they are set at different levels, as shown in Figure 9.7.

FIGURE 9.7

Create a nested set of bookmarks to organize and structure them.

Task: Creating Nested Bookmarks

In this task, we'll move some bookmarks so that they are nested and have a better organization and structure.

1. Open a PDF document that contains multiple bookmarks.

2. Click and hold down on a bookmark that you want to move to a different location.

3. While holding down the mouse button, drag the bookmark so that the mouse pointer is positioned underneath the bookmark where you want to position the bookmark you are dragging. It must be positioned slightly in and to the right of the bookmark. Look for a small, solid line to appear underneath the bookmark, as shown in Figure 9.8.

4. Release the mouse button when the bookmark is appropriately positioned.

FIGURE 9.8

Drag a bookmark underneath and to the right of a bookmark where you want it nested.

▲

Viewing Nested Bookmarks

After you have nested several bookmarks, you can click the plus symbol to the left of the top-level bookmark to view its nested bookmarks. On the Macintosh you will see a triangle rather than a plus symbol. As an alternative, click the Expand Current Bookmark button or select Expand Current Bookmark from the pull down menu.

Setting a Document to Show Bookmarks When Opened

One of the greatest shortcomings of bookmarks is that most users don't know about them. If you go to the trouble of creating bookmarks, you'd like your readers to use them. But most casual users of Acrobat don't know about the Navigation pane. You can easily overcome this issue by causing the Bookmarks palette to appear whenever the document is opened. Setting up your PDF file to operate in this manner is handled by the document's properties settings.

Task: Setting Bookmarks to Open with the Document

▼ TASK

In this task, we will force the bookmarks to open when the document containing them opens.

1. Open or create a PDF document that contains bookmarks.

2. Select File, Document Properties, Open Options. The Document Open Options dialog box opens.

3. In the Initial View section of the dialog box, enable the Bookmarks and Page option, as shown in Figure 9.9.

4. Click OK.

5. Save the PDF document.

FIGURE 9.9

The Document Open Options dialog box lets you force the PDF document to show the Bookmarks palette whenever it opens, making bookmarks easy to find.

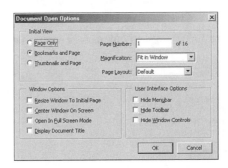

▲

Bookmark Properties

All bookmarks do not have to look the same. Change the color of your bookmarks or the style of type in which they appear by right-clicking a bookmark and selecting Properties from the context menu. In the Properties dialog box, choose a color and type style to apply to the selected bookmark, as shown in Figure 9.5.

Deleting Bookmarks

It's easy to delete bookmarks you no longer need. Select the bookmark you want to delete from the Bookmarks palette and click the trash can icon at the top of the palette. Alternatively, right-click the bookmark (Macintosh users should control click) and then choose Delete from the context menu to delete the bookmark.

Summary

After completing this hour, you should be able to create bookmarks that link to other pages within a PDF file, link to specified portions of a PDF page, or even link to other PDF documents. You should also be able to link to Web pages and be able to create bookmarks that cause actions such as printing or playing a movie. You should be able to arrange your bookmarks in a logical order, nesting them if necessary. You should also be able to change the appearance of a bookmark by adjusting its color and type style.

Workshop

To finish this hour on bookmarks, we'll look at several questions about their use and then provide some exercises to increase your skills with this useful feature.

Q&A

Q Creating bookmarks is time consuming. Are there any time-saving tips?

A Always try to create your bookmarks in the file's original program. Bookmarks can be based on styles used in programs such as Word, PageMaker, and InDesign. If this is not possible, try to use text that already exists in the document for the titles of your bookmarks. Select the text with the Text Selection tool and press the keyboard shortcut Ctrl+B (Command+B on the Macintosh) to create the bookmark using the selected text as the title.

Q Why should I bother with bookmarks?

A Online reading habits are very different from those associated with reading paper documents. Readers like to skim important topics, and they expect links to take them right to sections of importance. Bookmarks help highlight the main sections of a document and quickly access the information readers need.

Q Can I nest more than one level of bookmarks?

A Yes. Acrobat allows you to create multiple subsections of bookmarks. If you have a document with Section 1, subsection A, Subsection 1, and then subsection a, Acrobat can create bookmarks that are nested four levels deep to accommodate this outline.

Quiz

1. **Which of the following is a bookmark *not* capable of doing?**

    a. Linking to a specific PDF page.

    b. Linking to a Web site.

    c. Linking to a specific page within a Microsoft Word document.

    d. Linking to a Microsoft Word document

2. **If your Bookmarks palette disappears each time you select a bookmark, why is this occurring?**

    a. The Bookmark Properties are set to close the palette after the user clicks a specific bookmark.

    b. Hide After Use is selected in the Bookmarks palette menu.

    c. The bookmark's preferences are set to close the palette.

    d. This behavior occurs when bookmarks are set to link to internal pages within the same PDF file.

Quiz Answers

1. **c**   Although it is possible to link to other types of files, it is not possible to link to a specific page within these other documents.

2. **b**   The Hide After Use option causes the palette to collapse after each use.

Exercises

Get a better understanding of using and creating bookmarks by trying the following exercises.

1. Download the document titled `catalog.pdf` from the `AcrobatIn24.com` Web site. Arrange the bookmarks into different sections; nest some bookmarks. Delete the bookmarks. Add a bookmark that links to a Web site.

2. Create a document using Word or PageMaker that includes multiple styles. Use the options in these programs to create the bookmarks automatically. Then convert the file to a PDF and open the file and the Bookmarks palette in Acrobat to view and use the converted bookmarks.

9

HOUR 10

Using Links to Add Interactivity to PDF Files

Increasingly, more people are reading documents online over the Internet. The way people read documents online is different from the way they read offline. When reading documents online, viewers have come to expect interactive documents. Readers want to see information on their computer screen that links to related pages. They don't want to scroll through pages of information. Fortunately, Acrobat allows the easy creation of interactive links. These links can take you from one portion of a PDF file to another. These same links can also be used to navigate to other PDF documents or even to Web sites.

In this hour, you'll learn the following:

- How to create links to specific PDF pages
- How to create links between PDF files
- How to create links to Web pages and e-mail addresses
- How to edit and modify existing links

Using Links

Links are geographic regions of a page that, when clicked, cause an action to occur. Often links are intuitive. A link might be part of an index: You click a topic and are taken to the related pages. Or you click a URL and are taken to a Web page. Some links are visible and stand out from surrounding areas, such as blue text or a blue frame around a graphic. But other links are invisible, so you might not be able to tell them apart from other areas of a document. You can tell you have found a link when the mouse pointer changes from an arrow to a pointing finger. The finger will have a *W* attached to it if the link is a Web link that will launch your Web browser; the finger will have a + if the link is for a Web page that will launch within Acrobat. Figure 10.1 shows an invisible link on a PDF page.

FIGURE 10.1

Links on a PDF page change the shape of the mouse cursor. The link area may be visible or invisible.

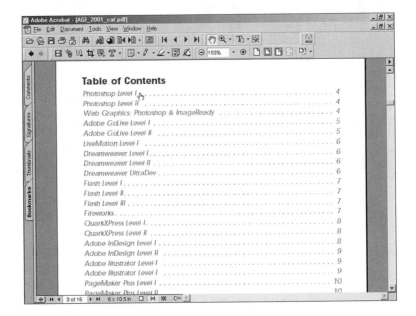

You can change the color of text to make it blue, and then add a link to it. Change the color of your text by using the Text Attributes palette (choose Tools, TouchUp Text, Text Attributes).

When you build a PDF file, you control whether the links are visible and what occurs when the links are clicked. Although most links are created manually, there are some utilities used to create links automatically. Some software utilities work in conjunction with Distiller and can build links at the time the document is converted to PDF. Acrobat also includes an option that locates Web addresses within a PDF file and automatically converts those URLs to PDF links.

Creating Links Within PDF Files

Links can be added to any page on a PDF file by using the Link tool, shown in Figure 10.2. Before adding a link, you must consider where on the page you want to place the link and where the link will take you when it is clicked.

FIGURE 10.2
The Link tool is found in the toolbar and is used to add links to PDF pages.

Link tool

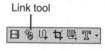

10

Task: Creating a Link

In this task, we will create a link from one page in the document to another page in the same document.

1. Open a PDF file in which you want to add a link.

2. Using the navigation tools, move to the area of the page where you want to add a link.

3. Select the Link tool from the toolbar by clicking it or by pressing the L key on your keyboard. This tool is shown in Figure 10.2.

4. Drag a rectangle around the area where you want readers to click to activate the link. The Link Properties dialog box will appear. Select the Go to View option and then ignore this dialog box temporarily.

5. With the Link Properties dialog box still open, navigate to the page that will be the destination for the link. Select a zoom level and a magnification that shows the portion of the page you want.

6. Click the Set Link button in the Link Properties dialog box. Acrobat returns you to the location where the link was created.

7. Switch to the Hand tool and click the link you just created to test the link. The Link tool is used to create and edit links and cannot be used to test links.

You can check a link without switching back to the Hand tool. Use the link's context menu (right-click the link—Ctrl+click for Macintosh users—and select Follow Link.

Link Properties and Actions

The Link tool creates a default link you can use to navigate between pages in a single PDF file. As you saw in the preceding task, you simply select the source of the link and its destination. By default, Acrobat assumes that you want to link from one location in a document to another in the same document, and it creates an invisible link. But links do not have to be invisible, and they can be used to initiate a variety of actions other than jumping to another page in the same document. To modify the appearance and action of the default link created with the Link tool, you use the Link Properties dialog box (see Figure 10.3). After you change these attributes, they are applied to all future links that you create.

FIGURE 10.3

The Link Properties dialog box appears when you drag out a new link with the Link tool.

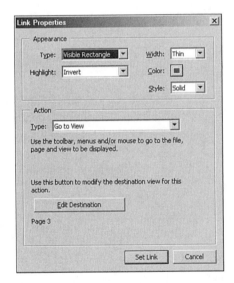

You access the Link Properties dialog box by creating a new link or by editing an existing link (which is discussed in the next section). Modify the properties and attributes before clicking the Set Link button, but don't forget to select the destination for the link.

Link Appearances

The following link attributes can be applied to links. Attributes do not change how a link operates, but they modify how the link appears on a page. They are found in the Link Properties dialog box shown in Figure 10.3.

- **Type**—Select whether you want the link to have a visible rectangle surrounding the area where the reader clicks to activate the link, or if the link should be invisible.

- **Width**—If the link Type is visible, you can set the thickness of the line surrounding the link with the Width option.

- **Color**—If the link is visible, you can also change the color of the line that surrounds the link. This option is useful if you want to make your links blue so that they look similar to the default hyperlink color in most Web browsers. The link color can be customized to any color you prefer. By default, links are invisible, but Acrobat will remember this selection after you change it.

- **Style**—Visible links can have solid lines or dashed lines. If you have chosen to make the link visible, use the Style option to select either a solid or a dashed line for the link.

- **Highlight**—When the user clicks a link, the appearance of the link can change momentarily. The Highlight option allows you to set how a link will appear when it is being clicked with a mouse. The link itself is not affected by this option, only the appearance of the link at the time it is being clicked is affected. Here are the options listed in the Highlight drop-down list:

  - **None**—When the link is clicked, it does not change appearance.

  - **Invert**—When the link is clicked, dark areas become light and light areas become dark for the length of time that the mouse button is being pressed.

  - **Outline**—When the link is clicked, a thin line appears around the perimeter of the link for the length of time that the mouse button is being pressed.

  - **Inset**—When the link is clicked, the portion of the page that is the link appears to be pressed into the page (much like a real-life button) for the length of time that the mouse button is being pressed.

Link Actions

The following sections describe the actions that can be applied to links using the Type drop-down list in the Action portion of the Link Properties dialog box.

Go to View

As is the case for bookmarks, the Go to View option is the default action for links. It is used to take you to a specific view on a specified page. Unlike the process for defining a bookmark, however, you must specify where the link will exist on the page, and you must also specify the destination of the link.

Execute Menu Item

The Execute Menu Item option is found above the Go to View option in the Action Type drop-down list box in the Link Properties dialog box, so it is easy to miss. It is the most versatile of any of the link properties because it allows your link to perform any command from the menu items with one simple click, regardless of whether that menu command involves printing, closing the PDF file, or changing the page magnification. Anything you can accomplish from the menus can be assigned to a link by selecting the Execute Menu Item option.

Import Form Data

Use the Import Form Data action to import form data from other PDF files or form data that has been exported to .fdf files. Form data is described in more detail in Hour 16, "Creating and Using Interactive Forms."

JavaScript

Acrobat supports JavaScript actions. The JavaScript can be written right into the PDF file. Select this option and then click the Edit button. Type your JavaScript. If you usually write your JavaScript using a text editor, you can copy and paste it from the text editor into this window.

Movie

Select the Movie option from the Type drop-down list to have a link start, stop, or pause the playing of a movie that has been placed on a PDF page. You must import a movie onto your page before you can use this command. Movies are not embedded into the PDF file, so you must include the movie along with the PDF if you send this file to someone and you want the link to work. Hour 17, "Enhancing a PDF with Multimedia," discusses how to add multimedia components such as movies to your PDF files.

Open File

You can direct links to other types of documents that are not PDF files. Use the Open File option to create a link to some other file type. Whether the file you want to link to is a Microsoft Word document, a spreadsheet, or a movie, Acrobat can link to it. When you use the Open File option to create a link to the file, you are not embedding the file into the PDF document. If readers are to use this link successfully, you must provide access to the linked file along with access to the PDF file. Also remember that people will need whatever software was used to create the linked file. If you are linking to a PageMaker file, for example, readers will need PageMaker on their computers if the link is to work successfully.

Read Article

Use the Read Article option to create a link that will take the reader to an article. An article is a structured way of presenting data on a page and makes it easier for readers to view data that links between columns and pages.

Reset Form

After a form has been filled out, the Reset Form action provides an easy way to clear all the data in the form fields. Hour 16, "Creating and Using Interactive Forms," is devoted to PDF forms.

Show/Hide Field

You can make form fields visible and invisible. The Show/Hide Field option allows a link to change the appearance of the fields in a form. See Hour 16 for more details on this option.

Sound

To add your favorite sound to a PDF file, use the Sound option. When the link is clicked, you can have the sound play. Like movies, sounds are not embedded in PDF files and must be sent along with the PDF file if the link is to work successfully.

Submit Form

After a form is filled with data, you use the Submit Form action to submit the data to a specified recipient. If you already have the word "submit" on the form, you can add a link to that word, applying an action to that text. Details on this option are discussed in Hour 16. Alternatives to creating links that perform actions include creating buttons using Acrobat's forms capabilities or using a bookmark to create a Submit Form action.

World Wide Web Link

You can create a link directly to the Web using the World Wide Web Link option. This is a great way to take text that references a URL and make it link to the Web.

Task: Creating a Web Link

Creating a link to a Web address is just as easy as creating a link in a PDF file, as we will see in this task.

1. Open a PDF file in which you want to add a link.
2. Using the navigation tools, move to the area of the page where you want to add the link.
3. Select the Link tool from the toolbar.
4. Drag a rectangle around the area where you want readers to click to activate the link. The Link Properties dialog box opens.
5. Select World Wide Web Link from the Type drop-down list in the Action section at the top of the dialog box.
6. Click the Edit URL button, type the Web address, and click OK.

7. Back in the Link Properties dialog box, click the Set Link button (see Figure 10.4).

8. Test the action of the link by clicking the link with the Hand tool.

FIGURE 10.4

*After adding a URL to
a Web link, confirm the
Web address and click
the Set Link button.*

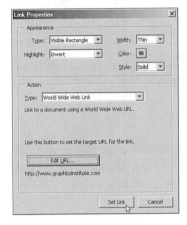

Editing an Existing Link

When you click the Link tool in the toolbar, all links on the PDF page become visible
with a thin black line surrounding the area of the link.

You can edit an existing link by selecting the Link tool and double-clicking an existing
link. You can also edit the properties of a link by clicking the link with the right mouse
button (Ctrl+click for Macintosh users) and selecting Link Properties from the context
menu. Either of these methods opens the Link Properties dialog box, where you can
change the destination, appearance, and type of link.

Automatically Creating Links to Web Sites

Acrobat can review the text in a PDF document and automatically add links to any
URLs it finds in the text. To use this time-saving feature, choose Tools, Locate Web
Addresses, Create Web Links from URLs in Text. A dialog box opens, asking which
pages you want to scan for Web links. Specify the appropriate pages. Acrobat then scans
the text and alerts you to the number of links it has added to the document. Creating
Web links automatically is the easiest way to add links based on Web addresses to the
text of a PDF file. This works only with complete Web addresses—including the
http://.

The Locate Web Addresses command can also be used to remove Web links from a
document.

Setting Page Actions

Page actions are similar to links and bookmarks in that they execute a command. But page actions differ in that they do not require the reader to click any particular element. Instead, page actions occur when the reader opens or navigates to a certain page or leaves a certain page. For example, when someone opens a page of a document, you can arrange for a sound to play or a movie to begin playing.

You can apply multiple page actions to a single page. It is possible to have several actions occur when a page is opened and to also have several actions occur when the same page is closed. To set up the page actions for your PDF file, you use the Page Actions dialog box (see Figure 10.5).

FIGURE 10.5

The Page Actions dialog box allows you to set actions to occur when pages are open or closed.

10

Task: Setting a Page Action

In this task, we'll examine how to cause an action to start when a page within a document is opened:

1. Open a PDF file in which you want to create a page action.

2. Using the navigation tools, move to the page where you want the action to occur.

3. Select Set Page Action from the Document menu. The Page Actions dialog box opens.

4. From the When This Happens list, select whether you want the action to occur when the page opens or closes.

5. Click the Add button on the right of the dialog box; the Add an Action dialog box appears, as shown in Figure 10.6.

6. Select an action from the Type pull-down list. After choosing the action, click the Set Action button to return to the Page Action dialog box.

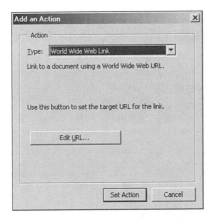

FIGURE 10.6

The Add an Action dialog box allows you to specify the type of action that will occur when a page is opened or closed.

7. If you want to apply multiple actions, repeat steps 4, 5, and 6 to assign additional actions to the opening or closing of the page.

8. When you are done applying actions, click the OK button to close the dialog box.

9. Test the action you just defined by opening or closing the page to which you applied the action.

Creating and Modifying Destinations

A *destination* is a specified location on a page. Although it can be used in a manner similar to a link or bookmark, its real purpose is for creating links across multiple PDF files. A list of destinations in the PDF are found in the Destinations palette (shown in Figure 10.7), which can be opened from the Window menu.

If you know you will be linking to a certain destination within a PDF file, you may want to create the destination before building the link. Links to destinations are not affected by the adding or deleting of pages—which is not the case with traditional links. Traditional links specify that you navigate to a certain page number, regardless of the content on that page. Destinations attach themselves to a certain page, not to a page number. By using destinations, you can always link to the content of a page, even if you add or delete pages from within the document.

Adding and Linking to a New Destination

A destination can help you create a link from one PDF file to a specific location within another PDF document.

FIGURE 10.7

The Destinations palette shows a list of the destinations that have been defined within a document.

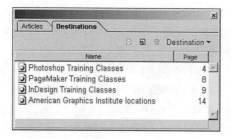

Task: Creating a Destination

In this task, we'll build a destination so that a link can be attached to it.

1. Open a PDF file in which you want to create a destination.

2. Navigate to the page and zoom magnification where you want to create a destination.

3. Open the Destinations palette from the Window menu.

4. From the Destination palette menu, choose Scan Document or click the Scan Document button at the top of the palette, to the far left of the palette menu. You must always scan a document before setting the first destination.

5. From the Destination palette menu, choose Set Destination. You can also use the New Destination button, to the left of the palette menu; it looks like a dog-eared document.

6. Type a name for the destination and press Enter or Return.

Task: Linking to a Destination

After you have built a destination, you will probably want to use it by creating a link to it from another PDF file. Follow the steps in this task to link to an existing destination from another PDF file:

1. Open a PDF file in which you want to add a link to the existing destination.

2. Using the navigation tools, move to the area of the page where you want to add a link.

3. Select the Link tool from the toolbar.

4. Drag a rectangle around the area where you want readers to click to activate the link. The Link Properties dialog box opens. Ignore this dialog box temporarily.

5. With the Link Properties dialog box still open, open the document that contains the destination to which you want to link, and navigate to the page containing the destination to which you will be linking.

6. For the second PDF file, open the Destination palette from the Window menu and select the destination to which you want to create a link. You might have to rescan the document for destinations to appear in the palette.

7. Make sure that the Link Properties dialog box lists the link type as Go to View.

8. Click the Set Link button in the Link Properties dialog box. Acrobat returns you to the location where the link was created.

9. Switch to the Hand tool to test the link to the destination.

Using Articles

If you have ever started to read a document on the front page of a newspaper or a magazine and then followed the story to another page, you understand how an article works. *Articles* are designed to make it easier to follow a document as it links across columns or pages of a PDF file. Articles are built into a PDF file by the person creating the file. A list of the articles in a PDF file is shown in the Articles palette, which you can open from the Window menu (see Figure 10.8).

To read an article, double-click its name in the Articles palette or by right-clicking (Ctrl+clicking if you are a Macintosh user) the article name and selecting Read Article from the context menu. Acrobat then zooms to a magnification that centers the article on the page, showing only the article on your screen and not the other parts of the document.

You can also read an article by moving the mouse over text that is part of an article. The mouse pointer changes to a hand with an arrow pointing downward. Click within the article text, and your screen will adopt a view that shows only the article on the screen. Press the Page Down key to scroll through the article, or click with the Hand tool to scroll.

FIGURE **10.8**

The Articles palette lists any articles that have been defined in a PDF file.

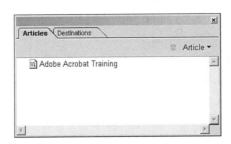

Task: Creating an Article

To create an article, you must start by opening a PDF file that has stories flowing across multiple pages or columns. Then follow these steps:

1. Locate the starting point for the article. The "starting point" could the first paragraph of a story or any section of a story where someone would start reading.

2. Choose the Article tool from the toolbar by clicking it or by pressing the A key on your keyboard. The tool is shown in Figure 10.9.

FIGURE 10.9

Use the Article tool to define how articles read across a PDF file.

Article tool

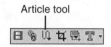

3. Using the Article tool, drag a box around the first portion of the article. This will be the first section that the user will read.

4. Scroll or navigate to the next portion of the article and draw a box around this portion using the Article tool. This is the next section of the document that will be viewed by the reader of the article. Repeat this process until you have reached the end of the article.

5. When you have reached the end of the text of the article, click the End Article button, which will appear at the bottom of the document window.

6. Switch to the Hand tool and test the article by reading it. When you first click on the article with the Hand tool, you should be taken to its beginning (the first section you defined). Then you should progress to the next section of the article, and so on until you reach the end of the article (see Figure 10.10).

FIGURE 10.10

The Hand tool will show an arrow inside the hand when it is placed over an article. Click on the article and Acrobat will center it on your screen at the appropriate magnification.

As with bookmarks, articles can be created automatically when producing PDF files from many word processing software packages and desktop publishing software packages. When possible, use the features included with your design software, such as Microsoft Word or QuarkXPress, to expedite this process.

Changing Existing Articles

The article number and reading sequence for articles is displayed at the top of the article box that is visible around articles when you use the Articles tool, as shown in Figure 10.11. The first number represents which article this is within the document, the second number represents which portion of the article the box contains. In the figure, you can see the fourth and fifth sections, or portions, of article number one.

FIGURE 10.11

When creating or editing articles, use the article number and reading sequence that appears in the boxes surrounding the article.

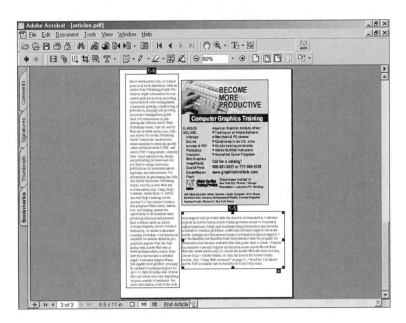

To delete a portion of an article, select the Article tool and move your cursor over an existing article. Click in the box containing the portion of the article to be deleted and press the Delete key on your keyboard. You can then choose to delete either that potion of the article or the entire article.

Task: Adding More Pieces to an Article

▼ TASK

You may find that, after building an article, you have additional parts of a story you want to include. You do not have to re-create the entire article; instead, you can add new sections to an existing article, as we will do in this task.

1. Open the PDF file that contains the article to which you want to add more information.

2. Select the Article tool and click the portion of the article *after which* you want to insert additional article pieces.

▼

3. Click the plus symbol in the lower-right corner of this portion of the article.

4. Draw additional portions of the article. These new article boxes will be inserted into the article following the portion of the article you selected in step 2.

5. If you click the page instead of dragging new article sections, a dialog box appears, telling you to drag out additional boxes to define the article. Click OK to close the dialog box and then drag over additional sections of the document where the article will continue.

6. When you are finished, click the End-Article button that appears at the bottom of the page. This button is only visible when you use the Article tool.

> To combine two articles, select the Article tool and click the plus tab at the bottom of the first article you want to combine. Press and hold the Ctrl key on your keyboard (Macintosh users press the Option key) and click in the box that contains the start of the second article. The two articles will then be combined.

10

Summary

After completing this hour, you should be able to create links from one page to another page within a PDF file. You should also be able to create links that magnify a certain portion of a page, take you to a Web site, or execute any menu command. Additionally, you should be able to create a destination and link to that destination when linking from one PDF file to another. You should also be able to change the appearance of a link by adjusting its color, visibility, and other attributes. You should also be able to create articles so that readers can more easily navigate through the content in PDF files—especially if the content jumps over pages.

Workshop

With the variety of options for creating and using links, you might have some questions. In this workshop, we address some of those that we've been asked in the past and wrap up the chapter with some exercises.

Q&A

Q When creating links, is it possible to view a list of all the links within a PDF file?

A No. Acrobat does not contain a "links palette" or any other method for viewing all the links in a consolidated location.

Q Why would I want to change the color of a link?

A If your audience is not familiar with hyperlinks, placing a blue box around a hyperlink in a PDF file is intuitive. Most readers will understand that the blue box signifies a link—even if they are not familiar with using links in a PDF file. Many readers assume that hyperlinks are limited to Web use.

Q Many link actions are similar to bookmark actions; is one better than the other?

A Links, bookmarks, and even forms overlap in functionality. One is not necessarily better than another. Although bookmarks provide a running index of links you can use to jump around in the PDF, the standard links discussed in this hour require you to be on the page that contains the link before you can activate the link. In many cases, it is best to create both links and bookmarks to make your documents easy to read and navigate.

Q The End-Article button is not visible when I draw articles. Why?

A If any of the Navigation panes are open, such as the Bookmarks or Thumbnails palette, they often take up so much space on your screen that you cannot see the End-Article button. Either reduce the size of the Navigation panes or close them entirely to make the End-Article button visible.

Quiz

1. **Which of the following actions can be achieved using a link?**

    a. Linking to a specific portion of a PDF page in another PDF document.

    b. Linking to a Web site.

    c. Linking to a specific page within a Microsoft Word document.

    d. Linking to a Microsoft Word document.

2. **If you open a page and a sound plays each time you open the page, what is happening?**

    a. A link has been created to play a sound.

    b. The page has a sound embedded in it.

    c. The Sound tool was used to create a sound action for the page.

    d. A page action was applied to play a sound when opening the page.

3. **If you have a story that goes across multiple pages, what is an easy way for readers to follow the various sections of the story?**

    a. A link between each section.

    b. An article linking the sections.

    c. A bookmark listing the sections.

    d. Having the reader scroll using thumbnails.

Quiz Answers

1. **a, b, and d** You can use links in a PDF file to link to all these locations except to a specific page in a file that has not been converted to a PDF.

2. **d** Page actions can be used to play sounds or have other actions occur whenever a document page is opened or closed.

3. **b** Articles linking various sections of a story are often the easiest method for structuring how a story should be read. Creating links between sections using buttons and the Forms tool is also possible, but is more time consuming to set up. The details surrounding forms are covered in Hour 16.

Exercises

Get a better understanding of using and creating links by trying the following exercises.

1. Take several PDF files that have related information and create links to and from each PDF file using the Link tool.

2. Open a PDF file that includes Web addresses and have Acrobat find the URLs and automatically convert them to PDF links.

3. Take a PDF file that has stories reading across several pages and create articles that link the pages.

10

PART IV

Reviewing and Editing PDF Files

Hour

Hour 11

Extracting Text and Graphics

Having the ability to share PDF documents across more than a dozen computer platforms comes at a small price. The price you pay is limited editing and extraction capabilities. PDF files are great for distributing documents, and they do let you make minor changes (see Hour 12, "Editing a PDF File," for details). But if you need to completely rewrite a document or edit several pictures, you will quickly find that Acrobat is the wrong tool for editing. To edit documents, you will want to go back to the original file whenever possible—whether that file was created in Word, PageMaker, or whatever software you used to create the file.

Because you might not always have access to the original file that created the PDF, Adobe has created methods for extracting text and graphics from PDF files. You can then take these extracted elements into other software programs and edit them.

In this hour, you'll learn the following:

- How to convert an entire PDF document to editable text
- How to extract portions of a PDF document for editing
- How to retain text formatting when exporting text for editing
- How to convert PDF files to HTML and XML
- How to extract images from PDF files

Extracting Portions of Text

When you have a PDF file that contains several sentences or paragraphs that you want to use in another document, Acrobat makes it easy to copy the text from the PDF file. To do this, you need the correct tool: the Text Select tool or the Column Select tool. These tools are shown in Figure 11.1.

FIGURE 11.1
The Text Select tool can be used to select ranges of text for copying or modifying. The Column Select tool is similar to the Text Select tool but is used to select text on a page that contains multiple columns.

Text Select Tool

Use the Text Select tool to highlight text that spans an entire page. This tool is not used for text editing, only for selecting the text. You can access this tool by selecting it in the toolbar or by pressing the V key on your keyboard to select it. Use this tool to highlight the text you want to copy or move to another program for editing. Because you will not edit the text in Acrobat, select the Copy command from the Edit menu, or press Ctrl+C from the keyboard to put the selected text on the system Clipboard. Move into the program you use for editing text, such as Microsoft Word, open the file into which you want to paste the extracted text, and select the Edit, Paste command or press Ctrl+V.

After selecting the text you want to extract, right-click the selected text to open the context menu; then select the Copy command. (Mac users can Ctrl+click to access the context menu.) When you get into your word processing software, right-click (or Ctrl+click) to access the Paste command.

After you remove text from a PDF file for editing, there is no way to reinsert the text back into the PDF document. If you have to edit more than a few words and keep the document as a PDF file, you should extract the entire document for editing. Refer to "Extracting Entire PDF Files for Editing," later in this hour.

Column Select Tool

Pages that use columns of text are more difficult for Acrobat to select. If you try to use the standard Text Select tool to select columns of text, you will discover that it selects lines of text across the columns—even if the text does not read across the columns. To address this issue, you will want to click and hold the Text Select tool in the toolbar to display the menu of associated tools. Choose the Column Select tool from the menu shown in Figure 11.1. Use this tool to draw a box around the range of text you want to select for editing, as shown in Figure 11.2. After the text is selected, copy it, move to a word processing software, and paste the extracted text in the document.

FIGURE 11.2

Use the Column Select tool to select a column or a portion of a column of text.

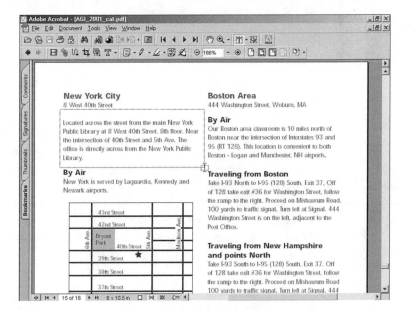

Text that is removed from Acrobat using the Text Select tool or the Column
Select tool is not formatted. Unformatted text loses its association with any
particular font name, size, color, indents, and other attributes it might originally have held.

Drag and Drop

After selecting the text you want to extract from the PDF file, you can drag and drop it
into the software program where you want to edit the text. You can drag and drop text as
an alternative to the Copy and Paste commands; both methods produce the same results.

Task: Dragging and Dropping Text from Acrobat

In this task, we will move text from a PDF file into another program. Note that this feature is not available on the Macintosh.

1. Launch the editing application and open the file in which you want to insert the
   text extracted from the PDF file. This cannot be another PDF file. It must be a document that can be used for text-editing, such as Microsoft Word.

2. Adjust the windows on your computer screen so that both the PDF file from which
   you will be copying the text and the document into which you will be inserting the
   text are both visible, side by side.

3. Select the text you want to copy in the PDF file using one of Acrobat's selection
   tools.

4. Click the selected text and hold the mouse button down.

5. Continue to hold the mouse button as you drag the selected text into the other
   document.

6. When the text insertion point is at the desired location in the new document,
   release the mouse button to drop the text at that location.

Saving a Range of Text Directly in Acrobat

After selecting a block of text that you want to edit, you can save just that part of the
PDF file. Right-click the selected range of text (Mac users can Ctrl+click) and then
choose Save As from the context menu, as shown in Figure 11.3. In the Save As dialog
box that opens, name the text file and specify a location on your hard disk drive or computer network. The file you have just created will be a text file that can be opened or
imported into a word processing document or a page-layout document.

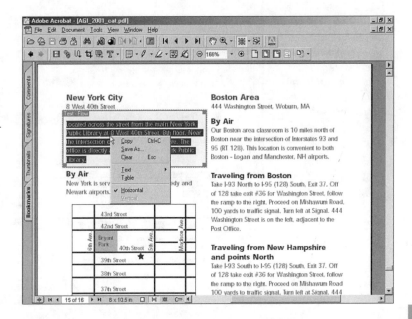

FIGURE 11.3

Access the context menu for selected text by right-clicking (Ctrl+clicking on the Mac) the selected text. Use this menu to save selected text to a separate file for editing or importing into other programs.

Extracting Tables and Formatted Text (Windows Only)

Retaining the formatting of text that is copied from a PDF file requires that you use the Table/Formatted Text Select tool, shown in Figure 11.4. This tool is found on the menu that appears when you click and hold down the Text Select tool in the toolbar. Note that the Table/Formatted Text Select tool is available only in Windows versions of Acrobat; the Macintosh version of Acrobat lacks this feature.

FIGURE 11.4

Use the Table/Formatted Text Select tool to copy text or tables from a PDF file while retaining its formatting.

Text that is selected with the Table/Formatted Text Select tool will be listed as either text or a table, as shown in Figure 11.5. You can have Acrobat automatically attempt to determine what the selected text is, or you can manually identify the text. After you select the text, Acrobat will place a label identifying the text at the top of the box outlining the selection.

FIGURE **11.5**

Text selected with the Table/Formatted Text Select tool is marked as Table or Text in the box that surrounds the selected text.

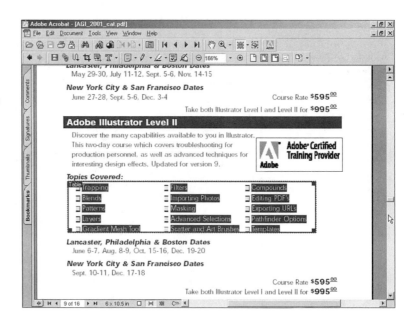

You can change the way Acrobat views the text by switching between the following three options, available from the context menu. (Access the context menu by right-clicking text that has been selected with the Table/Formatted Text tool.) The context menu is shown in Figure 11.3. After you select and identify the text, copy and paste it into another document as described earlier in the hour.

- **Text, Flow:** This option causes the text to be exported without regard to the way the lines of text ended in the PDF file. The line breaks from the PDF file are not maintained, but paragraph breaks *are* retained.

- **Text, Preserve Line Breaks:** This option causes the text to look identical to the way it was in the PDF file. Paragraph breaks are also retained.

- **Table:** Use this selection to maintain the format of an original table, including rows and columns.

Changing Preferences for Extracting Tables and Formatted Text

You can access the preferences for extracting tables and formatted text from the Edit menu: Choose Edit, Preferences to display the Preferences dialog box. From the list on the left side of the dialog box, select Table/Formatted Text. The Table/Formatted Text Preferences dialog box that appears is divided into two tabs; the General tab is shown in Figure 11.6.

FIGURE 11.6

The general preferences for extracting tables and formatted text.

The General tab of the Table/Formatted Text Preferences dialog box allows you to set several options, including

- **Default Selection Type:** This option specifies whether Acrobat automatically determines the kind of text that has been selected (a table or a text flow). If you do not want Acrobat to make this determination automatically, choose the Text or Table option. Acrobat will then assume that all text selected with the Table/Formatted Text Select tool is the type of text you identify here.

- **Default Text Layout:** Use this option to identify vertical text (such as Japanese) or horizontal text (such as most European and Roman-based languages, including English).

- **Preserve Line Breaks:** Select this option only if you want Acrobat to remember how each line of text ends in the PDF file and to export these line breaks with the selected text. If you plan to flow the text into another document, it is usually best to deselect this option.

- **PDF Document Language:** Select the language of the PDF document.

- **Table Border Color and Text Border Color:** These options allow you to set the color of the box that will surround tables or text when you select them using the Table/Formatted Text Select tool.

The RTF Export tab of the Table/Formatted Text Preferences dialog box allows you to specify which attributes will be maintained when you select and copy formatted text from a PDF document. The RTF Export tab is shown in Figure 11.7. If you want Acrobat to retain an attribute, enable the check box next to its name. For example, if you want Acrobat to copy the font name that was used in the PDF file so that the text will use the same font when you paste it into a word processing document, enable the check box next to the Font Name option.

FIGURE 11.7

The RTF Export options for tables and formatted text determine which attributes are copied with the text when you use the Table/Formatted Text Select tool.

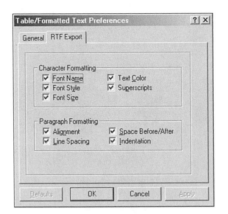

Extracting Entire PDF Files for Editing

There are several ways you can extract an entire PDF file for editing. The following sections describe these several ways.

Selecting and Exporting Multiple Pages of Text

To select multiple pages of text for exporting, you should first determine whether you want to export formatted or unformatted text. After choosing the appropriate selection tool (the Text Select, Column Select, or Table/Formatted Text Select tool), change your page-viewing mode to Continuous. To do this, choose View, Continuous from the menu bar or click the Continuous icon at the bottom of the page (see Figure 11.8). Then select and copy the text as described earlier in this hour.

To select multiple pages of text, start by selecting the Text Select tool, the Column Select tool, or the Table/Formatted Text Select tool. Choose Tool, Continuous or click the Continuous button at the bottom of the Acrobat window. Select all the text you want to export and choose Edit, Copy. Paste the copied text onto a word processing page.

Exporting the Entire Document for Editing

Select the Save As command from the File menu to save a PDF file as RTF text. Rich Text Format (RTF) is a formatted text file. Selecting this option retains most of the attributes of the text contained in a PDF file. An RTF can be opened by most word processing software programs such as Microsoft Word.

FIGURE 11.8

Switch to the Continuous viewing mode to select text from multiple pages.

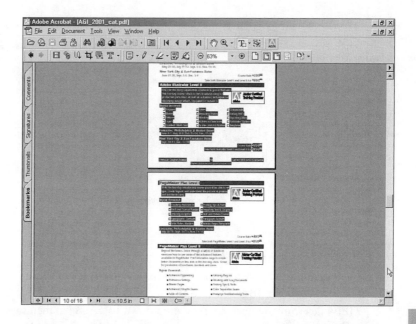

Sometimes, all the text formatting is not carried over to the new document even if you export the text as an RTF file. This is part of the trade-off for having an ultra-portable file format. You will also notice some inconsistencies that appear when you export text. None of these inconsistencies are regular enough to note here, but they do occur, and you should be aware that the export process is not perfect.

11

Acrobat can also export the entire document as HTML or XML. These options require you to download the XML export filter from the Adobe.com Web site. These filters add a variety of formats to the Save As dialog box: You can select the XML, HTML, Plain Text, or RTF file type when saving the selected text (see Figure 11.9).

Plain text is unformatted text; text attributes such as font name, type size, and color are discarded when the file is saved. The Plain Text option is best if you want to remove all the formatting in the PDF file but still want to use the text in another document. Any word processing software can open a plain text document. *XML* and *HTML* are coded text files used by Web browsers.

FIGURE **11.9**

XML and HTML are added options in the Save As dialog box that are made available when you download the Save as XML plug-in from Adobe.com.

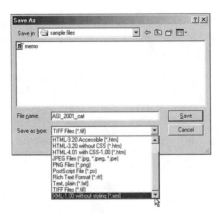

Extracting Images

Acrobat allows you to save entire PDF pages as images or to simply save the images from the PDF file. To save entire PDF pages as images, select File, Save As, and choose TIFF Files from the Save As Type drop-down list. Acrobat then saves each page as a TIFF file. TIFF files are bitmap graphic files; you cannot edit the text in these files, and the text typically looks more jagged.

If you want to export just the images from a PDF file, select File, Export, Extract Images As, and then choose the desired file format (JPEG, PNG, or TIFF). JPEG is a good format to choose if the images are photographic in nature and you will be posting them on a Web site. TIFF is a better option if you will be using the images for printed materials. The extracted images can then be opened in an image-editing program such as Photoshop. Use the PNG format for illustrations or line art that will be posted to a Web site. Although many modern browsers support it, the PNG format is not widely used. Note that the images contained within the PDF file are not affected by extracting the images; they remain intact in the PDF file.

Acrobat also includes a Graphic Select tool, shown in Figure 11.10. Use this tool to select a portion of a page or a picture that you want to copy from Acrobat so that you can paste it into another document, such as a word processing file. The Graphic Select tool always captures graphics at the resolution of the screen, so even high-resolution pictures tend to be captured as grainy and jagged. To improve the quality of images you extract from PDF files, either extract the images as just discussed or use the editing steps covered in Hour 12. The Graphic Select tool uses a lower-quality method for copying and pasting graphics than what is achieved by extracting the images.

FIGURE **11.10**

Use the Graphic Select tool to select images or pictures of a portion of a PDF page that you want to copy and paste.

Graphic Select tool

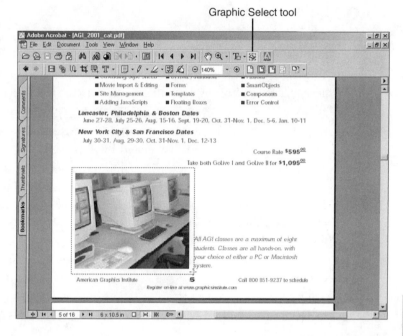

Summary

After completing this hour, you should be able to extract selected portions of a PDF file. You can then place the extracted text into a word processing document or a page layout document. If you want to retain some or all of the formatting from the original PDF file, you should be familiar with the options to control this. If the text you want to export is contained within columns, you should know how to select only the text you need. You should also understand how to save all the text from a PDF file in an editable format, such as RTF. Similarly, you should understand how to extract entire pages as graphic files or to extract just the images from PDF files so that they can be used individually.

Workshop

If you thought that PDF files were "untouchable," you've undoubtedly learned a few things in this hour. We wrap up this hour by looking at common questions and their answers, along with some quiz questions to make certain that you picked up the key concepts from this hour. We conclude with some exercises to improve your skills.

Q&A

Q **When extracting a small portion of formatted text, is it possible to save only that text to a separate file?**

A Yes. This is possible only in the Windows version of Acrobat. Use the context menu that is available by right-clicking the selected text with the Table/Formatted Text Select tool. Choose the Save As option from the context menu.

Q **If I select text with the Table/Formatted Text Select tool and Acrobat incorrectly labels it as a table, what should I do?**

A To change only one location where Acrobat incorrectly identified the selected text, right-click the selected text and choose the appropriate label for the text: Table or Text. If this happens frequently, open the Preferences dialog box by choosing Edit, Preferences, Table/Formatted Text; make certain that the Default Selection Type option is set to Automatic.

Q **If I want to extract formatted text on my Macintosh computer, do I have any options?**

A Although Acrobat on the Macintosh does not have a Table/Formatted Text Select tool, you can still use the Save As command to save the PDF file as Rich Text Format (RTF).

Quiz

1. **Which of the following is Acrobat unable to export?**

   a. An individual table.

   b. An individual picture.

   c. A paragraph of text.

   d. All the pictures in a document.

2. **What is the advantage of selecting text with the Table/Formatted Text Select tool?**

   a. It retains the font and size of the text.

   b. It retains the color of the text.

   c. It retains paragraph spacing and alignment.

   d. All of the above.

Quiz Answers

1. **b** Acrobat cannot export individual pictures from a PDF file. It can only export all the pictures or all the pages in the file as graphics. You could use the TouchUp Object tool to extract an image, as is explained in the next hour. The Graphic Select tool is also an option for copying and pasting a low-resolution version of a graphic from a PDF file, but you might not be satisfied with the quality.

2. **d** Both character attributes (such as font, size, and color) and paragraph attributes (such as alignment and spacing) are retained when using the Table/Formatted Text Select tool.

Exercises

Learn more about the text selection tools by trying the following exercises.

1. Open a PDF file and select text in the file using the various selection tools in Acrobat. Then copy the text you've selected into a word processing document.

2. Open a PDF file that contains a table. Select the table text and copy it into a word processor using both the Table/Formatted Text Select tool and the Text Select tool. Note the differences in how the text is carried between the programs based on which tool you use.

11

Hour 12

Editing a PDF File

PDF files sometimes contain mistakes that require editing. You might have forgotten a period at the end of a sentence or you might have noticed that photographs and images must be corrected. Fortunately, Acrobat has tools that allow you to modify PDF files. The touch-up tools are correctly named because they allow you to touch-up minor mistakes. You can edit text in a limited way, but graphics-editing capabilities are somewhat more robust. However, keep in mind that these are not full-fledged editing tools; they are *touch-up tools*. The last part of this hour also discusses software you can purchase from third parties to enhance Acrobat's editing capabilities.

In this hour, you'll learn about the following:

- Editing text with the TouchUp Text tool
- The limitations to Acrobat's text-editing capabilities
- Editing graphics with the TouchUp Objects tool
- Using third-party editing tools
- Editing entire PDF files

Editing Text with the TouchUp Text Tool

Use the TouchUp Text tool to edit text in a PDF document. For example, if you have a typographic error or have forgotten a punctuation mark, the TouchUp Text tool can be used to fix these problems. The TouchUp Text tool is shown in Figure 12.1.

FIGURE 12.1

The TouchUp Text tool is used to edit text within a PDF file.

 Task: Using the TouchUp Text Tool

In this task, we'll use the TouchUp Text tool to make changes to a PDF document.

1. Open a PDF file that contains text you want to edit.

2. Select the TouchUp Text tool.

3. Use the mouse to click in a line of text than contains text you want to edit.

4. Delete any unwanted text and add any new text.

5. After you complete the editing, switch to the Hand tool. Doing so ensures that you will not accidentally edit other type and allows you to navigate throughout the document or confirm your corrections.

> The TouchUp Text tool allows you to edit one line of text at a time. It does not allow you to edit multiple lines of text concurrently. If you add text on one line of a PDF document using the TouchUp Text tool, that line of text will not reflow to another line. Each line of type is edited in isolation from the other lines.

> If you create PDF files that you do not want to be modified or edited, use Acrobat's security features. These features are discussed in Hour 4, "Creating PDF Files from Your Electronic Documents," and Hour 14, "Creating and Applying Digital Signatures."

Limitations to Text-Editing Capabilities

Acrobat allows you to edit text in documents to which security has not been applied and also in documents where Acrobat can access the fonts necessary for editing the text. If a PDF document is created, and Acrobat does not have access to the complete font used in the text being edited, Acrobat cannot add or change the text. Acrobat can always delete text, but it might not be able to add or change text if the font necessary is not available.

When a PDF file is created, it is possible to include a subset of the font containing only the characters used in the PDF file—not the entire font family. This process, called *subsetting*, is discussed in Hour 4. If the fonts needed to edit a PDF file are subsetted, Acrobat cannot edit the text using that font. If you try to edit such text, you will receive a warning message, as shown in Figure 12.2.

FIGURE 12.2

When you attempt to edit text in a PDF file where the fonts have been subsetted, a warning message appears.

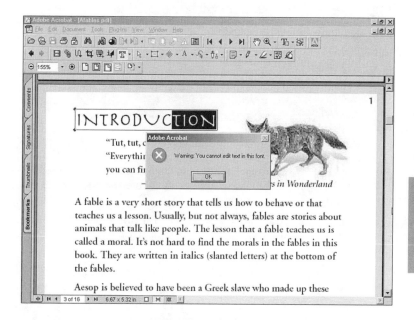

12

Fonts that are embedded in their entirety, and not as subsets, do not have this editing limitation. If a font is embedded in a PDF file but is not installed on your computer, Acrobat can "unembed" the font from the PDF file so that you can edit the text.

It is still possible to edit text that uses a font that has been subsetted within a PDF file. To do this, you must change the font that has been applied to the text you want to edit. You must change it from a font that is an embedded subset to a font that is installed on your computer. Although this process might cause the appearance of the text in the PDF to change slightly, it is required if you want to edit text that has an embedded subset font applied to it. The following section explains how to change the Font attribute of the text in a PDF document.

Changing Text Attributes

To change the characteristics of type used in a PDF file, you must access the Text Attributes palette by selecting Tools, TouchUp Text, Text Attributes. The Text Attributes palette opens as shown in Figure 12.3; this palette contains the options described in the following sections. As you would expect, you must highlight the text on the page before you can apply any of the options in the Text Attributes palette.

FIGURE 12.3

The Text Attributes palette provides the capability to change most of the character-istics of type used in a PDF file, including font, color, and type size.

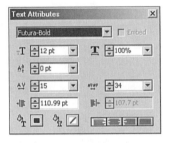

Font

The Font drop-down list in the Text Attributes palette lists all the fonts you can apply to the selected text in a PDF file. Several fonts may be listed at the top of the pull-down menu, separated by a line from a longer list of alphabetically listed fonts (see Figure 12.4). The fonts at the top of this drop-down list are the fonts already used in the PDF file. Fonts following the line are those that are installed on your computer. If you select any of these fonts, you will have complete editing capabilities; fonts above the line might be embedded subsets installed in the PDF that can not be edited.

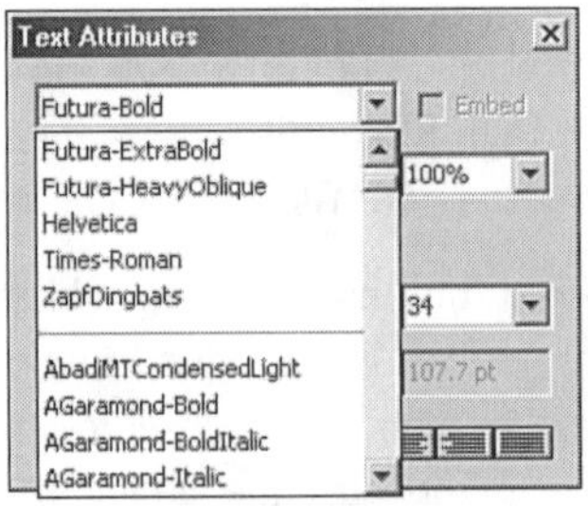

FIGURE 12.4

Select a font that's installed on your computer if you want complete editing capabilities in the PDF file.

Embed

Select the Embed option if you are switching to a new font and want to embed that new font in the PDF file. Font embedding and its advantages and drawbacks are discussed in Hour 3, "Where Do PDF Files Come From?," and Hour 4.

Size

The Size option changes the size of selected type. Use this option to make the type larger or smaller.

Horizontal Scaling

Choose the Horizontal Scaling option to take selected text and make it wide or thin. This option maintains the height of the text but stretches or compacts it horizontally.

Baseline Shift

The Baseline Shift setting allows the selected text to be moved up or down from the baseline on which it normally sits. Use this option to elevate footnote numbers or registered trademark symbols.

Left and Right Indent

The Left and Right Indent options push text in from the left and right edges of the paragraph.

Kerning and Tracking

The space between individual character pairs and between a range of characters is controlled with the Kerning and Tracking controls. *Kerning* adjusts the space between a character pair. If you want to adjust the space between a range of characters, select the entire range and use the kerning controls. Similarly, *tracking* adjusts the amount of space between a range of characters. This value is measured using one-thousandth of an em space increments. A full em space is defined as the width of the character m using the typeface and size being edited. This means that an em space of 12-point Times type differs from an em space for 10-point Helvetica.

Fill and Stroke Color

The *fill color* is the color that will be applied to the selected text. If you decide to change the color of text, use the Fill Color option. If the text had a border color applied to it in the original file, the Stroke Color option allows you to modify to color applied to the border. If a border color has not been defined, you can add one. However, Acrobat does not let you control the thickness of the border color.

Additional Text-Editing Capabilities

The way a PDF file looks on the average computer screen or on a laser printer may be your first concern. But advances in technology now allow PDF files to be read by screen-reading software that assists visually impaired readers and to be transferred onto hand-held computer devices. Consequently, it is important to understand how your PDF file will be viewed and read on devices other than a standard computer screen. Access the following commands by choosing Tools, TouchUp Text.

Text Breaks

The Text Breaks option is found in the Tools, TouchUp Text menu. It lets you see how Acrobat will represent the breaks between words and lines to screen-reading software or another device that might have to reflow the text in the PDF. Using the TouchUp Text tool, select the text in which you want to confirm the line breaks. A separate Text Breaks window appears, as shown in Figure 12.5. Acrobat places a large space between every word and places a blank line between each line. If you do not see a space between words or a blank line where one should be represented, you can use the editing tools described in the following sections.

FIGURE 12.5

The Text Breaks window lets you preview how a PDF file will be represented to screen-reading software or how it may be reflowed on handheld computer screens.

Insert: Line Break, Soft Hyphen, Non-Breaking Space, Em Dash

Use the Line Break, Soft Hyphen, Non-Breaking Space, and Em Dash options to add these elements in locations where they are needed—as you have identified using the Text Breaks window. Although the Line Break option only affects the way a document will be read or will reflow on other computers, the remaining commands affect how the document will look on traditional computers and when printed—as well as how the document will be read or reflowed.

Fit Text to Selection

When changing text attributes, it is possible that the text you are inserting might not be the same size as the text you are replacing. Use the Fit Text to Selection option to force any new text that you insert to take up the same amount of space that the old text occupied. The space between words and characters may be exaggerated to make it fit when using this option.

Show Line Markers

To change how text is positioned horizontally across the page, use the Show Line Markers command. It provides a box around a selected line of text, as shown in Figure 12.6. After selecting a line of text to edit, click the diamonds that appear in the corner or center of the line of text depending on the justification setting in the Text Attributes palette (in this figure, the diamonds are on the left side of the box, so the text is left justified). You can then drag the line of text further left or right on the page to establish a new location for the line.

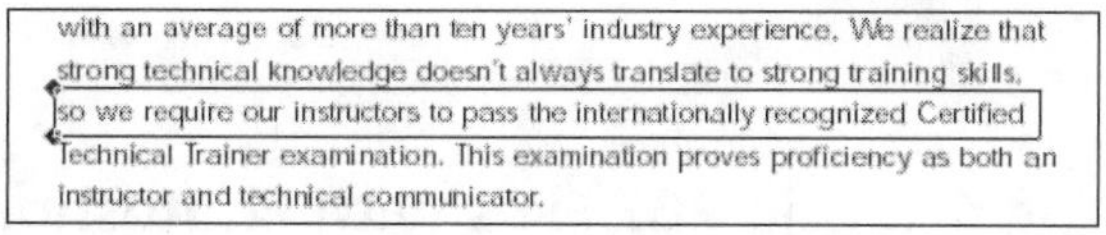

FIGURE 12.6

Line markers appear as a thin box around the line of text being edited with the TouchUp Text tool.

with an average of more than ten years' industry experience. We realize that strong technical knowledge doesn't always translate to strong training skills, so we require our instructors to pass the internationally recognized Certified Technical Trainer examination. This examination proves proficiency as both an instructor and technical communicator.

Editing Graphics with the TouchUp Object Tool

12

To move graphics such as photos to new locations in a PDF document, use the TouchUp Object tool, shown in Figure 12.7. After selecting this tool, click on a graphic and drag it to a new location in the PDF file.

Moving graphics to new locations is not the only editing option you have for graphics. If you have Photoshop and Adobe Illustrator, you have access to more extensive editing functions for graphics.

FIGURE **12.7**

The TouchUp Object tool provides the capability to move graphics in PDF files or to change the position of most objects on a PDF page.

TouchUp Object Tool

Task: Editing Scans in PDF Files with Photoshop

Graphics used in PDF files can be brought into Photoshop for retouching and saved back into the PDF file with any edits. This task explains how.

1. Open a PDF file that contains photographs that have been scanned or are from a digital camera.

2. Select the TouchUp Object tool.

3. Right-click a scanned graphic that you want to edit. If you are a Macintosh user, Ctrl+click the scanned graphic.

4. From the context menu that appears, select Edit Image.

5. The image will open in Photoshop.

6. Edit the graphic as desired in Photoshop and select the Save command.

If the Edit Image option is not available from the context menu for the selected graphic, you may have to modify your preferences. Select Edit, Preferences, General. In the Preferences dialog box, choose the TouchUp option and then select Choose Image Editor to identify where Photoshop is located on your computer. Similarly, select Choose Page/Object Editor to identify the location of Adobe Illustrator on your computer.

Editing illustrations such as graphs and charts used in PDF files involves the same process as editing graphics. The only difference is that computer illustrations are typically divided into multiple segments after they are converted to a PDF file. This happens even if all of the pieces are from the same file. Because of this, you will sometimes end up editing just a portion of the graphic and not the entire file when trying to modify it using Adobe Illustrator.

The best method for ensuring that you will edit the entire graphic rather than some of its parts is to drag a box around the graphic you want to edit. Then right-click the selected graphic and choose the Edit Objects command. Notice that the context menu lists Edit Object when only one component is selected, but it changes to the plural—Objects—when multiple items are selected.

If, after identifying the location of Photoshop or Illustrator on your computer, you are still unable to edit images, reinstall Adobe Acrobat. Acrobat looks for these programs when it is installed. If Photoshop and Illustrator are installed after Acrobat, Acrobat is sometimes unable to locate them to use for editing purposes.

You can also edit a text block using the TouchUp Object tool if you have Adobe Illustrator software. The text opens in Adobe Illustrator, where you can manipulate a large range of text—often a bit more fluidly than you can using the TouchUp Text tool.

12

Using Third-Party Editing Tools

You can expand the software tools available for editing PDF files by purchasing some additional components from third-party software developers. These programmers have created software that operates within Acrobat and adds additional editing functionality to Acrobat. Two of the more popular options are Enfocus PitStop and Quite a Box of Tricks.

Enfocus PitStop

PitStop is available from Enfocus software (www.enfocus.com) and adds several editing tools to the Acrobat toolbar palette along with several dialog boxes for additional editing functionality (see Figure 12.8). The additional editing options include:

- Editing illustrations and paths within Acrobat. This feature eliminates the need to go into Adobe Illustrator to modify graphics. You can change the color, size, and shape of objects used in a PDF file using PitStop.

- Editing text, one paragraph at a time. This enhancement expands on Acrobat's text-editing capabilities. Acrobat allows you to edit only one line of text at a time without this feature.

FIGURE 12.8

The Enfocus PitStop Inspector palette provides additional editing functionality within Acrobat.

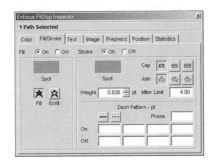

We discuss additional editing features of Acrobat as they relate to printing and prepress features in Hour 24, "Printing with Acrobat."

Quite a Box of Tricks

Although the name of this software sounds a bit odd, it starts to make sense when you understand the developer's name: Quite Software. Where PitStop lets you edit individual items on a page, Quite a Box of Tricks focuses on additional page-editing capabilities (see Figure 12.9). It allows you to modify all of the images in a document to reduce the file size or to scale the page so that it is larger or smaller. You can learn more about this software at www.quite.com.

FIGURE 12.9

Quite a Box of Tricks provides options for modifying and editing pages beyond those capabilities provided within Acrobat.

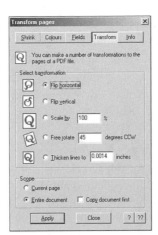

More Third-Party Editing Tools

If you are looking for additional third-party editing tools to help you modify your Acrobat files, try the Power Xchange at www.thepowerco.com. They have dozens of tools to help you work more efficiently with PDF files, including the tools from Enfocus.

Editing Entire PDF Files

If you want to edit an entire PDF document, try opening it using Adobe Illustrator. After you launch Illustrator, open the PDF file by using the File, Open menu command—not by double-clicking the PDF file. It may take a while for the PDF to open, but after it does, you will have the ability to edit text and graphics using the various tools Illustrator offers, as shown in Figure 12.10.

FIGURE 12.10

PDF files such as this one can be opened and edited using Adobe Illustrator.

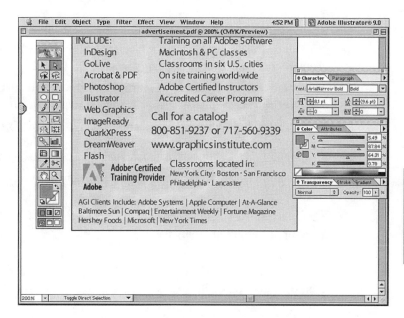

Summary

After finishing this hour, you should be able to edit text and graphics contained in PDF documents. You should know how to edit individual lines of type or make use of third-party utilities to edit text across an entire paragraph. You should also be able to move graphic files to new locations on a PDF document how to edit photographs using Photoshop, and how to edit graphics and illustrations using Illustrator (if you have these software tools).

Workshop

We finish this hour by looking at some issues you may encounter when trying to edit objects in PDF files. Following the Q&A section are several quiz questions to confirm your understanding of the process of editing PDF files. Finally, you'll find some exercises to practice what you've learned.

Q&A

Q When I edit text, Acrobat sometimes displays a message that text cannot be edited in the selected font. How can I tell which fonts are embedded subsets and are therefore not available for editing?

A As discussed earlier in the hour, fonts that are embedded subsets cannot be used for editing text unless you also have the entire font installed on your computer. To determine which fonts are embedded subsets, select File, Document Properties, Fonts. This command provides a list of all the fonts used in a document and whether they are embedded, embedded subsets, or not embedded. You can find more information about embedding fonts in PDF files in Hour 4.

Q Sometimes when I try to select a graphic with the TouchUp Object tool, I end up selecting several nearby items as well. Is there any way to avoid this?

A Unfortunately not. When PDF files are created, items are often grouped together for display purposes. It can become difficult to separate them. Similarly, you will sometimes encounter items that should be grouped but find that you can select only individual elements. Acrobat does not have any commands for grouping or ungrouping.

Q Can I adjust the stacking order of objects on a PDF page so that one item is in front of or behind another item?

A To do this, you will want to make the adjustment in the original software package that was used to design the PDF. If this is not possible, you can try to open the PDF file using Adobe Illustrator and adjust the stacking order in Illustrator.

Quiz

1. **Editing photographs and scans used in PDF files requires what tools?**

    a. The TouchUp Object tool and Adobe Photoshop.

    b. A third-party plug in: Enfocus PitStop.

    c. The TouchUp Object tool and no additional software.

    d. Graphics used in PDF files cannot be edited.

2. Which attributes cannot be changed by Acrobat in a PDF file?

    a. Fonts used on text in a PDF file.

    b. Colors applied to text.

    c. The page size of the document.

    d. All of the above.

Quiz Answers

1. **a** Acrobat requires a photo-retouching software that can open PDF files (such as Adobe Photoshop) to edit the images and save them back into the PDF. Use the TouchUp Objects tool and right-click an image to edit it using Photoshop.

2. **c** Acrobat does not allow you to change the size of the PDF pages without additional software plug-ins. All the other options—such as changing font and color—are available by using the TouchUp Text command from the Tools menu.

Exercises

Learn more about the text-selection tools by trying the following exercises.

1. Open a PDF file that contains multiple illustrations, charts, and tables. Practice moving and selecting the individual items and the entire group. Practice opening the entire group of selected objects for editing using Adobe Illustrator.

2. Try changing the font, color, and size of text using the Text Attributes palette. Also try modifying individual words and lines of type using the TouchUp Text tool.

12

HOUR 13

Adding Comments and Annotations

Now that you have some practice getting around in PDF files, let's focus on ways you can add comments to your PDF files. We will explore some of the many uses for the comments and markup tools and the different ways to use these most important features.

In this hour, you will learn about the following:

- The similarities and differences between the comments and markup tools
- How to add comments to a PDF file
- How to create custom comments with the Stamp tool
- How to change the basic look and properties of comments
- How to export, import, and summarize comments
- How to filter comments using the Tools menu
- How to spell check comments
- How to share comments using a shared folder

A Few Facts About the Use of Comments

Sometimes, the need arises to add information to a PDF file: an observation or remark, perhaps a note about a change that should be made. Adobe has included a series of tools within Acrobat, called the Comments and Annotations tools, for just such purposes. These tools allow you to include text pertinent to a particular portion of the PDF document; the text appears inside a text box that the viewer can open using the Hand tool. On the document, an icon or other form of graphic "mark-up" character appears, indicating that there is copy to be read. When the viewer double-clicks the icon or graphic, the text box opens, revealing the information you wanted them to see.

Here is one possible scenario for using the Comments and Annotation tools: You are preparing a document that must be approved—and possibly changed—by several others in your office. Instead of passing an interoffice memo from person to person or distributing a series of copies throughout the office, you can simply create a PDF from the original document and e-mail it to everyone on the list.

Each person can then use Acrobat to mark up the document with his or her comments and changes. They can return the document to you with their changes in place, or they can export the changes and e-mail just the changes. If you receive a file with just the changes, you can import the changes into the original PDF file, and those changes will appear exactly where the reader intended them to be located.

Here is another scenario: Suppose that you have to get a client's approval on a particular document, and time is of the essence. You can simply e-mail the document in PDF format to the client, who in turn marks up any necessary changes or additions to the document, using the Comments or Graphic Markup tools. Your client returns the original file with the changes added or exports the comments and e-mails them to you.

Think of the time and money using these Acrobat features will save! No more manila interoffice envelopes being passed around with the risk of being lost. No more courier fees to send the documents to someone in another location. And instead of having to read through numerous marked-up copies of the same document, you can import *all* the comments into a single PDF document and see them all at the same time.

In addition to the Comments tools, Acrobat offers a group of Graphic Markup and Text Markup tools. These tools work similarly to the way the Comments tools work but appear differently in the document. Graphic Markup tools allow you to draw a shape or marking to highlight the area in question. Text Markup tools offer features such as strikeout, underline, and highlight to call attention to selected text.

The scenario we have been alluding to is more commonly known as the *PDF Workflow*. It is, simply put, a way to add speed and accuracy to the normal office workflow using PDF files. PDF Workflow is changing the way businesses operate. The PDF file format—and its native application, Acrobat—help to eliminate paper waste and unnecessary time spent waiting for documents to be returned. Documents are distributed instantaneously through e-mail, and the sender has a record of when the documents reach their destination. The sender can also save or print all the comments on a document for record keeping and other purposes.

Comments Tools

Comments are on a separate "layer" of the PDF document. Adobe keeps the comments separate from the actual contents of the PDF file so that the comments can be deleted, exported, and imported without affecting the original items on the page. Let's begin to explore the different Comments tools and how to use them. Figure 13.1 shows the Comments tools in the toolbar.

> For easier access to the Comments tools, expand the Comments portion of the toolbar. To do this, click the black triangle to the right of the Notes tool on the left end of the toolbar. Choose Expand This Button from the menu that drops down to add the hidden tools to the toolbar. To put the tools away again, simply click the black triangle a second time to tuck the tools away.

FIGURE 13.1

The Comments tools are located in the toolbar at the top of the Acrobat screen.

Comments tools

13

Notes Tool

The Notes tool places an icon on the document, which, when clicked, opens to a text window. The viewer uses the Hand tool to open the window and read the message.

Task: Using the Notes Tool

▼ TASK

The Notes tool is the first tool we will experiment with to begin working with comments. Before you start this task, open a PDF file to which you want to add comments.

▼ 1. Choose the Notes tool from the toolbar.

2. Click in the PDF document where you want to add a note; a window opens, allowing you to insert text. Notice the current date at the top right of the window and the author's name at the top left (see Figure 13.2). Later in this hour, we will explore how to change properties for the Comments tools (such as changing the color of the top bar and the author name), but for now, just type the text of the note you want to add in the box. When you're done, click the × in the upper-left corner to close the window (Macintosh users can click the white box in the upper-left corner of the notes to close the text window).

3. Select the Hand tool and double-click the comment icon; the comment window
▲ opens. This is how the reader views the text you have added to the PDF.

FIGURE 13.2

Double-click the comment icon to open the comment window, which shows the current date, author's name, and text of the comment.

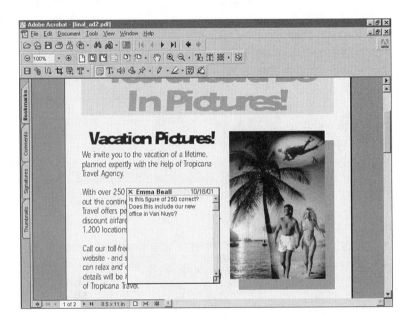

With the comment window closed, you can change attributes by using either the Hand tool or the Notes tool to select the note; then choose Edit, Properties (Ctrl+I for users of IBM-compatible computers, Command+I for Macintosh users). The Note Properties dialog box opens (see Figure 13.3). Here, you can change the icon that will appear when the window is closed, the color of the icon, and the color of the bar at the top of the comment window. You can change the author name that appears in the top bar of the window, as well.

After you make these changes, multiple users can use the Notes tool to add comments to the document, and the comments will appear differently (if a different color is chosen in the properties).

FIGURE 13.3

Use the Note Properties dialog box to change the attributes of the comment window.

You can reposition the comment on the PDF page by dragging it with either the Notes tool or the Hand tool. You can move the comment when it's either open or closed.

Acrobat provides a preference setting that overrides the computer's identity name as the author name for comments in future documents. Choose Edit, Preferences, General (Ctrl+K for users of IBM-compatible computers, Command+K for Macintosh users) and click the word Comments in the list on the left side of the pane. If the check box next to the Always Use Identity For Author option is deselected, your author name as specified in the Note Properties dialog box will appear on all subsequent comments. Select this option to allow Acrobat to pick up the computer's identity name as the comments' author in the future.

Free Text Tool

The Free Text tool is located on the toolbar next to the Notes tool. Although you can use the Free Text tool to add a comment to the PDF, instead of the icon and hidden text window that you get when you use the Notes tool, the Free Text tool simply displays a line of text. The rest of tool's features work the same as those for the Notes tool. You can change attributes for the text (font size, outline color, and background color) in the Properties dialog box. Select the text field by clicking once to highlight it, and choose Edit, Properties (as shown in Figure 13.4).

In other words, the Notes tool allows you to see a simple icon that you can double-click to reveal the message. By contrast, the Free Text tool displays the text right on the page. If the message the user wants to add is a few short words, the Free Text tool is a good option. For lengthier messages, it might be a better choice to use a comment tool that has its text box "hidden."

You can move the text you create with the Free Text tool by dragging it with the Hand tool or the Free Text tool. You can resize the text area by dragging the corner handles.

FIGURE 13.4

Change properties for the text created by the Free Text tool in the Properties dialog box.

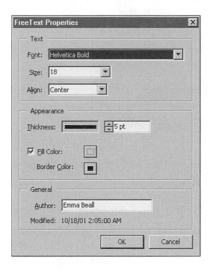

Sound Attachment Tool

The Sound Attachment tool allows you to use a recorded sound as a comment. You can record the sound on your computer in Acrobat (provided that you have a microphone), or you can click the Choose button to pick a prerecorded sound.

After you have identified the sound you want to use as a comment, you choose the Sound Properties, such as color of the icon the viewer clicks, a short description of the sound, and the author name. To open the Sound Properties dialog box, click once on the sound icon to highlight it and then choose Edit, Properties. Click OK to close the Sound Properties dialog box when you are finished. See Figure 13.5.

To play the sound, the user double-clicks the speaker icon with the Hand tool. To hear the sound properly, make sure that the user has the proper speaker and sound card equipment installed. If you are unsure that the users of the PDF file have the proper equipment, it might be better to use a different comment tool so that the users are not hampered by not being able to hear the sounds you have included for them.

FIGURE 13.5

You can use sounds as comments in a PDF file by recording them or choosing an existing sound file after you select the Sound Attachment tool.

Audio comments are saved as WAV (.wav) files on Windows computers and as AIFF (.aiff) files on Macintosh computers. The sounds are embedded into the PDF document, so there is no need to send the original sound file when transporting the PDF; it is contained within the PDF file.

Any Comment, Graphic Markup, or Text Markup icon can be deleted. First select the icon (click the icon, shape, or text markup once with the Hand tool or the tool used to make the comment) and then press the Delete key on your keyboard.

Users of IBM-compatibles can right-click, and Macintosh users can Ctrl+click to find the Delete command.

Stamp Tool

The Stamp tool allows you to use a predesigned stamp, which you can choose from a variety of categories. The text window appears when you double-click the stamp on the PDF page.

Select the Stamp tool and click the PDF page; the last-used stamp appears as a "mark" on the page. Double-click the mark with either the Stamp tool or the Hand tool to open a window in which you can add the text note. The window that displays looks like the Notes window: It shows the author and the date the note was created. An example of a stamp created with the Stamp tool is shown in Figure 13.6. You can choose from a variety of predefined icons for the stamp or create custom stamps in Adobe Illustrator.

13

Click once on the stamp you placed on the page with the Hand tool or Stamp tool to select the stamp. Choose Edit, Properties to view the Stamp Properties dialog box. Here, you can select a category (such as Faces) and view the stamps for that category. You can also change the color of the text window's top bar and can change the author name. Click OK to close the dialog box when you are finished.

Creating Custom Stamps

Not only can you apply the stamps provided in the Stamp tool's categories, you can create custom stamps as well.

Examples of how custom stamps can prove useful include stamps of your signature or of your company logo. Customizing stamps for your particular purpose is easy with Acrobat.

Task: Creating a Custom Stamp

Let's create a custom stamp. Custom stamps are stored in the Plug Ins, Annotations, Stamps folder of Adobe Acrobat. Follow these steps to create a custom stamp and save it for use within Acrobat.

1. Using a illustration or image-editing program such as Adobe Illustrator or Adobe Photoshop, create your custom stamp. Save the stamp document in PDF format. Both Illustrator and Photoshop allow you to save directly to PDF by choosing File, Save As and choosing Adobe PDF as the file format.

2. After creating the custom stamp, open it in Acrobat. Create a page template by choosing Tools, Forms, Page Templates. Name the template (choose a name related to the stamp, such as your company name, your name, the shape of the custom stamp, and so on). Specify a category name for the stamp by typing the category in the Title field of the Document Properties dialog box (choose File, Document Properties, Summary to open this dialog box (users of IBM-compatible computers

▼ press Ctrl+D, Mac users press Command+D). The name you enter in the Title field is the category the stamp will appear under when you view the stamp categories in the Properties dialog box.

You can choose to use an existing category or create one of your own (such as company logos, a "sigs" category in which your own handwritten signature could appear, and so on).

3. Save the page template file to the Stamps folder of Adobe Acrobat (Acrobat, Plug-Ins, Annotations, Stamps).

Now when you use the Stamp tool, you can choose the new category and the new ▲ stamp to use on your document for comments.

In the preferences you set for your comments (choose Edit, Preferences, General to open the Preferences dialog box and then choose Comments from the pane on the left), you can specify that you want to have the pop-up text windows open automatically when the mouse moves over them.

You may want to set up your file this way to make it faster for users to view the comments. In the Preferences dialog box for the file, choose the Automatically Open Pop-Ups When Mouse Over option.

File Attachment Tool

Embedding a file in the PDF for the viewer to open and read is an option the File Attachment tool offers. To use the tool, simply click with it and choose the file to attach (see Figure 13.7). Here are some points to keep in mind concerning the use of this tool:

- The user must have an application that can read the attached document. For example, a Word document can be read in a word processing application.

- After the file is attached to the PDF, right-clicking (Ctrl+clicking for Macintosh users) allows you to save a copy of the embedded file to disk. Doing so saves a copy of the file, separate from the PDF file, in addition to the file embedded in the PDF document.

- After the file has been attached to the PDF document, the name of the attached file appears as a ToolTip when you pass the mouse pointer over the icon.

13

FIGURE **13.7**

The File Attachment tool gives you the option of attaching an actual file to the PDF document. When you click with the File Attachment tool, a dialog box prompts you to choose the file to attach.

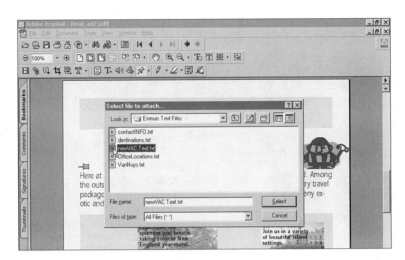

Task: Attaching a File with the File Attachment Tool

Follow these steps to experiment with the File Attachment tool.

1. Open a PDF document and choose the File Attachment tool from the toolbar.

2. Click on the document page; Acrobat prompts you to select the file you want to attach. Browse to find the file you want to attach and then click the Select button to open the Properties dialog box.

3. Next, you will apply File Attachment Properties. Choose the file icon you want to show on the PDF page. For instance, if the file you are attaching is a spreadsheet document or a graph, you might want the Graph icon to appear on the PDF page. In this dialog box, you can also choose a color for the icon by clicking the colored square next to the word Color.

4. The filename of the file you attached appears in the Description box. You can change this to a brief description of the file, if desired, and change your author name as well. To do this after the file has been attached, use the Hand tool to select the icon. Then choose Edit, Properties and change the description. The description is what appears when the user hovers the mouse pointer over the icon on the page. Click OK when you are finished.

5. Using the Hand tool, double-click the File Attachment icon you just added to the PDF file. A dialog box appears, where you can click Open to view the file in its native application.

6. After you finish viewing the attached file, close it in the usual way; the original PDF file remains open in the background.

Graphic Markup Tools

As you can see in Figure 13.8, another way to annotate a PDF file is by using the Graphic Markup tools. These tools include the Pencil, Square, Circle, and Line tools. This series of tools allows you to mark up a document using graphic elements, but also provides a text window like the one you get with the Notes tool. You can make the text window visible by double-clicking the graphic element. (If you cannot see the different graphic markup tools, remember to expand the button in the toolbar to show the hidden tools.)

The cursor turns into an arrow when it passes over the graphic markup tools, alerting the user that this is a comment.

FIGURE 13.8

Graphic Markup tools let you call attention to a particular area of a PDF by drawing shapes on the page; double-click the graphic element to display its associated text window.

Graphic Markup tools

Pencil Tool

You can use the Pencil tool to draw a freehand shape around a particular area of the PDF page you want to point out to someone (see Figure 13.9). You can then add text to the text window; when viewers double-click the shape, they can view the text.

FIGURE 13.9

The Pencil tool gives you the freedom to draw a freehand shape to alert the user that a comment is attached here.

13

Select the Pencil tool from the toolbar and draw around the area you want to call out. Using either the Hand tool or the Pencil tool, double-click the line you drew. The text window opens, displaying the author name and date. Type the text you want to add, close the window by clicking the × in the upper-left corner of the window (Macintosh users can click the white box at the top of the window).

When you click once on the line, the control handles appear, enabling you to resize the shape. Choose Properties from the context menu (or choose Edit, Properties from the menu bar) to display the Pencil Properties dialog box (see Figure 13.10). Choose the thickness and color of the line and change the author, if necessary. Click OK to close the dialog box.

FIGURE 13.10

Use the Pencil Properties dialog box to adjust the appearance of the line you draw or to change the author name for the comment associated with the line.

Square Tool

To draw a box around something on the PDF document page, use the Square tool (see Figure 13.11), located next to the Pencil tool on the toolbar.

Press and hold the Shift key as you drag the Square tool to constrain the shape to a square. You can also use the Square tool to draw a rectangle or square that calls attention to an element or area of text on the page.

Double-click the shape with the Hand tool or Square tool to open the text window associated with the square, just as you did with the Pencil tool. Type any text you want in the box and then close it.

Click the square or rectangle once with the Hand tool or Square tool to select the graphic. Choose Edit, Properties to open the Properties dialog box for the graphic, where you can change the graphic's appearance, or drag the control handles after the square is selected.

FIGURE 13.11

The Square tool.

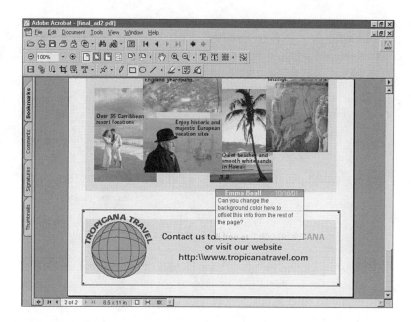

Circle Tool

The Circle tool works just like the Square tool; instead of drawing rectangles, you use the Circle tool to add ovals and circles to the PDF document. Press and hold the Shift key as you draw with the Circle tool to constrain the shape to a perfect circle.

Double-click the circle with the Hand tool or Circle tool to open the text window associated with the shape. Type any text you want in the box and then close it.

Edit the properties for the circle in the same way you change the properties for the Square tool (see Figure 13.12).

Line Tool

Use the Line tool to add a rule to the document. The rule can have a text window attached to it in the same way the other graphic markup tools do.

Press and hold the Shift key as you draw with the Line tool to constrain the line to multiples of 45 degrees. For example, if you want the line to be perfectly horizontal or vertical, press and hold the Shift key as you draw the line.

Double-click the line with the Hand tool or Line tool to display the text box in which you can type a comment.

13

FIGURE 13.12

FIGURE 13.12

Change the appearance of the circle by selecting it and choosing Edit, Properties to open the Circle Properties dialog box.

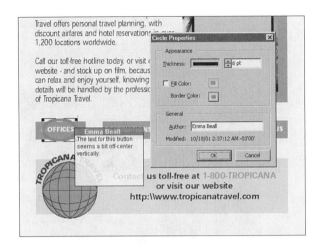

Click once on the line with the Hand tool or Line tool to select it and choose Edit, Properties to open the Line Properties dialog box. Change the appearance of the line using this dialog box. Figure 13.13 shows some of the effects you can achieve using the Line tool.

FIGURE 13.13

The Line tool creates rules and arrows you can double-click to view comments.

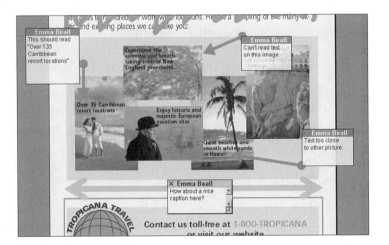

Text Markup Tools

The Text Markup tools are the final set in the triad of comments tools. Text Markup tools give you the ability to mark up the text directly, using three different looks, depending on the purpose of the comment. Figure 13.14 shows the Text Markup tools in the toolbar.

For instance, if you are indicating text to be removed from the PDF document, you may want to use the Strikeout tool, which causes the selected text to appear with a line through it. This common proofreader's symbol indicates text to be deleted.

FIGURE 13.14

The Text Markup tools let you mark changes directly in the text of a PDF document.

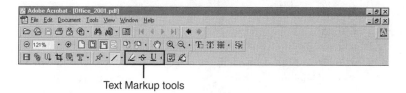

Text Markup tools

Highlight Tool

The first of the Text Markup tools is the Highlight tool. This tool gives the underlying text the look achieved by running a highlighter marker over text on a page. You can change the color of the highlight in the Highlight Properties dialog box.

To use the Highlight tool, select it from the toolbar. Click and drag the tool across the type you want to draw attention to. When you release the mouse, the selected type will be highlighted.

To attach the text of a comment, open the text window by double-clicking the high-lighted area with the Hand tool or the Highlight tool. By default, the selected text appears in the text window. To change the text comment, select the text and retype. Close the window by clicking the × in the upper-left corner of the window (Macintosh users can click the white box at the top of the window).

Click the highlighted area once with the Hand tool or Highlight tool to select it. Then choose Edit, Properties to open the Highlight Properties dialog box. Change the color of the highlight using this dialog box. Delete the highlight by selecting the highlight and pressing the Delete key on the keyboard. Figure 13.15 shows how the highlight appears in the PDF file.

13

FIGURE 13.15

Use the Highlight tool to highlight text on the PDF page in the same way you use a high-light marker on paper.

Strikeout Tool

Useful for indicating text to be removed, the Strikeout tool draws a line through the selected area of text.

To use the Strikeout tool, first select it from the toolbar. Drag the tool over the text in the PDF document you want to mark for deletion. The text appears with a line through it. To add comments to this highlighted text, double-click the selected text with the Hand tool or Strikeout tool to open the text window. Type the text in the window and close the window by clicking the × in the upper-left corner of the window (Macintosh users can click the white box at the top of the window).

To change the color of the strikeout characters, first select the affected text by clicking it using the Hand tool or Strikeout tool. Choose Edit, Properties to open the Strikeout Properties dialog box. Choose a new color for the strikeout character and click OK to close the dialog box. Figure 13.16 shows how the strikeout appears in the PDF file.

FIGURE 13.16

Use the Strikeout tool to mark text intended for deletion.

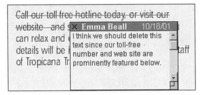

Another Preference setting you may want to experiment with is the transparency of your comment windows. Open the Preferences dialog box by choosing Edit, Preferences, General. Select Comments in the pane on the left side of the dialog box. Figure 13.17 shows the Comments page of the Preferences dialog box.

The Pop-Up Opacity field near the top of the page allows you to control the transparency of the text windows associated with your comments. Experiment with different settings to find the look that suits you best.

Underline Tool

You can mark text you want to emphasize in some way by underlining it. Choose the Underline tool from the toolbar and drag it over the text in the PDF document you want to underline. To add comments to this underlined text, double-click the selected text with the Hand tool or Strikeout tool to open the text window. Type the text in the window and close the window by clicking the × in the upper-left corner of the window (Macintosh users can click the white box on the top of the window).

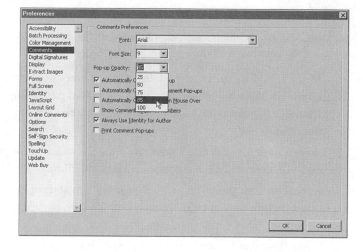

FIGURE 13.17

Choose preset transparency options from the Pop-up Opacity drop-down menu or enter an amount in the text box.

To change the color of the underline, first select the affected text by clicking it using the Hand tool or Strikeout tool. Choose Edit, Properties to open the Underline Properties dialog box. Choose a new color for the underline and click OK to close the dialog box. Figure 13.18 shows how underlined text appears in the PDF file.

FIGURE 13.18

Use the Underline tool to underline text to which you want to call attention.

Other Things You Can Do with Comments in Acrobat

Now that you have a basic understanding of adding, editing, and accessing comments, let's explore the options you have for managing the comments in a PDF document.

Summarizing Comments

After comments have been added to a PDF document, you can choose to prepare a report detailing each of the comments by summarizing the comments.

13

Task: Summarizing Comments in the PDF File

Summarizing your comments allows you to see all the comments in the PDF file at a single glance. To summarize comments, follow these steps:

1. Open a PDF document that contains different types of comments. These comments can include those added with the Notes tool, Stamp tool, Line tool, and so on. Opening a file that contains several different authors' comments will give you a better understanding of how the summarizing feature works.

2. Choose Tools, Comments, Summarize from the menu bar or press Ctrl+Shift+T for users of IBM-compatible machines (Command+Shift+T for Macintosh users).

3. Acrobat prompts you to choose how you want to sort the comments: by date, by author, and so on. You can also choose to filter the comments, as described later in this section. Click OK to close the dialog box.

4. Acrobat displays an onscreen list of the comments in the document (see Figure 13.9) separated into the categories you selected. You can choose to save this document as a PDF file (so that you can e-mail it to someone else, for example), print out the summary document, or close it without saving it.

FIGURE 13.19

Summarizing the comments in a PDF file allows you to view all the comments at once.

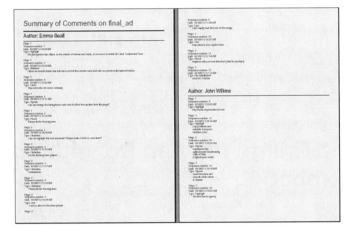

Exporting Comments

As mentioned earlier in this hour, you can export the comments in a PDF file into a small, portable format that you can e-mail to someone else who has the PDF file. That person can then import your comments into the copy of the PDF he or she has. E-mailing just the exported comments results in faster upload and download times for you and your recipient.

To export comments, start by opening a PDF document with multiple comments, preferably with multiple authors. Choose File, Export, Comments. Browse to find the location on your hard disk where you want to store the export file, specify a filename for the export file, and click OK to export the comments. Notice that the file has an .fdf extension, which indicates a forms data file. Note that you are not exporting a PDF document, you are exporting only data that can be used within another PDF document.

Deleting All Comments from a PDF Document

Now that you have saved the comments from a PDF file into a portable file, you can delete all the comments from the original file. In the following section, you learn how to import the comments back into the PDF file.

To delete all comments from a PDF file, choose Tools, Comments, Delete All. Make sure that you really want to delete the comments before you select this command because Acrobat deletes them without asking you for confirmation! (Of course, you can undo this function immediately after performing it by choosing Edit, Undo Multiple Deletes.)

Now you have a clean, uncommented PDF document into which you can import the FDF (exported comments) data file. As you will see in the next section, the comments will fall back into the exact spot where they were placed when they were originally created.

Importing Comments into a PDF Document

Importing comments into a PDF document is easy. You can import multiple comment files into a single PDF document so that you can view all the comments at once.

Consider this example: You have prepared a brochure that is being readied for the printer. You want to send it to several people for proofing purposes, so you e-mail the PDF document to each of these people. Each person reviews the document and adds comments to the file using his or her author name and a chosen color. These people then export their comments and send them to you in the FDF format. You import each FDF file into the original PDF document. When you import each of these FDF files, the comments fall into the exact place where they were originally intended to fall. You can then view all the comments from all the reviewers simultaneously.

To import comments into a PDF file, open the PDF file into which you want to import the comments and choose File, Import, Comments. Browse to select the FDF files you want to import and click OK. The comments fall into place into your open PDF file. To read the text window associated with each comment icon or mark, double-click the icon or mark with the Hand tool.

13

Filtering Comments

When you have received and imported several sets of comments into a single PDF file, it's likely that you will want to manage the comments instead of working with all of them at once.

Acrobat includes a feature that filters comments so that you can work with particular sets of comments sorted by author or by a particular type of comment.

To filter comments, choose Tools, Comments, Filter. In the Filter Comments dialog box that opens as shown in Figure 13.20, you can choose which authors' comments you want to view as well as which particular comment types you want to see. You can also choose a modification time to see only those comments that were made within a particular time period or select Anytime to see comments made at all modification times.

FIGURE 13.20

Display only particular comments by using the Filter Comments dialog box to specify which comments you want to see.

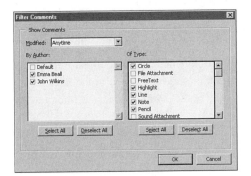

Finding Comments

To find data within a particular comment, use Acrobat's Find Comment feature. Choose Tools, Comments, Find to open the Find Comments dialog box. Type the information for which you are searching. You can also select from three options to help customize your search: Match Case (to search for text exactly as you typed it, matching uppercase and lowercase characters), Find Backwards (to search backwards through the file from the current location of the cursor), and Match Whole Word Only (to prevent the search from turning up comments in which the word you specified is contained within another word, as *the* is contained in the word *together*). Click OK to continue with the search.

Spell Checking Comments

You can use Acrobat's spelling checker to check comments and form fields (which we will cover in Hour 16, "Creating and Using Interactive Forms"). You can spell check only information added to these two areas.

To perform a spell check, choose Tools, Spelling, Check Form Fields and Comments. The spelling checker works like spelling checkers in other applications. You can make changes all at once, individually, or ignore the suggested changes. Click Done when you are finished spell checking the form fields and comments.

If you want to add words to the dictionary Acrobat uses to spell check, you can do that as well. Examples of when you might want to add words to the dictionary are for medical or legal terms that are used frequently in your documents or for proper names that are often added to comments. Adding words to the dictionary cuts down on the number of spelling "errors" Acrobat encounters. To add words to the dictionary, open the spelling checker dialog box and click Add.

Sharing Comments Online

You can share comments over network and Web servers, greatly increasing their flexibility. A Web browser and Acrobat 5 are required for either type of server to use Acrobat comments.

You can share comments online if your PDF documents are stored at a central location where others can access them. As discussed previously, comments are stored as FDF files (forms data format), which makes them accessible to others. A user can make changes to his or her own comments and can add or delete comments, but cannot make changes to others' comments.

To share Acrobat comments on either network or Web servers, both the Web browser and Acrobat must be configured to allow access to comments. Let's begin by configuring Acrobat.

From within Acrobat, choose Edit, Preferences, General to open the Preferences dialog box. Choose Online Comments from the pane on the left side of the window. To configure Web servers to share comments, consult your Webmaster for details on the preference settings and URL necessary.

For more information about sharing comments online, consult Adobe's Web site at `http://www.adobe.com/products/acrobat/`.

Local servers can be set up without a Webmaster's assistance. First, set up a shared folder on the server and give access to all users. Move the PDFs you want to share into the shared folder. Then open the Preferences dialog box, choose Online Comments from the pane on the left side of the dialog box, and enable the Network Server option. Browse to find the shared folder and click OK.

13

Summary

Comments are an integral part of Acrobat, as you have seen in this hour. Multiple sets of comments can be imported into one PDF file, and the comments will fall exactly where they were placed in the original files.

A variety of comments tools, as well as your ability to change author names and colors, gives you great freedom in personalizing the comments. Many users can have their comments distinguishable on the same PDF document.

Workshop

In this workshop, we will review the information covered in the hour, beginning with a few questions of related interest. After you take the short multiple-choice quiz, you can practice with a few hands-on exercises to give you some working experience with comments.

Q&A

Q What happens when I print a document with comments?

A You have control over how the comments are printed, if at all. Settings within the Comments Preferences and the Print dialog box allow you to control how the comments print: as icons, with the windows open, or hidden completely.

Q When I summarize comments, is the generated PDF already saved?

A No. The summary appears in PDF format, but it is not actually a saved file. You must choose File, Save to secure the document, or the document will be discarded when you close it.

Q How can I control the size of the stamp produced with the Stamp tool?

A Clicking on the PDF page with the Stamp tool produces the stamp at the default size. Clicking and dragging an area resizes the stamp to the area you define; you can also change the size afterward by selecting the control handles and dragging them

Quiz

1. **What file formats can be used with the Sound Attachment tool?**

    a. WAV for Windows users, AIFF for Macintosh users.

    b. Sounds are saved as PDF format from within Acrobat.

    c. MP3 is the universal format for sounds used in Acrobat.

2. **How can you change the appearance of a comment?**

   a. You can't. There is only one look for each comment tool.

   b. Select the comment and then choose Comments, Attributes from the Tools menu.

   c. Select the comment and choose Edit, Properties.

3. **Spell checking an Acrobat document checks which aspects of the file?**

   a. All text within the document.

   b. Only comments created with the Notes and Text Markup tools.

   c. Form fields and comments only.

Quiz Answers

1. **a** The formats used for sound attachments are WAV for Windows users and AIFF for Macintosh users.

2. **c** Select the comment and then choose Tools, Comments, Attributes to change the appearance.

3. **c** Spell checking affects form fields and comments only.

Exercises

1. Open a PDF document and add multiple types of comments. Use the Comments Filter dialog box to remove certain types of comments (by author or by specific comment type).

2. Use the Text Markup tools and become accustomed to how the text is selected. Experiment with Graphic Markup tools, which can be used to draw around specific areas, including columns.

3. Practice using some of the different settings for comments (choose Edit, Preferences, General, and click the Comments tab). For instance, change the opacity, show comment sequence numbers, and the change font and type size of the comment text.

13

PART V

Document Security and Digital Signatures

Hour

Hour 14

Creating and Applying Digital Signatures

If you receive electronic documents, why should you print them just to add your signature? After you print it, you then have to sign it and either fax, mail, or courier the document back to the sender. All these steps eliminate any advantages associated with distributing a digital PDF file. All the preceding comments are true—unless you use a *digital signature* to identify your files. Acrobat creates digital PDF files that can be approved and signed digitally, using a secure method to guarantee legitimacy. Unfortunately, many people still send PDF files to clients and co-workers whom then print and sign them, returning them by way of fax or overnight courier. But with what you will learn in this hour, you may never have to print a PDF file again.

Because federal law and many state laws now consider digital signatures valid, Adobe Acrobat makes it easy to confirm that you have viewed, approved, or reviewed a digital file by applying your unique digital signature to a PDF file.

In this hour, you'll learn the following:

- How to use digital signatures
- How to verify digital signatures
- How to apply a digital signature
- How to determine whether a document has been modified after it was signed

Using Digital Signatures

Digital signatures work in the same way that signing a check does. Before you can sign a check, you open a bank account; the bank keeps a copy of your signature on file so that it knows that your signatures on your checks are legitimate. Similarly, before you sign a PDF document, Acrobat will create an account for you. The type of account you create to sign documents is called a *profile*. The profile is a unique verifier that confirms the identity of the signature.

Creating a Profile

To get started with digital signatures, you must first create a profile. The profile consists of two components: One is a private signing key that is encrypted using 1024-bit encryption. This sits only on your computer and remains private. This private key is required for you to digitally sign documents; accessing it requires a password. The second part is a public key, sometimes referred to as a *certificate*, which you share with those people who will receive your digitally signed files. The public key is used to confirm the validity of documents signed with the private key.

Task: Creating a Digital Signature Profile

Before we start signing documents, we'll need to create a digital signature profile.

1. From the Tools menu, select Self-Sign Security and then select Log In. The Log In dialog box appears.

2. Click the New Profile button to display the Create New User dialog box shown in Figure 14.1.

3. Type your full name in the Name field. In the Organization Name field, type your company's name; in the Organization Unit field, type a department name (such as marketing). From the Country drop-down list, choose your country.

4. In the Choose a Password field, type a password that is at least six characters in length. Your password should also include at least one number to keep it more secure. Passwords *are* case sensitive.

Figure 14.1

The Create New User dialog box appears when you build a new digital signature profile to digitally sign PDF files.

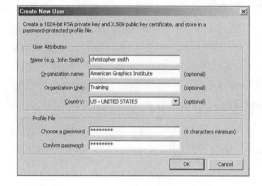

5. Confirm your password by retyping it and then click OK.

6. A dialog box will appear, asking you to select the location on your hard disk where you want to store the profile. Select an appropriate location and click the Save button.

Acrobat accesses this digital signature profile whenever you want to sign a file. The recipient of a signed file can compare any signatures you apply to documents to be certain that they have all been issued by the same signature profile. This arrangement ensures against others misappropriating your identity. Later in this hour, we discuss how you can share a public version of your signature certificate so that others can prove that your signature is legitimate.

After you have created a digital signature profile, you may want to place a copy of the file on any other computers you use, such as your laptop computer. Doing so ensures that your digital signature is identical regardless of which computer you use. To copy your profile to another computer, simply locate the signature file you created in the first task in this hour. Copy this file onto a disk or e-mail it to yourself. You can place the signature file in any location on the second computer.

Similarly, you can create multiple profiles on one computer if you share the computer with others (as is frequently true with home computers). If you copy a profile to another computer, or have more than one profile on your computer, you will have to access your profile before you can sign documents with it.

Task: Accessing a Digital Signature Profile

Before you digitally sign a document, you will have to log in to your digital signature profile, as explained in this task.

1. From the Tools menu, select Self-Sign Security and then select Log In. The Log In dialog box appears.

14

2. Click the Find Your Profile File button.

3. Navigate through your computer's hard drive to locate the signature file you want to use.

4. Enter the password you assigned to that profile, and you are ready to begin signing documents.

Sharing Your Public Profile

When you created your signature, a private encrypted key was created. It was saved on your computer as a file with the .apf extension.

Along with the private key, you also created a public signing key. Your public signing key is used by those with whom you share documents to verify the authenticity of your signature. You will want to share your public key with anyone who receives signed documents from you. The public key allows recipients of your documents to verify that the signature you applied on a document matches the information in the public key.

Although this sounds complicated, Acrobat takes care of most of the technical details for you. You share your public signing key with co-workers and associates who will later be receiving signed documents from you. People who receive your signature key place it in Acrobat's address book, and Acrobat automatically verifies signed documents they receive against the public signature keys stored in their address book.

Task: Sharing a Digital Signature Certificate

To send your public digital signature certificate, follow the steps in this task. The certificate is used by those who receive your signed files to confirm the validity of your signature.

1. From the Tools menu, select Self-Sign Security and then select Log In. The Log In dialog box appears.

2. Select your profile from the User Profile File drop-down list (see Figure 14.2), type the password associated with this profile, and click Log In.

FIGURE 14.2

The Self-Sign Security—Log In dialog box allows you to select your profile and enter your password so that you can begin to sign documents.

3. An alert dialog box may appear to inform you that You Are Now Logged In. If you do not want to see this dialog box in the future, enable the Do Not Show This Message Again option.

Click the User Settings button in the dialog box. If you have disabled the dialog box from appearing, choose Tools, Self-Sign Security, User Settings to make the User Settings dialog box appear.

4. In the User Information section of the User Settings dialog box, you will see the information associated with your digital signature certificate such as your name and the digital identifiers of your profile.

5. Click the Email button to send your public key certificate to another person as an attachment to an e-mail message.

6. Type the recipient's e-mail address and your contact information and then click the Email button.

Acrobat creates a new e-mail message using your e-mail software and automatically adds the certificate as an attachment.

7. If you want to manually attach the certificate to an e-mail message, or to copy the file to a floppy disk (so that you can transfer the public key the old-fashioned way), click the Export to File button in the User Settings window. You might have to take this step if Acrobat cannot communicate with your e-mail software to successfully create a new e-mail message with an attachment.

To give you an idea of the level of security involved in an Acrobat signature, typical Web browser encryption used for purchasing items online uses 128-bit encryption. Acrobat signature security is eight times more secure than what's involved in such online transactions.

Importing Signature Certificates

After receiving a digital signature certificate, you will want to verify the authenticity of the sender to make certain that it is accurate. After confirming its authenticity, you can add it to your address book.

▼ TASK Task: Adding a Certificate to Your Address Book

In this task, we will take a certificate file that has been sent to us and add it to our address book.

1. Locate the certificate file you have been sent. If the sender used Acrobat to e-mail the public signature key to you, the key will typically start with CertExchange and end with an .fdf extension.

14

▼ 2. Double-click the file. The Self-Sign Security—Certificate Exchange window opens, as shown in Figure 14.3

FIGURE 14.3

The Self-Sign Security—Certificate Exchange window alerts you to the fact that you are about to add a signature to your Acrobat list of trusted signature profiles.

3. Enable the Verify Identity When Adding check box and click Add to List. If you are not logged in to sign Acrobat documents, Acrobat requires you to log-in before adding the certificate to your address book.

   The Verify Identity dialog box opens, as shown in Figure 14.4.

4. After confirming that the certificate was sent to you by the correct person, click Add to List. This certificate is added to your Acrobat address book.

FIGURE 14.4

The Verify Identity dialog box provides the name and contact information for the person who sent you the certificate along with verification information about the certificate.

Verify the authenticity of a digital signature certificate by calling or sending an e-mail to the person who sent you the certificate asking whether that person did indeed send it. If you want to be extra safe, you can compare the fingerprint of the signature file you received with the fingerprint information in the sender's signature file. The fingerprint number for your version of the signature file is shown in the Verify Identity dialog box. The sender must check the certificate details by choosing Tools, Self-Sign Security, User Settings to provide you with the fingerprint information. By comparing the fingerprint on the certificate you received with the fingerprint on the sender's computer, you can be assured that the certificate is valid and accurate.

Verifying Digital Signatures

After receiving a digitally signed document, you will want to verify the signature to ensure that it is accurate and legitimate. You will also want to be certain that the document has not been edited since the signature was applied to it.

TASK

Task: Verifying a Signature

In this task, we will verify that a signature is legitimate. This process includes comparing it to any signature profiles in your Acrobat address book that contains a list of trusted certificates.

1. Open a PDF document that has been signed. Access the Signatures palette in the Navigation pane to see a list of any signatures in the document. The digital signature can also be identified by the words "digitally signed by" followed by the signer's name.

   If the document has been signed and the signature is visible, the PDF file opens to show you the signature and a question mark adjacent to the signature, which indicates that it has not yet been verified (see Figure 14.5). Some signatures may not be visible; these options are discussed later in this hour.

2. Move the mouse pointer over the unverified signature and click once on it. Acrobat verifies the authenticity of the signature.

   - If the signature matches with one of those in your address book, Acrobat informs you that it has matched the signature in question against your list of trusted certificates in its address book (see Figure 14.6).

   - If Acrobat does not find the signature in question in your list of trusted certificates, it informs you that the validity of the signature is unknown (see Figure 14.7). You can then click the Verify Identity button to obtain contact information about the signer of the document, as shown in Figure 14.8

14

*An unverified
signature.*

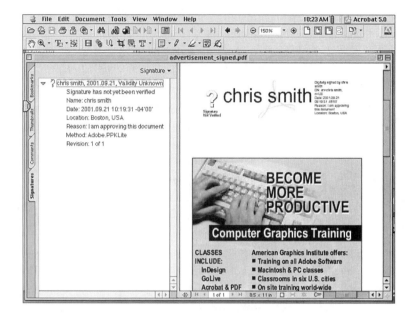

A verified signature.

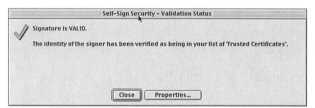

*Acrobat could not ver-
ify the authenticity of
the signature of a doc-
ument because the sig-
nature key was not in
your address book.*

Using the Signature Palette

You can also verify the signatures on PDF files using the Signatures palette, which is part of the Navigation pane on the far left side of the document window. The Signatures palette is adjacent to the Bookmarks and Thumbnails palettes. Click the Signatures tab to see a list of all the signatures that have been applied to the open document.

Select a signature in this list by clicking it once. Then use the Signature pull-down menu at the top of the palette to select the Verify Signature command (see Figure 14.9). Alternatively, you can access this command by right-clicking (Macintosh users should Ctrl+click) a selected signature to see the context menu, as shown in Figure 14.10.

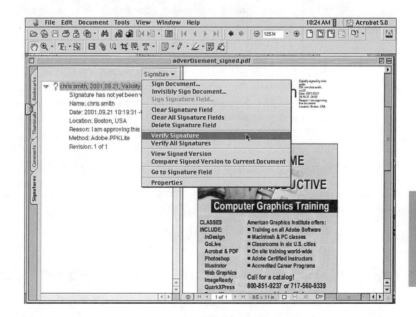

14

FIGURE 14.10

Access the context menu by right-clicking (Ctrl+clicking on the Macintosh) a selected signature.

Every time you receive a signed document, Acrobat includes encrypted information to verify the authenticity of the signature; Acrobat also includes a
public key. If you receive a digitally signed document and are certain of the
authenticity of the signature, you can add the public key to your address
book right from the signed document—even if the sender did not send you
their public key separately.

Do this by verifying the signature as described in the preceding task. When
the signature validity is reported as unknown because the sender is not in
your address book, click the Verify Identity button. Then click the Add to List
button. The certificate will be added to your address book, and future
signed documents from the same sender will be compared to the signature
in your address book to assess their validity.

The Signatures palette lists the signatures in a document and also lists the following
traits:

- When the document was signed
- Where the document was signed
- Who signed the document
- Whether the document was modified since the signature was applied

This last item is probably the most significant and is one of the more compelling reasons to use digital signatures in Acrobat. If someone uses Acrobat's editing tools to modify a document after a signature was applied, Acrobat alerts you to the fact that the document was changed by displaying an alert message: `Document Altered After Signing`. This message is displayed under the signature in the Signatures palette.

If a document has been modified after a signature was applied, Acrobat can provide you with an original version of the file that shows what the document looked like at the time it was signed. Access the original version of the document by selecting the signature that shows that modifications were made following its application. Using either the Signature menu or the context menu (right-click the signature to see the context menu; Ctrl+click on a Mac), select the View Signed Version command. Acrobat opens a copy of the document that shows what the PDF looked like at the time it was signed.

Additionally, Acrobat can show you which items on a page have changed since the document was signed. After opening a document that was altered after a signature was applied, select the signature that shows that modifications were made. From either the Signature menu or the context menu, select the Compare Signed Version to Current Document command. Acrobat creates a separate document that outlines areas where the pages differ. If multiple signatures have been applied to a document, you can compare how the document looked at the time each signature was applied by selecting Tools, Compare, Two Versions within Signed Document.

Applying a Signature

Acrobat makes it very easy to apply a digital signature. You can even apply multiple digital signatures to a document if the file requires multiple reviewers or signatures. These signatures allow others to confirm that the signer has authored, reviewed, or otherwise approved a document.

Task: Applying a Signature

In this task, we will apply a digital signature to a PDF file. The process is the same whether you are applying the first signature to the file or any subsequent signatures to a previously signed file.

1. Select the Digital Signature tool from the toolbar (see Figure 14.11). Alternatively, choose the Sign Document command from the Tools, Digital Signatures menu to access the Digital Signature tool.

14

FIGURE 14.11
The Digital Signature tool.

2. Locate an area on the page where you would like to sign the document. You can place the signature anywhere on the document. Note that the signature will overlap elements on the page. If you do not want the signature to be visible, use the Invisibly Sign Document option discussed in the following section.

3. Click and drag with the Digital Signature tool to apply the signature. Be certain that you make the signature large enough for others to read.

4. The Self-Sign Security—Sign Document dialog box appears, as shown in Figure 14.12. Click the Show Options button and then type your password, your reason for signing the document, and your contact information. (The contact information is useful for those who want to verify the authenticity of your signature if your public signature key is not already part of their address books.)

5. Click the Save button to sign and save the document with the same name. Click Save As to create an alternate, signed version of the document, leaving the original unsigned version untouched

FIGURE 14.12
The Self-Sign Security—Sign Document dialog box, showing the options fields you can fill out.

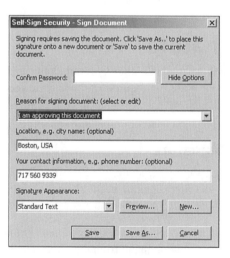

Invisibly Signing Documents

Signatures applied to a document do not have to be visible. Invisible signatures allow you to approve a document or project without defacing the final version. To apply an invisible signature to a document, choose Tools, Digital Signatures, Invisibly Sign Document. Acrobat requires you to enter your password and then provides you with the same options for saving the document as described in the preceding "Applying a Signature" task. The signature will not be visible on the document itself, but will appear in the Signatures palette. Recipients of the document will also be able to see whether the document was modified after the signature was applied.

To prevent others from changing a signed document, apply security settings to the document before signing it. Security settings are discussed in Hours 4, "Creating PDF Files from Your Electronic Documents," and 15, "Protecting Your PDF Files."

Changing the Appearance and Properties of Your Signature

You can customize your digital signature so that it displays only information you specify, such as your name and the date you signed it. You can even add a picture of your real signature if you want your digital signature to look more like a traditional signature.

To customize your signature, select Tools, Self Sign Security, User Settings.

Password Timeout

The Password Timeout section of the Self-Sign Security—User Settings dialog box is shown in Figure 14.13. From the drop-down list box, select how frequently you want Acrobat to ask for your password when you are signing a document. The most secure option is Always.

FIGURE 14.13

You can control how frequently you must enter your password when signing documents.

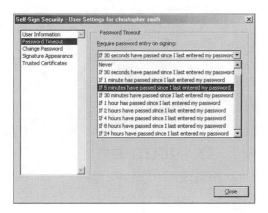

14

Change Password

The Change Password section of the Self-Sign Security—User Settings dialog box allows you to establish a new password for signing documents.

Signature Appearance

The Signature Appearance section, shown in Figure 14.14, lets you customize how your signature will look. Click the New button to establish a customized appearance for your signature. Provide a title, such as Custom Signature, and then select which elements you want displayed when the signature is applied by enabling the check boxes at the bottom of the page (such as name, date, location, and reason). If you want to add your own picture of a signature, click the Import Graphic from PDF File button. The graphic of your signature must be in the form of a PDF graphic, which can be made from any graphic file format using the instructions in Hours 4 and 6, "Converting Paper Documents to PDF."

Trusted Certificates

This section contains Acrobat's address book, which lists all the certificates you have received and stored from people who may send you digitally signed files. From this section, you can select Import from File to add a trusted certificate to this list, if you have received one on disk. You can also double-click a signature profile to add it to this list after a brief confirmation process (as described earlier in this hour). You can also remove signature profiles from this list by using this section of the User Settings dialog box.

FIGURE 14.14

Customize the appearance of your signature when you sign documents by using the Configure Signature Appearance dialog box.

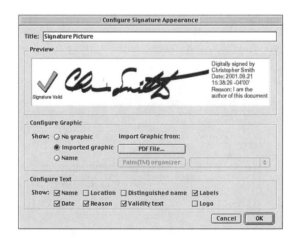

Summary

After completing this hour, you should be able to send and receive digitally signed documents. You should be able to verify the authenticity of a digitally signed document. Additionally, you should understand how to send and receive signature certificates so that you can verify the accuracy of signed documents. You should be able to identify whether a document has been altered after it was signed and then restore the document to its original appearance. You should also be able to customize the appearance of your signature, even adding a scanned version of your actual signature.

Workshop

To wrap up this hour, we address some common questions about digital signatures, followed by some exercises for you to use as practice.

Q&A

Q Do digital signatures increase the size of the file?

A Yes, but only marginally. A digital signature typically adds less than 10KB to the size of the file. The increase may be larger if you have added a customized scan as a part of your signature.

Q Are digital signatures safe and reliable?

A Yes. The technology used for signatures, the X.509 standard has been around for many years and is a standard for creating trusted relationships between parties who have to exchange information. It is based on the same standard used for Web browser security. Adobe has also partnered with RSA to implement this technology and create a 1024-bit encrypted private signature file. RSA is one of the leading suppliers of digital security software.

Q How can I be certain that a signature hasn't been created by someone pretending to be the signer of the document?

A The best way to ensure against a fraudulent signature is to check with the person who sent you the document. If you send signed documents, you should also take the time to send your public signature key to all recipients so that they can confirm the validity of your signature each time it is received. The person signing documents should take care to safeguard the password used to sign documents and use a password that contains a mixture of letters and numbers so that it cannot be misappropriated.

14

Quiz

1. **Digitally signed documents cannot be altered?**

    a. True

    b. False

2. **How many people can digitally sign a document?**

    a. Only one

    b. Only two

    c. More than one if you select the Sign Multiple command

    d. An unlimited number of signatures can be applied

3. **How does Acrobat return to the original version of a document?**

    a. By deleting the signature, the document returns to its original state.

    b. By selecting the Revert command from the File menu.

    c. By selecting the View Signed Version command from the Signature palette menu.

    d. Acrobat cannot return to the signed version of a document after it is altered.

Quiz Answers

1. **b**   Acrobat allows you to modify the signed version of a document unless security has been applied to it. You must apply security settings before signing the document if you want to prevent changes from being made after you sign it.

2. **d**   An unlimited number of people can sign a document. Each time a signature is added, Acrobat remembers what the document looked like at the time the signature was applied.

3. **c**   Selecting a signature in the Signatures palette and then choosing View Signed Version from the context menu or the palette menu causes Acrobat to produce a version of the document that is identical to what it looked like at the time the signature was applied.

Exercises

Learn more about applying signatures by trying the following exercises.

1. Create your own signature profile and customize it to contain an image of your signature. Try applying the signature to documents. Share your public signature key with others.

2. Apply a signature to a document and then use Acrobat's editing tools to modify the document. Try the Compare Signed Version to Current Document and View Signed Version commands to see how Acrobat can show you how the document originally looked and how it has changed.

14

HOUR 15

Protecting Your PDF Files

When posting files online or distributing them through e-mail, you might be concerned about people modifying or even stealing the text and graphics contained within a PDF file. Fortunately, Acrobat makes it possible to keep even the most prying eyes from accessing or editing your critical documents. Adobe Acrobat allows users to define the type of security applied to a PDF file—limiting access to a PDF file by way of passwords or eliminating editing or other capabilities. Acrobat also provides options for various levels of security that can be applied to a document.

In this hour, you'll learn about the following:

- Applying security to a document
- Using standard security options
- Allowing users to disable editing, printing, and so on
- Allowing users to password-protect files
- Using self-sign security
- Understanding Digital Rights Management and eBook security

About Document Security with Acrobat

PDF files can be protected using multiple levels of document security:

- Standard security
- User-level security
- eBook security

Standard Security

This basic level of security allows you to restrict access to a document by requiring a password to open the document. The standard security option also allows you to disable certain features unless the user knows the password to gain full access to the document. You also can disable access to certain features without requiring a password to open the document. The password is required to remove the restrictions. The features that can be disabled through standard security include:

- Printing
- Editing the document
- Selecting or copying items on a page
- Adding or modifying annotations or forms

User-Level Security

User-level security provides the option of distributing PDF files to individuals with whom you have established a trusted relationship by exchanging public digital signature keys. Using this option, you can specify exactly which people can access a document. If people who have this type of security clearance attempt to access a PDF file, they are required to log in using their self-sign security settings. If the creator has not granted them access to the document, they cannot open the file.

Each person receiving the file may have a different level of access. For example, one person may be able to open the file but not print it. Another person may have printing access, but may not be able to edit or select elements on the page. And anyone not on the distribution list for the document will not be able to open the file.

eBook Security

eBook security is highly secure. This security level is applied to PDF files by using Adobe Content Server, which is a separate software package. Adobe Content Server makes it possible to add security and then deliver PDF-based eBooks. This security level can control the number of computers on which the file can be read, for how long it can be read, and even whether the file can be shared and placed on another computer. eBook

15

security also allows for all the controls provided in standard security and user-level security, such as disabling access to printing. The Adobe Content Server then delivers the secured PDF files to the recipients over the Web.

The most unique security aspect of using eBook security is its capability to attach the file to a specific computer. If desired, you can specify that the file be opened only on the computer used to first download the file. If this setting is used, the file will not open on other computers.

We discuss Adobe Content server and eBooks in further detail at the end of this hour.

Applying Password Security for Opening a Document

Security can be applied to a PDF file at the time the file is created (as introduced in Hour 4, "Creating PDF Files from Your Electronic Documents"). But you can also add security to a PDF file using Adobe Acrobat. We'll start by adding the security feature that requires a password to open a PDF file. Figure 15.1 shows the dialog box that appears when you try to open a PDF file that has this security setting applied.

FIGURE 15.1
You can make PDF files that require the user to enter a password before they can be opened.

Task: Requiring a Password to Open a PDF File

In this task, we will restrict access to a PDF file by adding a password to the file.

1. Open the PDF file to which you want to restrict access with a password.
2. From the File menu, select Document Security. The Document Security dialog box opens, as shown in Figure 15.2.

FIGURE 15.2
The Document Security dialog box lets you determine what type of security, if any, should be applied to a document.

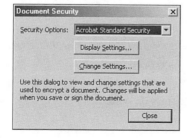

▼   3. From the Security Options drop-down menu, select Acrobat Standard Security. The
            Standard Security dialog box, shown in Figure 15.3 should open. If it does not
            open automatically, click the Change Settings button.

FIGURE 15.3

Start applying security options to an existing PDF file using the Standard Security dialog box.

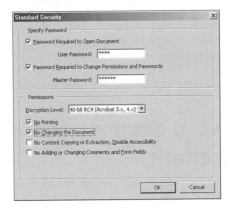

        4. Enable the Password Required to Open Document option and type the password
            you want to apply to the document and click OK.

        5. Re-enter the password when prompted.

        6. Click OK.

▲   7. Save the file for the security settings to take effect.

Using Security to Restrict Access to Features

Passwords are not the only way to protect your PDF files. You can restrict access to specific features—with or without applying password protection to the entire document.

▼ TASK

Task: Disabling Printing in a PDF with Security

You can distribute a PDF file without allowing recipients to print the file by following the steps in this task.

        1. Open a PDF file that you do not want printed.

        2. From the File menu, select Document Security. The Document Security dialog box
            opens.

        3. From the Security Options drop-down menu, select Acrobat Standard Security. The
            Standard Security dialog box should open. If it does not open automatically, click
▼   the Change Settings button.

4. In the Permissions area of the dialog box, enable the No Printing option.

   If you want, you can also require that a password be entered to open the file by enabling the Password Required to Open Document option, as explained in the preceding task.

5. Enable the Password Required to Change Permissions and Passwords option in the top half of the dialog box. *This step is very important.* If you do not require a password to change permissions, anyone will be able to access the Change Permissions dialog box and remove any restrictions you placed on the file. Click the OK button.

6. Re-enter the password when prompted to do so and click OK.

7. Save the file for the security settings to take effect. No password is required for anyone to open this document, but a password is required if you want to eliminate the restriction on printing.

8. Reopen the file. Open the File menu and notice that the Print option is disabled, as shown in Figure 15.4.

FIGURE 15.4

Printing is one of the features that can be disabled using the standard security options in Acrobat.

Although we have only discussed how to disable printing, there are a host of other restrictions you can apply to protect your PDF file. The following sections describe these options.

Encryption Level

In the Standard Security dialog box, you can specify the level of encryption you want to apply to the PDF file. From the Encryption Level drop-down list, select 40-bit RC4 or 128-bit RC4. This is more than a choice of how secure the file will be because only Acrobat 5 supports 128-bit encryption. If you select 128-bit encryption, even users who know the password will not be able to open the document unless they have the most current version of Acrobat.

No Changing the Document

Selecting the No Changing the Document option in the Standard Security dialog box disables all the editing tools—including the Touch Up Text tool and the Touch Up Object tool. Even third-party editing tools such and Enfocus Pitstop cannot be used to edit a file where security has been set to disallow editing.

No Content Copying or Extraction

The No Content Copying or Extraction option disables the tools for highlighting text or graphics so that the text and graphics in the document cannot be copied and pasted into other documents or saved to disk.

No Adding or Changing Comments and Form Fields

If the No Adding or Changing Comments and Form Fields option is chosen, you cannot use any of the commenting and annotation tools in Acrobat. Additionally, any form fields in the file will be inaccessible.

How Secure Is It?

When you choose 64-bit encryption from the Encryption Level drop-down box in the Standard Security dialog box, you are providing 20 billion possible keys to decipher the encrypted information, but only one of the keys is the correct one. If the PDF file fell into the wrong hands, the person receiving it would have to find the right key—a nearly impossible task. With 128-bit encryption, the number of possible keys is the square of the number of 64-bit keys. For all practical purposes, it is impossible for someone to decipher the information contained in an encrypted PDF file. The only way to access the encrypted data is by knowing the correct password. Remember to use passwords that mix letters and numbers and are not easy to guess. Also mix between uppercase and lowercase letters in the same password to enhance security.

Be aware that there are some unscrupulous software developers who are working on creating software that will "crack" the default security features discussed earlier in this hour. Updated information about this topic is available at the companion Web site for this book, AcrobatIn24.com.

Applying User-Level Security with Digital Signatures

By exchanging digital signature certificates with other users, you can establish a trusted relationship. You can share documents with these users so that only they will be able to open them. Digital signature certificates use a very high level of security: Not only do they require a password, they also require that the encrypted PDF file be opened on a computer that has a specific digital signature security certificate that uses 1024-bit encryption.

▼ TASK

Task: Applying User Specific Security

In this task, we will to apply separate security options for individual recipients of a PDF file.

1. Open a PDF file to which you want to apply a digital signature.

2. From the File menu, select Document Security. The Document Security window opens.

3. From the Security Options drop-down menu, select Acrobat Self-Sign Security. If you have not logged in using your own Self-Sign Security user name and password, Acrobat requires you to do so at this time. If you have already logged in by selecting Tools, Self Sign Security, Log In, proceed to the step 4.

4. The Self-Sign Security—Encryption Settings dialog box opens, as shown in Figure 15.5. The left side of the dialog box shows all the trusted certificates you have received from other people or have imported from digitally signed documents.

FIGURE 15.5

The Self-Sign Security—Encryption Settings dialog box lets you decide who can access a file and what level of access each person will receive.

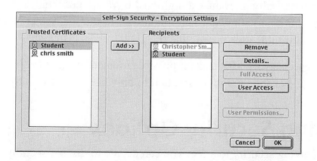

5. From the Trusted Certificates list, select all the people to whom you will be sending the document and click the Add button.

The names you selected move to the Recipients list on the right side of the dialog box. By default, all Recipients have full access to the PDF file. They are the only

▼

▼ people who can access the file. They must log in using self-sign security on a
computer that has the security certificate. That security certificate must be from
the creator of the public certificate that was sent to you.

6. To specify specific settings for an individual user, click the user's name in the
   Recipients list and then click User Access. Clicking this button tells Acrobat that
   this user will not be provided with full access to the file.

7. Click the User Permissions button; the User Permissions dialog box appears,
   shown in Figure 15.6.

FIGURE 15.6

*User permission set-
tings let you determine
the exact privileges a
user will have when
you apply user-specific
security settings with
self-sign security.*

8. Disable the Allow Content Copying and Extraction option if you do not want this
   user to be able to remove text or graphics from the PDF file for use in other documents.

9. From the Changes Allowed drop-down list, select any restrictions you want to
   apply. Select None if you do not want this user altering the file in any way.

10. From the Printing drop-down list, choose whether you want this user to be able to
    print the document in Low Resolution (if you do not want this user to be able to
    commercially reproduce a high-quality version of the document). Select High
    Resolution to allow normal print access to the file; select Not Allowed if you do
▲   not want this user to print the file at all.

All these security options make it possible to guard against the inappropriate use of your
PDF file and enable you to distribute it to only certain individuals.

Changing Security Options

After applying security to a file, you can decide to disable security or change the privileges that are allowed with the file—as long as you know the password to change the
security options. At any time, you can change the security options for a file by selecting
File, Document Security and clicking the Change Settings button in the Document
Security window.

Digital Rights Management and eBook Security

15

If you want to distribute your PDF files as eBooks, as shown in Figure 15.7, there are some amazing security options to help protect your information. These options require the use of Adobe Content Server, which is used to both prepare and then sell eBooks. Content Server is a separate software product from Adobe that enhances the security features of PDF files and modify them so that they can also be read using eBook readers.

FIGURE 15.7

The most popular form of an eBook is a version of PDF. Here, an eBook is displayed using Adobe's free eBook Reader.

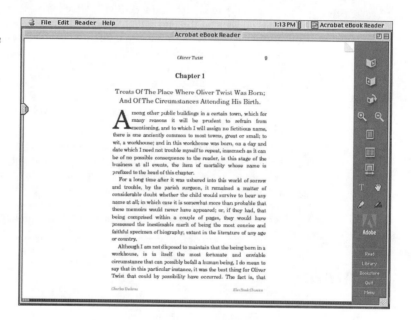

Each eBook is encrypted so that only the legitimate owner of the eBook can read it. When it is purchased or downloaded, it is attached to a specific computer or eBook reader. The owner of the file can restrict the number of computers on which the file can be read.

Adobe Content Server lets you choose what privileges to enable in each eBook, including the number of computers on which it can be opened and for how many days it can be viewed.

- **Printing:** You can set how much and how often the customer can print the eBook.
- **Lending and Rights Assignment:** You can decide whether the file can be temporarily or permanently transferred to another computer or eBook reader.

- **Time-out:** You can have a file expire after a certain period of time. Alternatively, you can allow access to an eBook for a predetermined length of time with an option to purchase the book after that time.

More information about Content Server is available under the products section of the Adobe.com Web site.

> **eBook Security Without Hassles**
>
> It is possible to set detailed security for Adobe PDF files that include time limits on viewing the files without having to purchase and implement Adobe Content Server. Although Content Server is the best professional solution, if you have only a small number of files you want to share, and you do not mind sending them manually to people and establishing the user privileges on a case-by-case basis, try Adobe Studio. The Studio service is available online at studio.adobe.com (note that there is no www at the start of this address). Set up an account and use the Delivery option to send files.
>
> PDF files sent through the Adobe Studio service can be set to time-out or to be opened only on one computer, among other options. The PDF file remains on the studio.adobe.com server until it is picked up by whomever you direct to the site. That person only has access to the file at the level you specify. There is a fee for this service, but it allows a small firm to provide secure, restricted access to PDF files without investing in Content Server.

Summary

After finishing this hour, you should be able to confidently control access to your sensitive PDF files. You should be able to restrict access to the file itself or to specific features, such as editing or printing. You should also be able to establish user-specific security settings that enable each reader of a PDF file to be granted unique permissions on what they can do with the file. Anyone who has not been specifically granted access to the PDF file will not be able to open it. You should also understand the concepts behind eBook security.

Workshop

As you have seen, there are a number of ways to protect your data after you have converted it to a PDF file. We conclude this hour with some questions and clarifications about using security, a quick quiz, and then some exercises associated with securing PDF files.

15

Q&A

Q Can I restrict printing or editing on a file that also uses password protection?

A Yes, but you will have to use two passwords. Set one password for opening the document and set a separate password for changing permissions and passwords. You will want these to always be separate passwords when they are used together. Otherwise, anyone with the password to open the document will also be able to modify the security restrictions.

Q Can user-specific security settings using digital signatures be used with the free Acrobat Reader?

A No. The user-specific security settings require the recipient to have created a digital signature certificate and to have sent you a copy of their public certificate key. These features are not supported in the free version of Acrobat Reader.

Q Does it matter whether I set the security options when I create the PDF file or use Acrobat after the file is created?

A Acrobat Distiller lets you add security restrictions at the time you create PDF files; these are the same security options available from within Acrobat. It is often more efficient to set the security when creating the PDF file. But many users don't set the security settings until they are finally ready to distribute the PDF file.

Quiz

1. **How can you open a PDF file that requires a password to open it if you don't know the password?**

    a. Call Adobe customer service for a secret password that opens all documents.

    b. Open the file in Adobe Illustrator and resave the PDF.

    c. PDF files that use security to restrict opening cannot be opened unless you know the password.

2. **User-level security lets you send PDF files to whom?**

    a. Any user who has the full version of Acrobat.

    b. Any user who has either the free Reader or the full version of Acrobat—but it must be version 5.

    c. Any Acrobat user who has sent you his/her digital signature public certificate key.

    d. Any Acrobat user on your local area network.

3. How can you apply eBook security to a PDF file?

    a. Select eBook from the Document Security settings.

    b. Select eBook from the User Level Security dialog box.

    c. Use Adobe Document Server to turn the PDF into an eBook PDF.

Quiz Answers

1. **c**   Do not forget your password. If you forget your password, the odds of opening your file are stacked heavily against you. The high level of security used in PDF files makes the files impossible (for all practical purposes) to open.

2. **c**   Users of Adobe Acrobat who have sent you their digital signature security certificates can receive a file from you with user-specific security settings. Digital signatures have only been available since version 4 of Acrobat and are not a part of the free Reader software.

3. **c**   Adobe Document Server is one method for converting PDF files to eBooks. If you want to do this on a limited basis, consider using an eBook processing service—several are listed on the Adobe.com Web site. If you simply want to restrict access to the PDF to tie it to one computer or limit its use for a specified time period, try the distribution features available at studio.adobe.com.

Exercises

Learn more about securing PDF files by trying the following exercises.

1. Open a PDF file that does not have security. Apply security that restricts access to certain features. Save and then reopen the file. Notice which tools are disabled or which menu commands are disabled.

2. Add a password to open a PDF file. Save and reopen the file.

3. After receiving digital security certificates from other Acrobat users, try to establish security that limits access to only specific users. If you do not have anyone to send you a digital security certificate, download the one posted on AcrobatIn24.com.

PART VI
Forms and Buttons

Hour

Hour 16

Creating and Using Interactive Forms

As you have learned in the previous hours of this book, PDF documents are a powerful tool for increasing speed, accuracy, and successful communication in the workplace.

Now we are ready to begin using the files we have formatted as PDF documents to create interactive forms for interoffice use and for use on the Web.

In this hour, you will learn about the following aspects of forms in Acrobat:

- PDF forms versus HTML forms
- Different types of buttons and how to create them
- Setting and changing the tab order
- Aligning form elements using the Layout Grid
- Adding actions to buttons
- Submitting form data

The Power of Creating Forms in Acrobat

Interoffice forms such as vacation forms, travel expense forms, and so on can be created. Text fields are used on forms for the user to enter the necessary data. Acrobat can spell check the form field data, if necessary.

You can put together the form in any program. By designing the form in a page layout program, you can determine the look of the form and its features. But you could create the form in an image-editing or illustration program as well, such as Photoshop or Illustrator. In these instances, graphics in the native document could have "invisible" fields over them. The fill-in fields, added in Acrobat, can be invisible if you have accounted for that in the design, or you can give them a custom appearance—a ruled, beveled, or shaded look, to name just a few options.

Different types of form fields include text boxes (for the user to fill in), combo boxes (with a pull-down menu to choose from), radio buttons (which allow the user to select only one item from a series of options), and check boxes (which enable the user to choose multiple items from a list of options).

You can specify a particular format for certain types of data; for example, you can specify that dates be displayed as 01/22/01 or Jan 22, 2001. If you specify a particular format for a form field, the user is prompted if he or she does not enter the data in that format.

You can apply actions to your forms as well. Actions you can apply to a form include, but are not limited to, playing a movie, submitting or resetting the form, and activating a World Wide Web link.

PDF Forms Versus HTML Forms

Interactive forms can be created in HTML, the programming language used for formatting Web pages. Actions as well as other features can be applied to an HTML form, but HTML forms pale in comparison to PDF forms.

The most obvious difference is this: The look of HTML can vary depending on the browser used to view the page, the version of the browser used, and the platform (IBM-compatible versus Macintosh), to name a few of the variables.

PDF forms, on the other hand, look the same regardless of the browser used, regardless of the browser version used, and regardless of the computer platform used to view the document. With PDF, What You See *Is* What You Get (remember WYSIWYG?)

Creating Form Fields

So let's explore the many aspects of creating forms in Acrobat. We will begin by becoming familiar with the different types of form fields.

Adding Text Fields to Your Form

The first type of field we will create is a text field. A *text field* is a box on the form in which the user types information, such as a First Name field in which the user types his or her first name. Text fields can be invisible (if you have accounted for them in the design of the form and have defined an area for the field, such as a shaded box). You can also add simple appearance attributes to make the form fields more visually appealing.

> Here's an example of a situation in which a form field could be invisible: You create a document that contains graphics you want to use as Print or Submit buttons (that is, the graphics have the words *print* or *submit* on them before the document is converted to PDF). Then, in Acrobat, you add an invisible form field over the graphic. By "invisible," we mean that the form field has no appearance but the actions associated with a form field can still be added. This means that when the user clicks the button, the button will cause the document to print or be submitted.

Task: Adding a Form Field

In this task, we explore the use of form fields by adding different elements to a form. Note that it is important to plan your form before converting the file to PDF and beginning to add form elements. Although the Form tool is a powerful feature of Acrobat, planning ahead is essential to produce a successful form.

Add text or graphics that will be complimented by the form elements. For instance, in your native document, you use text or graphics to ask the questions you want answered; in Acrobat, you add the form fields to allow the user to enter the necessary data.

1. Open a PDF document into which you want to add form elements. Select the Form tool from the toolbar and click and drag an area on the page where you want the text field to appear. When you release the mouse, the Field Properties dialog box opens.

2. From the Type drop-down list in the Field Properties dialog box, choose Text to create a text field. In the Name box, type a name for the field. All form elements must be named because the information the form provides will be returned as a script, and the field name will identify the information.

3. In the Short Description text box, you can type a short description if you want; doing so is not necessary.

4. On the Appearance tab at the bottom of the dialog box, choose options to define the look you want for the element. You can choose a ruled, beveled, shaded, or dashed look for the style of the border rule, to name a few options. Change the color of the border rule or shaded background by clicking on the corresponding color box (see Figure 16.1.)

   If you do not want to give the form field an appearance, that is, if you want it to be invisible, do not enable the border or background box. Remember that invisible form fields are useful if the native document has a graphic or text element that will be used as a button, and you just want to apply the action to it. In this case, you would draw the form field, make it invisible, and assign the required action to it.

5. You can change the text style and color by selecting options in the Text area of the Appearance tab. These options control the look of the type the user will enter in the field.

6. Also on the Appearance tab, you can indicate additional attributes, such as requiring this field to be filled in before the user can continue.

FIGURE 16.1

You can change the border and background colors of the text field you create on the Appearance tab of the Field Properties dialog box.

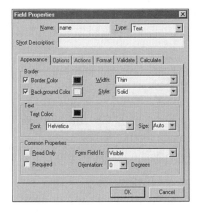

To add precision to your forms, use the layout grid. Access the grid by choosing View, Grid. You can change settings for the grid by selecting Edit, Preferences, General. When the General page of the Preferences dialog box opens, choose Layout Grid from the pane on the left.

Among the settings you can personalize are the number of subdivisions, the grid line color, and the grid offset.

You can also choose the View, Snap to Grid command, which "snaps" the edges of your form elements to lines in the grid to ensure the precise lineup of the elements on your form.

▼ 7. Click the Options tab of the Field Properties dialog box to move to that tab (see Figure 16.2). In the Default text box, type the text you want to appear in the text box you are creating until the user types in a real answer. For example, you might want to use the text box to display the text Last Name, First Name, to indicate that the user should enter the data in that order. You can leave the Default box empty if you do not want any default text to appear there.

FIGURE 16.2

You can supply default text that will appear in the text field you are creating on the Options tab of the Field Properties dialog box.

16

8. Other features you can enable on the Options tab include the Align feature, which aligns the text the user types inside the box. (The default alignment is left.) You can also limit the number of characters the user can enter in the field, request a password, and add multiline capability, among other options.

> If you enable the Password option, the data the user enters in the field will appear as a series of asterisks. This feature prevents the data being entered from being seen while it's onscreen.

9. Enable the Multi-line option if the text field is to contain more than one line of text. An example of a multiline field is a question that requires a lengthy answer (such as "Why do you wish to join our organization?").

The Limit Number of Characters option is useful when you want to control the format for the data entered by the user. If you are asking the user to enter a four-digit password, limiting the answer to four digits can help prevent erroneous answers. A warning beep alerts the user if they try to enter too many digits in the

▼ field.

You can also apply actions to the field you are creating. Actions are set up on the Actions tab of the Field Properties dialog box. We will skip the Actions tab for the text field we are creating and cover that topic later in this hour.

10. Click OK to close the Field Properties dialog box and create the text field on the PDF page. To see the final appearance of the text field, select the Hand tool; click in the box to add type. If you want to edit the attributes of the field, select the Form tool and double-click on the field to open the Field Properties dialog box again.

Adding Radio Buttons to Your Form

Next we will explore the use of radio buttons on a form. *Radio buttons* are a set of responses to a specific question from which the user can choose only one. For example, if the question is Gender?, radio buttons that provide the answers Male and Female are appropriate because the user can select only one of those responses.

Task: Working with Radio Buttons

▼ TASK

In this task, we'll add a series of radio buttons to our form. Remember that the radio buttons belong to the same group, but each will have a separate export value.

1. Open a PDF file to which you want to add form fields and identify the area where you want to add the radio buttons. Select the Form tool and click and drag a small area where you want the first radio button to appear. When you release the mouse button, the Field Properties dialog box opens (see Figure 16.3). From the Type drop-down list at the top of the dialog box, choose Radio Button.

FIGURE 16.3

The Field Properties dialog box looks different depending on the type of form field you are adding. Here are the choices on the Options tab for the radio button.

▼ 2. Name the field. The sample form we are creating in this hour is to be used online by a travel agency. The radio buttons will signify whether the traveler prefers smoking or nonsmoking hotel rooms. Therefore, name the radio button field "smoking." On the Options tab of the Field Properties dialog box, choose the style of button you want to appear on the form. The default is Circle, but other options for the style of the button are Check, Cross, Diamond, Square, and Star.

3. The export value you enter is the "answer" to the question for the radio buttons. For example, the radio buttons we are creating here are named "smoking." The export value for the first radio button should be yes. If the user chooses this button, he or she prefers a smoking room.

4. Click OK to create the first radio button on the form.

5. Duplicate this radio button to preserve its appearance for the other button or buttons required. Use the Form tool to select the button (click once to highlight the radio button) and choose Edit, Copy. Then choose Edit, Paste to insert a duplicate of the radio button on the page; drag the new radio button to position it on the form. Double-click the new radio button with the Forms tool to open the Field Properties dialog box so that you can change the export value for the second button. Change the second radio button's export value to no. If the user chooses this second button, they prefer a non-smoking room.

Remember that all the radio buttons will have the same name, but their export values will be different. Radio buttons with the same name belong to the same group; their export values determine the information returned when the user selects a certain button.

The user can choose only one button in a group of radio buttons, so there is no chance of multiple answers for this option. To allow multiple answers, choose a form field such as check box.

6. See the finished radio buttons by selecting the Hand tool. Try out the radio buttons; you should be able to choose only one, as shown in Figure 16.4.

▲

16

FIGURE 16.4
Radio buttons allow the user to choose only one response from a list of possible responses. Each radio button in the group of radio buttons has the same name but different export values.

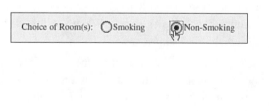

Radio buttons are for those times when you want the user to choose only one option from a list of possible responses. If you want the user to be able to choose multiple options, select another type of form element, such as the check box.

If you want a radio button to be selected by default, enable that option under the Options tab. For example, here's a question you might pose on a form: Do you want to be added to our mailing list? You can use radio buttons to provide the mutually exclusive answers yes and no. You might want the default answer to be yes, to encourage the user to be included on the list.

Radio buttons can, of course, provide multiple choices. You can use radio buttons to ask users for the year in which they were born; provided that they are willing share that information with you, they will select the one radio button from the list of radio buttons that corresponds to their birth year.

Remember that radio buttons are for those instances in which only one answer to the question is appropriate. If you want to allow multiple answers, use another kind of form field such as a check box.

Adding Check Boxes to Your Form

Check boxes are similar to radio buttons in that they are used to provide a list of possible responses from which the user can select an answer. But where radio buttons allow the user to select only one answer from the group, check boxes allow the user to select multiple answers. For example, you may want your users to indicate their favorite sporting events. Radio buttons would allow them to choose only one answer, but check boxes give them the option of choosing multiple items, such as golf, horse racing, *and* swimming.

Task: Creating Check Boxes

Let's create some check boxes on the PDF page that's currently open.

1. Select the Form tool from the toolbar. Click and drag a small area on the PDF page where you want the check box to appear. When you release the mouse button, the Field Properties dialog box appears.

2. On the Options tab, select Check Box from the Check Style drop-down list as the type of element you want to create and give it a name (see Figure 16.5). In this sample form, the check boxes will indicate favorite things to do while on vacation. The Name field for each check box should name the type of activity, and the export value for each check box will be yes. If the box is checked, the user is indicating that the activity is one they enjoy while on vacation.

FIGURE 16.5

Check boxes allow the user to select multiple items.

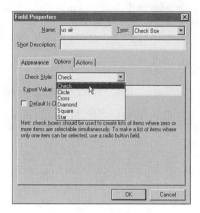

16

3. Click the Options tab and, from the Check Style drop-down list, choose the shape of the check box, such as diamond, check, or star, to name a few.

4. Click OK. Try out your check boxes by selecting the Hand tool and clicking in the boxes (as shown in Figure 16.6). If you want to resize the check boxes, select the Form tool, then click the check box and drag to resize.

Use check boxes on your form for those situations when multiple answers are appropriate. Copy and paste duplicates of the check box using the Form tool, as you did with the radio buttons in the preceding section. Remember that each check box must have a different name but the same export value. When the check box is selected, its export value is yes; if the box is not selected, it returns the value no.

FIGURE 16.6

Use the Hand tool to try out the check boxes; you should be able to select multiple answers.

Adding Combo Boxes to Your Form

Use combo boxes to give users a pull-down menu from which they can choose their answer. Combo boxes allow only one answer, but can be a viable option if you have a large number of answers from which the user can choose. Combo boxes take up less room on the form than check boxes because the choices remain hidden until the user clicks the drop-down arrow.

For the sample form we are developing, we'll use a combo box to provide a list of possible answers to the question, Are you traveling with children? The combo box we will create has only two answers, but your combo box can be set up to list more possible answers.

▼ TASK Task: Creating Combo Boxes

In this task, we will experiment with the use of combo boxes. Combo boxes use a scrollable window to display the choices. The combo box displays one item at a time, as opposed to the list box, which displays as many items as can fit in the form field.

1. Open a PDF file to which you want to add form fields and identify the area where you want to add the combo box. Select the Form tool and click and drag an area for the combo box. In the Field Properties dialog box that opens, choose Combo Box from the Type drop-down list.

2. In the Name field, type a name for the combo box. Click the Options tab to open that page. In the Item field, type the first answer you want the user to see in the combo box. As shown in Figure 16.7, the Export Value you provide can be the same or different from the item itself, but the Export Value is the data that is returned from the form.

   If you leave the export value blank, the item text is sent as the export value.

FIGURE 16.7

Combo boxes list selections from which the user can pick an answer. The Item is what the user sees in the list; the Export Value is the information returned from the form.

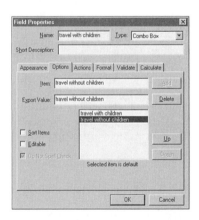

3. Click the Add button to add this item to the combo box list. The pane at the bottom of the Options tab shows the list of items as it will appear when the combo box is opened. Repeat step 2 to add more items to the list.

   In this sample form, we use the combo box to answer the question, Traveling with Children? The text of the first item in the list (what the user will see in the combo

▼ box) is Yes, and the export value is `travel with children`. The second item is No, and the export value is `travel without children`.

> The pane at the bottom of the Options tab lists the items as they will appear in the combo box itself. The item that is selected when you click OK to close the Field Properties dialog box is the item that will be the default, that is, the answer that will appear in the combo box window before the user makes a selection. (One answer must always be seen in the combo box.)

16

▲ The finished combo box will show one answer; the other answers are accessible by pulling down the menu (see Figure 16.8).

FIGURE 16.8

Combo boxes are an efficient way to present a large number of items from which the user can select only one. Open the combo box by clicking the arrow to the right of the box's window.

Traveling With Children: travel without children
travel with children
travel without children

Other options available with combo boxes include:

- **Editable**: Allows the user to edit items in the combo box. When this option is selected, there is no determining that some items may be edited and others not. All items are subject to editing. This option is not available for list boxes, only combo boxes.

- **Sort Items:** Choose this option to alphabetically sort the items in ascending order. If you keep the option enabled, new items added to the list will also be sorted in the same manner.

- **Up/Down**: Use this option to manually move items around in the list order. This option enables you to move up or down items in the list, one level at a time. To use this option, you must first disable the Sort Items option because it will override the Up/Down option.

Adding List Boxes to Your Form

Another form element you can choose with the Form tool is the list box. The list box allows you to choose one answer from multiple items, as does the combo box, but the list box displays as many answers as the size of the field will permit (see Figure 16.9).

When the list of items in a list box exceeds the space allowed in the form field, the box contains scrollbars at the top and right. These scrollbars enable the user to move through the list with ease.

FIGURE 16.9

List boxes are similar to combo boxes, but list boxes allow the user to see multiple answers, depending on the size of the box you created.

Task: Adding a List Box

▼ TASK

In this task, we will create a list box using the Form tool. In this example, the list box will provide possible responses to the question, Favorite Destinations. Be sure to allow enough vertical space for your list box when creating the native document. Remember that you can choose only one answer from the list of answers provided in the list box.

1. Open the PDF file to which you want to add form fields and identify the area where you want to add the list box. Select the Form tool and click and drag the area where you want the list box to appear.

2. In the Field Properties dialog box that opens, choose List Box from the Type drop-down list. Type a name for this form field in the Name field. For this example, we give the field the name destinations.

3. On the Options tab, add entries to the list box in the same way that you did for the combo box in the preceding task: The Item is the answer your user will see in the list box, and the Export Value is the data returned from the form. Quite often, these two fields contain the same information, as in the example shown in Figure 16.10.

    Leaving the export value blank gives the item the same export value as its name, which is an acceptable alternative.

4. Click the Add button to add this item to the list box. The pane at the bottom of the Options tab shows the list of items as it will appear in the list box. Repeat step 3 to add more items to the list.

▼

▼   The item selected when the dialog box is closed is the default item—the first one
          the user sees.

    5. Click OK. Select the Hand tool from the toolbar and test your new list box. Select
        several items in the list by Ctrl+clicking to select (on IBM-compatible machines)
        or Command+clicking (on Macintosh machines).

▲   To allow the user to select multiple items from the list box, be sure to enable the
          Multiple Selections option on the Options tab of the Field Properties dialog box.

FIGURE 16.10

*Most times, the Item
and Export Value for
an item in a list box
are the same. The
selected item is the
item that will be
selected by default
when the user first
views the list box.*

Using list boxes on your form requires enough space to show the multiple items, if that
is an option you want to use. Otherwise, the items will appear in a scrollable box, and
only the ones for which there is room to appear will be viewable at first glance.

Adding Signature Fields to Your Form

A *signature form field* gives the user the option of using digital signatures on the form.
Digital signatures are covered in greater detail in Hour 14, "Creating and Applying
Digital Signatures," earlier in this book. Here we'll give them a quick overview as they
apply to forms.

First, you must set up a digital signature profile, as described in Hour 14. Then, using
the Form tool, click and drag the area on the PDF page where you want the digital signature to appear. When you release the mouse button, the Field Properties dialog box
opens. Choose Signature from the Type drop-down list.

Name the field and click the Signed tab to open the dialog box to that page. You are
given three options:

  • **Nothing happens when the signature field is signed.** The field will be signed,
    but nothing else will occur (no action).

- **Mark as read-only.** You have the option to "lock" all fields or only selected fields.
- **This script executes when the signature is signed.** After the document is signed, you can assign a JavaScript to be activated (more on this option later in the hour).

You create the signature form field and assign the properties you want it to have. When the user clicks the form field, a dialog box prompts the user to apply the digital signature.

The user can choose User Profile File to select his signature from the list of possible signatures available from that computer. If the user has not already created a digital signature, he or she can create one at that time by choosing New User Profile and following the prompts.

Working with Form Fields

Now that you have the basics of forms and their elements, let's discuss some of Acrobat's form-editing features.

Resizing Form Fields

Resizing a form field is an easy task. Using the layout grid described earlier in the hour, you can assemble the form with greater precision. Occasionally, however, you'll have to resize a field.

Task: Resizing Form Fields

There may come a time when the form field you created has to be resized to better suit the form. In this task, we experiment with resizing a form field after it has been created.

1. Open the PDF file that contains form fields you want to edit. Select the Form tool and click once on a field to select it.

2. Drag the corner handles to resize both width and height simultaneously, or drag a center handle to alter the field in only one dimension.

3. Click inside the field and drag it to reposition the field; double-click the field to bring up the Field Properties dialog box where you can change or add to the form field on a more elemental level.

Duplicating Form Fields

When you want to create multiple fields that resemble each other (such as check boxes or certain text fields), it is easier to duplicate the field and change the attributes than to create each field from scratch. By duplicating the field, you can maintain the size and shape of the field so that the group of fields looks consistent.

To duplicate a field on the same page, select the Form tool and click the field once. From the menu bar, choose Edit, Copy; position the mouse pointer where you want to insert the duplicate and choose Edit, Paste. You can reposition the form field as described in the preceding task, and you can double-click the field to open the Field Properties dialog box.

Duplicating form fields can also be done document-wide. For instance, a button that takes the user to the first page of the document (an action) can be duplicated on all pages, instantly. Here's how to make a Home Page button for all the pages in your PDF document that returns the reader to the top of the document.

To duplicate a form field, Ctrl+drag (on IBM-compatible machines) or Option+drag (on Macintosh machines) the field with the Form tool.

Task: Duplicating Form Fields

▼ TASK

To simplify the process of creating a form in which similar fields are needed, duplicate the field and change the attributes as necessary. In this task, we will duplicate a button to demonstrate the process.

1. Let's begin by creating a button. Open the PDF file to which you want to add the Home Page buttons and identify the area where you want the first button to appear. Choose the Form tool and draw an area you designate to be the button. In the Field Properties dialog box that opens, choose Button from the Type field. Name the form element and, on the Appearance tab, select options to give the button a shaded or ruled appearance.

2. On the Options tab, choose Push from the Highlight list and choose Text Only from the Layout list. In the Button Face Attributes field, type the word **Home** as the label that will appear on the face of the button you are creating.

Highlight is one of the option categories you can select when making a button with the Form tool. Some people are confused by the wording of the category.

This option determines the look of the button when it is clicked. Following is a list of the choices available to you to determine how the button will appear when selected:

- **None**: There is no difference in appearance (such as a highlight) when the button is selected.
- **Invert**: The colors of the button are inverted when the button is selected.
- **Outline**: A border appears around the button when it is being selected.
- **Push**: The button takes the appearance of being "pushed in" on the Mouse Down event and "pushed out" on the Mouse Up event.

16

▼

▼ 3. Click the Actions tab where we can assign an action to the button we're creating (see Figure 16.11). We want the button to take the user to the first document page when it's clicked, so choose Mouse Down as the event. Click the Add button to display the Add an Action dialog box (see Figure 16.12).

4. Under Add an Action, choose Execute Menu Item. This command allows us to choose any item from the Acrobat pull-down menus as the action we assign to the button. We want this button to perform the Document, First Page command, located in the Acrobat menu bar.

FIGURE 16.11

The Actions tab in the Field Properties dialog box.

FIGURE 16.12

The Add an Action dialog box.

5. Click the Edit Menu Item button. For users of IBM-compatible computers, a facsimile of the Acrobat menu bar appears; choose Document from the list of menu headings and then choose First Page.

Macintosh users: In the Menu Item dialog box, select the menu items from the menu bar.

▼ 6. Click OK. Click Set Action. Click OK again.

7. Test the action of the button using the Hand tool. When you click the button, you should be taken to the first page of the document.

8. Using the Previous View icon on the menu bar, go back to the page where you created the button. Select the Form tool and click the button once to select it. Choose Tools, Forms, Fields, Duplicate from the menu bar. Indicate the page numbers on which you want this button to appear (typically, you don't put a Home button on the first page). Click OK to position the duplicate button or buttons.

The field is duplicated in the exact position on each page you requested. You can, if necessary, move the field around on the individual pages; unless you do that, however, the field falls into exactly the same position on each page.

▲ 9. Test the new buttons with the Hand tool.

By using the Tools, Forms, Fields, Duplicate command, you copy the button to each page you indicate, and the action you specified for the original button will work! This is an easy way to set up buttons to perform simple actions.

Another example of the usefulness of buttons is to create a Print, Reset Form, or Submit button. In the following task, we'll set up a Print button. You can choose to have the word Print appear on the default button Acrobat creates for you, or you can create an icon of your own and save it as a PDF, to appear instead of Acrobat's default button.

Task: Adding an Icon and Applying an Action to It

To use an icon you have prepared as a Print button that will appear on one or more pages of the PDF, and link that button to an action, follow these steps:

1. Open the PDF file to which you want to add the Print button and identify the area where you want the first button to appear. Select the Form tool and click and drag an area for the button. In the Field Properties dialog box that opens, choose Button from the Type drop-down list. Name the field and be sure that you do **not** have anything selected on the Appearance tab (because we are adding an icon you have created, there is no need to request a ruled or shaded appearance).

2. On the Options tab, choose Icon Only from the Layout drop-down list. Click the Select Icon button and browse to choose the icon file you want to appear as the button. Click OK.

3. On the Actions tab, choose Mouse Down as the event (you want the button to work when the user clicks it) and click Add to add the action.

4. For the action type, choose Execute Menu Item. Click the Edit Menu Item button. From the facsimile of the Acrobat menu bar that appears for users of IBM-compatible machines, choose File, Print.

▼

▼　　　　Macintosh users: In the Menu Item dialog box, select the menu items from the
　　　　　menu bar.

　　5.　Click OK.

　　6.　Test the new button with the Hand tool. As long as the user's computer is con-
　　　　nected to a printer, the document will print when he or she clicks the button.

　　7.　As we did with the Home button in the previous task, you can duplicate the print
　　　　button to appear on other pages. Select the button and choose Tools, Forms,
▲　　　　Fields, Duplicate. Indicate the pages on which you want to duplicate the button
　　　　　and click OK.

Aligning Form Fields

To align a series of form fields, select the Form tool and Shift+click to select the fields
one at a time. The Shift+click method enables you to select multiple fields.

Choose Tools, Forms, Fields, Align from the menu bar. Choose the alignment you prefer
from the list.

To distribute space evenly between fields, first use the Form tool to select multiple fields.
Then choose Tools, Forms, Fields, Distribute. Choose Vertically or Horizontally.
(Aligning the form fields affects only the elements we have added in Acrobat; the design
of the original document is unaffected.)

To size individual fields or multiple fields at the same time, select the field or fields you
want to resize and press Shift+up-arrow, Shift+down-arrow, Shift+left-arrow, or
Shift+right-arrow on your keyboard to increase or decrease the size of the fields.

Reordering Form Fields

The order in which you create the form fields is the order in which the user will enter the
data and move from field to field when he or she presses the Tab key to navigate through
the form.

If you want to change the order of the fields, choose Tools, Forms, Fields, Set Tab Order.
The PDF file changes to display the form with the number of each field in the corner of
the field box (see Figure 16.13). Click the field you want to be the first field the user fills
out; Acrobat renumbers that field to number 1. Click the field you want to be the second
field the user fills out; Acrobat renumbers it as number 2. Continue in this manner to
select all the fields. Click outside a field box to exit renumbering mode.

FIGURE 16.13

To renumber the order in which the user can tab through the form fields, choose Tools, Forms, Fields, Set Tab Order. The field box numbers appear; click the fields in the order you want to renumber them.

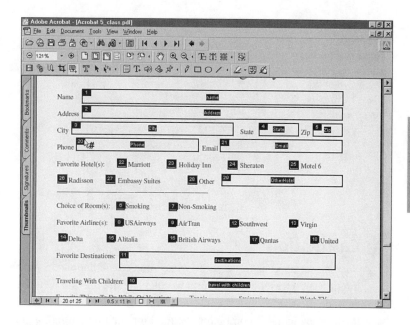

Validating and Calculating with a Form Field

Now that you understand the basics of creating and editing forms in Acrobat, let's talk about validation and calculation, two other features of the Form tool.

Validation

Acrobat can check the data the user enters in a field for correct content. For example, if you are requesting that the user enters the year of his or her birth, you can specify a range of years that is applicable (for example, 1900-1990). If the user attempts to enter a birth year of 1995, a warning dialog box appears to notify them that this number is not acceptable.

To set up the validation for the field, double-click the field to open the Field Properties dialog box. Click the Validate tab. You can enter a value in the Greater Than and Lesser Than boxes. For example, if you have designed a survey for people in their 40s and have asked for their age, you can enter the 10-year span in the two boxes. Anyone who was born less than 40 years ago or more than 50 years ago could not enter their age and continue with the survey (see Figure 16.14).

You can also choose to use a custom script for the validation process. A script is useful if, for example, the user has to enter a password. The script can check the password and allow or disallow the user to continue based on the value entered in the field.

FIGURE 16.14

Validating a form field ensures that the data returned will be in the correct format, as defined by you, the form creator.

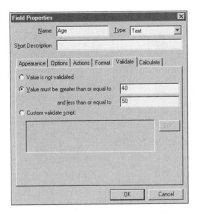

Calculation

You can set up your forms to do some simple calculations in Acrobat. For instance, you might want a travel expense form to calculate the miles traveled multiplied by the amount allotted for mileage. Or perhaps you are totaling the number of products sold in the last few months, combining the total for each month into a grand total. These examples of calculations can be easily performed within Acrobat.

Task: Performing a Calculation Within a Form

In this task, we perform a calculation within a form.

1. Begin by choosing the PDF you want to apply the calculation to. Figure 16.15 shows a simple PDF created entirely in Adobe Illustrator; we will add invisible form fields over the existing elements. To efficiently work through this exercise, we recommend that your calculation be the same or similar to the one in the example.

FIGURE 16.15

Choose the file to which you will be adding the calculation. Our example produces a simple result by adding two sums together.

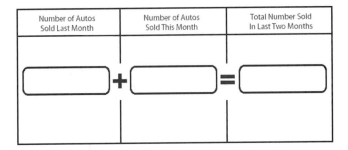

2. Set up the form fields for the calculation. Using the Form tool, draw a form field for the first number—in this case, the number of autos sold last month (see

Figure 16.16).

The fields do not have any appearance, that is, they are invisible fields. The rounded rectangles were drawn in the original file and the form fields were simply put over top of the rectangles.

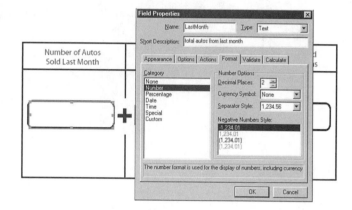

Be sure to assign each field as a text field; from the Format option, choose Number. In this example, the information will be added in the form of a number, so our fields must be set up to receive the information correctly.

After we set up the three fields, use the last field—in this example, it is the Total field—to calculate the total.

3. With the Field Properties dialog box still open, switch to the Calculate tab and choose the second option, Value Is The Sum Of, as shown in Figure 16.17.

4. To determine which numbers will add up to the total, click the Pick button; then select the fields you want to include, clicking Add after each selection (see Figure 16.18). Close the Field Properties dialog box by clicking OK.

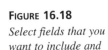

FIGURE 16.18

Select fields that you want to include and then click Add.

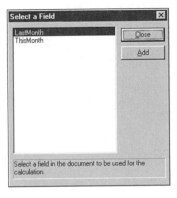

5. Test your calculation by using the Hand tool to click inside the first field. Type a number, press the Tab key or just click inside the second field, and type another number. Pressing the Tab key again or clicking inside the third field performs the calculation (see Figure 16.19).

Wasn't that easy?

FIGURE 16.19

The form calculating a sum.

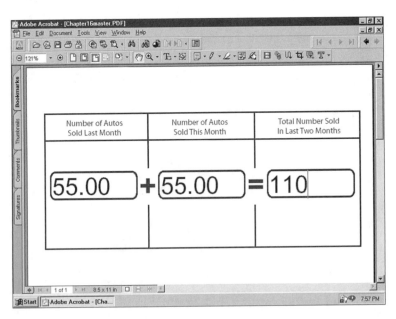

To set up a custom calculation, you must create some JavaScript code and enter it in the proper field in the Field Properties dialog box. To enter the code, click the Calculate tab and type the data in the box labeled Custom Validation Script.

Calculation Order

Acrobat's capability to calculate fields on a form also allows you to change the order of these calculations. If you have multiple calculations on a form, and a number determined from one calculation affects a later calculation, you can specify the order in which the calculations occur.

Let's use the scenario we created for our calculation as an example. Suppose that you had set up a form to calculate the total number of autos sold—daily, then weekly, then monthly. To get the exact number of autos sold for the month, you must first calculate the total for each week because those totals are what make up the monthly total.

To change the order of the calculations on a form, choose Tools, Forms, Set Calculation Order. In the dialog box that appears, reorder the calculations.

Importing and Exporting Form Data

After you have produced a working PDF form, you can export and import the data from the form for use in other PDF documents.

To export form data, open the PDF that contains the completed form. Choose File, Export, Form Data. This command saves the form data as a separate file, in .fdf (form data file) format.

To import form data, open the PDF file into which you want to import the data. Choose File, Import, Form Data. Select the FDF file you want to import and click OK. You can bring form data information into another PDF document, and the data will fall into place—provided that the fields in the new document have the same names as the form data's original document.

For an example of how form data is used, consider a corporate-wide questionnaire. The Human Resources department of a company can decide to e-mail the questionnaire in the form of a PDF to its employees. Perhaps the department is asking some slightly personal questions for use in a company newsletter, such as "What can be found in your refrigerator?" The employee fills out the form, exports the data, and e-mails the resulting FDF file back to the Human Resources department. The data file is small and easy to e-mail; the HR department simply imports the data to the original questionnaire and can view the results as they were intended.

Form Data Use Over the World Wide Web

The form data exported from the PDF file can be used in several ways. As already mentioned, it can be saved as an FDF file and e-mailed for use in another PDF document.

16

PDF forms can also be submitted over the World Wide Web using a Common Gateway Interface (CGI) application on the Web server. This CGI application gathers the data for use in a database. For this to work properly, the fields must all be named in accordance with the CGI script. (In other words, the names in the script must match the names in the form. The form field named `Total Autos for October` would not return the information correctly if the CGI script referred to that field as `October Total Autos`.)

Web server administrators usually set up these scripts. The scripts are not created in Acrobat; someone with extensive programming knowledge can write the scripts using the Adobe FDF Toolkit. Adobe's Web site at `http://www.adobe.com` is useful for finding CGI samples and contact numbers for the Adobe Developer Support program.

Summary

In this hour, we explored the powerful Forms tool and used some basic exercises to create the different kinds of form fields.

As we have learned, each type of field has characteristics that are useful in different situations. The radio buttons, for instance, are good when only one answer is correct. In comparison, the check boxes allow the user to select multiple answers.

We learned that forms are an integral part of the office workflow, and Acrobat's form features give you the ability to create interactive forms for online and office use. The form information can be imported and exported for use in other documents.

A variety of form field types give you flexibility and freedom when creating PDF forms. Fields can be invisible, as we have discovered, or can take on a custom appearance with appearance options such as shaded, ruled, or beveled.

We practiced duplicating form fields on multiple pages so that they appear on the new pages in the exact position as on the original page, with appearance, options, and action settings intact.

Each form will have its own set of requirements, but the many features of Acrobat's Form tool give us the flexibility to meet each challenge and give the form the necessary functions.

Workshop

To review the information presented in this hour, you will find a few questions and answers about related information. The multiple-choice quiz that follows is useful in reinforcing your newfound knowledge. Finally, you will find some hands-on exercises to give you another opportunity to use the hour's lessons in a practical way.

Q&A

Q What happens to the form data in an online form when the user clicks the Submit button?

A If you create a button on your form and apply an action (such as Submit Form), the data is sent to an Internet server as a text stream to a CGI script. The Internet Service Provider receives the data and returns it to the creator, where the information can be used for different purposes. One example is an online form requesting a catalog. The company receives the data from the form (the name and address of interested party) and can then send the catalog to the new customer.

Q Why would I want to enter a description of the form field, and is it necessary that I do so?

A No, it is not necessary to enter a description of the form field. The name of the form field, however, *is* required, and must be different for each field, (except in the case of a group of radio buttons). The description of the field makes it possible for a ToolTip box to appear when the user passes the mouse pointer over the field. The ToolTip can be useful when filling out the form.

Q What do the On Focus and On Blur options on the Actions tab mean?

A The On Focus option allows the action to occur when the user reaches that particular form field from a previous field by using the Tab key or moving the mouse. The On Blur option causes the action to occur when the user exits the field by using the Tab key or moving the mouse.

Quiz

1. **Which form element requires multiple answers to have the same name but different export values?**

    a. Combo box

    b. Radio button

    c. Text field

2. **How do you move a form field?**

    a. Click once to select it and then move the field with the handles.

    b. You cannot move a field after it is created.

    c. Click once to select it and then click inside the field and move it.

16

3. The layout grid is used to

   a. Allow easy alignment and consistency in the placement of form elements.

   b. Name the fields by typing the form field names directly onto the grid.

   c. Change the color and appearance of text for each form field.

Quiz Answers

1. **b**   Radio buttons have the same name but different export values, so the user can choose only one answer.

2. **c**   Click once to select it; click inside the field to move it.

3. **a**   The layout grid allows easy alignment and provides consistency in the placement of form elements.

Exercises

These hands-on exercises will reinforce the knowledge you have gained in this hour.

1. Prepare a PDF form using the various elements discussed in this hour, including a Reset button that deletes entered data from the fields. Export the data to an FDF format and import the data back into the PDF form. Notice that the data falls back into the same place because the fields are named to match the data.

   You can apply the Reset Form action to a button. When you choose Execute Menu Item as your action, you can choose this option from the menu list.

2. On a multiple-page PDF file, create a Home button on a particular page. Apply an action to the button so that the user goes to the first page of the file when the button is clicked. Use the Duplicate option to copy this button to each page in the file.

3. Shift+click to select multiple fields on the form and then align them. It may be useful to turn on the layout grid before aligning the fields.

PART VII

Using PDF Files for Multimedia and Presentations

Hour

Hour 17

Enhancing a PDF with Multimedia

For those situations in which information must be conveyed and visual appeal is of utmost importance, you can put together exciting and interesting presentations that contain multimedia components. Movies and sounds are easily incorporated into the PDF format, and you, the document creator, have a variety of options at your disposal to control the look and performance of the PDF.

Some of the exciting features we will cover in this hour include:

- Using movies and sound within PDF files
- Inserting movies
- Inserting sounds
- Adding buttons such as Stop, Play, and Pause
- Understanding multimedia file formats

Using Movies and Sound Within PDF Files

Think of the possibilities that adding movies and sounds to your PDF files opens to you! Adobe Acrobat can give your PDF document the power of a multimedia presentation and allow you to control how the movies and sounds perform. Let's explore some possible scenarios you may encounter and how the multimedia features in Acrobat can deliver the message you want to convey easily and effectively.

Let's examine some situations in which multimedia presentations would be helpful in getting your message across to others:

- You are preparing a CD for high school students to assist them in learning more about the history of the United States. A map of the country could be the first page they see, and a sound message could tell them to click a state to learn more about it. When the students click a state, a new page could be launched, with information about the state's government, major exports, terrain, and so on.
- You are putting together a presentation for a group of executives in a boardroom meeting. You will be speaking on the latest sales figures and want to deliver this data in an interesting and appealing way. By preparing the PDF in its native application and adding multimedia features in Acrobat, you can easily assemble the finished product with professional results.

One way you can apply an action such as playing a movie or sound to a file is with a "page action." Page actions are specific functions performed at the open or close of a particular page. Sounds and movies are just two of the actions that can be used as page actions. Others include reset form, submit form, and execute menu item.

As students in the first example link to various parts of the document to learn more about the individual states your presentation can include movies illustrating a particular portion of the state, or perhaps demonstrating the major exports of the state.

Figure 17.1 shows an example of a multimedia feature that has been added to a PDF document.

Limiting the amount of reading the user has to do in the PDF, by adding graphics with links, and now by including sound and movie files in the presentation document, we will make the PDF easy to navigate and understand—even for individuals with limited computer knowledge. It is not necessary that they have a grasp of Acrobat because the features we add to the document will walk them through it with ease. To review the addition of links to a PDF document, see Hour 10, "Using Links to Add Interactivity to PDF Files."

FIGURE 17.1

Multimedia added to a PDF document increases its visual impact and offers a variety of options for the user to navigate and easily use the document.

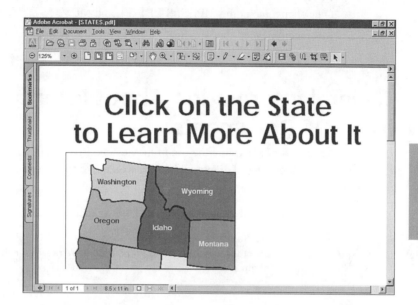

Let's explore another situation in which the use of multimedia can be an effective way to deliver a message. Let's use the scenario of the owner of a cookie company who has created a Web site to sell his or her products. To demonstrate the products and perhaps the way they are prepared, the business owner has created a QuickTime movie. On the Web site, users can click a link that starts to play the movie; users can also stop, start, and pause the movie at their convenience. Sound files can be used to explain the shipping of these products, or perhaps offer comments from satisfied customers.

As you can see, the benefits of using multimedia are far-reaching. Now, let's begin to demonstrate the ways to add these useful and exciting attributes to your PDF files.

Correct File Formats for Movie and Sound Files

Before you can add multimedia to PDF files, you must be acquainted with the guidelines for movie and sound files. To use movies and sounds within PDF documents, there are certain guidelines you must be aware of regarding file formats:

- Movies for IBM-compatible computers can be either QuickTime or AVI files.
- Movie files for Macintosh computers must be in QuickTime format.
- File formats for movies on the Macintosh can be in any format supported by QuickTime, including MPEG, SWF, AVI, and MOV.
- It is recommended that you install QuickTime 4.0 or higher for best results, regardless of your computer platform.

General Information About Inserting Movies into PDF Documents

Let's begin to further explore the use of movies in a PDF document. If you have a prepared movie file and a PDF into which you would like to place the movie, we are ready to begin.

Movie files can be prepared in a program such as QuickTime. Check out the AcrobatIn24.com Web site if you do not have movies or the capability to create them.

A point to remember: As mentioned earlier, movie and sound files are not embedded into the PDF file. They are *linked* to the PDF file, which means that the original files must accompany the PDF files.

Later in this hour, we will cover the different file formats and provide some details on how to save your movies for best use with PDF documents.

As mentioned earlier, sound and movie files are simply linked to the PDF. Therefore, the movie and sound files must accompany the PDF when you save them to disk, upload them to the World Wide Web, or put them on a CD-ROM. However, when sound files are added to a PDF as an action, they become part of the file and are embedded within the PDF file.

Task: Adding Movies to a PDF File

To add a movie to a PDF file, follow these steps:

1. Open the PDF document to which you want to add the movie. In the toolbar at the top of the screen, click the Movie tool to select it (see Figure 17.2). Click with the

▼   Movie tool on the location in the file where you want to add the movie; this will be
the center of the movie frame (you can move it later). When you release the
mouse, the Movie Properties dialog box appears (see Figure 17.3).

FIGURE 17.2

*The Movie tool makes
it easy to link to pre-
pared movies from
your PDF files.*

FIGURE 17.3

*Use the Movie
Properties dialog box
to control how the
movie behaves as well
as certain features
regarding the display
of the movie.*

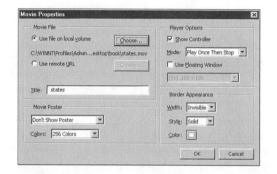

17

2. If the movie is on your local computer, select the Use File on Local Volume
   option; if the movie is on a remote computer, select the Use Remote URL option.
   Then click the active Choose button to navigate to the movie file.

3. In the Title field, type a title for the movie, usually the name of the movie or a
   short, descriptive title. (The movie's name appears as the default title.)

4. Enable the Show Controller check box if you want the user to be able to stop,
   pause, or restart the movie.

5. From the Mode drop-down list, choose how the movie is to be played, such as
   play once and then stop. The most common option here is to Play Once Then
   Stop, depending on the situation.

6. Enable the Use Floating Window check box if you want the movie to display in a
   separate window. Otherwise it will play directly on the PDF page you have chosen. If you choose Use Floating Window, you can choose the size of the window
   in which the movie will be displayed from the preset list of dimensions.

7. If you have not created a graphic that directs the user to click for the movie to
   play, you may want to select the Movie Poster option. This option displays the first
   frame of your movie as a sort of "poster" on the document. If you choose the
   Don't Show Poster option, there will be an empty block with no indication of the
▼   subject of the movie.

▼   If you select the Movie Poster option, you can choose the number of colors to display the poster. For 8-bit color images, choose the 256 Colors option; for 32-bit images, choose the Millions of Colors option.

8. After you have set the movie options, click OK and then play the movie. To play the movie, select the Hand tool and click the movie poster. This action triggers the movie to play—either within the frame or in a floating window, depending on the
▲   options you chose.

When you are placing a movie with the Movie tool, it is a good idea to click and not click and drag to add the movie.

The movie is set to a certain *resolution*, that is, a certain number of pixels (the little squares that make up the display) per inch. If you click and drag with the Movie tool, you will resize the movie and change the number of pixels per inch. This will result in a movie of lesser quality, and in some cases, a blurred image.

If the original movie is large, click and drag to make the movie appear at a reduced size. This may not be a problem for you, but you should know that sizing the movie to a larger dimension could produce that blurriness.

It is also important to note that resizing the movie does not affect it disproportionately. There will be no distortion, regardless of whether you enlarge or reduce the size.

An alternative to using the movie poster as a placeholder is to add a graphic or frame for the movie in the native document. Here are some tips for this procedure:

- First create the movie file. Keep track of the dimensions of the movie.

- Then, in the page layout application, add a ruled box or graphic that same size, as a placeholder for the movie. When you add the movie in Acrobat, choose not to add a poster in the Movie Properties dialog box. The movie is added, but the user clicks on the graphic or frame to play the movie.

Changing Movie Properties

After you have assigned the movie's properties, you can alter them easily by selecting the Movie tool and double-clicking within the boundaries of the movie. The Movie Properties dialog box opens, displaying all the currently specified settings. Make changes to the properties and click OK to save the new properties. You can then test the movie's new properties by selecting the Hand tool and clicking within the boundaries of the movie.

You can move the movie around on the page with the Movie tool. Simply select the tool and then click and drag the movie icon to the new location.

Here's an alternative way to play the movie: While the movie is still selected in the PDF file, Windows users can right-click it and choose Play Movie from the context menu. Macintosh users can Ctrl+click and choose the Play Movie option.

This shortcut saves you time and prevents you from having to switch from the Movie tool to the Hand tool.

Inserting Sounds into PDF Documents

Just as movies added to a PDF document can add visual interest, sounds can help get the message across and add functionality to the PDF file as well.

Sounds, when added to a PDF document, are linked to the file. This means that they are not part of the PDF document, still separate entities, and must reside with the PDF document. This information is crucial when you're uploading the PDF to the World Wide Web or saving it to a disk or CD-ROM. You must upload or save the sound and movie files along with the PDF file.

Why add sounds to a PDF document? Let's explore some reasons for using sounds and how they can improve your documents.

Suppose that you are creating a Web site for a public park or wildlife preserve. You may want to add sounds as page actions to demonstrate the subject of each page. For instance, from your home page, there is a link to a page describing a bird sanctuary. When the user clicks the link for that page, a sound file of birds singing plays while the page is loading.

As mentioned earlier in this hour, you can apply a page action to a particular page of the PDF file so that that action occurs when the page is opened or closed. The user doesn't click on anything; the action runs automatically.

Or maybe you have a form on your Web site that people can use to order a product or send for more information. Your sound page action could direct them to fill out the form and click the submit button at the bottom of the page.

Perhaps an audible inspirational message could greet a user, or a verbal description of a specific product. A sound can give the user direction on using a product, contacting you, or simply telling how to get to a specific page. The possibilities are limitless—and easy to achieve with Acrobat.

Task: Adding a Sound to Your PDF File

Let's begin to add sound files to an existing PDF file. Visit the `AcrobatIn24.com` Web site that complements this book for sound files you can use in this task.

1. Open the PDF document to which you want to add sounds. Choose the Movie tool.

2. Drag to define the area the user will click to play the sound (see Figure 17.4). When you release the mouse button, the Movie Properties dialog box opens.

FIGURE 17.4

Click and drag to define an area for the sound link and to display the Movie Properties dialog box, where you choose the sound file you want to add.

Using a graphic to create a link is a great way to add the sound files. When creating the original document in the native application, create a graphic that will appear as a button or link in the PDF file. Although you can create the button or link in Acrobat, the appearance options offered by Acrobat are limited. Creative features will be more available in the native application and can make appealing, eye-catching graphics for a professional look.

3. If the sound file is on your local computer, select the Use File on Local Volume option; if the sound file is on a remote computer, select the Use Remote URL option. Then click the active Choose button to navigate to the desired sound file. Change the Files of Type option to All Files to view the sound file formats. (The only other choice for Macintosh users is Sound Files.)

▼

▲

Macintosh users: Acrobat converts Sound Mover (FSSD) and System 7 sound files to QuickTime movies before it plays them. This may cause playback delays when the user clicks the link for the sound.

Adding Sounds Using the Form Tool

In addition to using the Movie Properties dialog box to add sounds to a PDF file, you can use the Form tool to add sounds. An advantage to adding sounds this way is that you can create the button, if one does not already exist in the file. You can also add movies to PDFs using the Movie tool, for much the same reason.

In other words, when the original document was prepared, if a button or graphic (such as one that says, *Click Here to Hear The Ocean*) does not exist, the Form tool gives you options to add such a button or graphic.

TASK

Task: Adding Sounds with the Form Tool

In Acrobat, let's add a button to which we can link the sound file for the sound action.

1. Open the PDF file you want to use for the sound action. Using the Form tool, click and drag an area to define the button. In the Field Properties dialog box that opens, under the Appearance tab, choose the options you want for the look of the button you are creating (see the example in Figure 17.5).

17

FIGURE 17.5

The Appearance tab of the Field Properties dialog box allows you to control the visual appearance of the button, such as text color, text size, button color, and button outline.

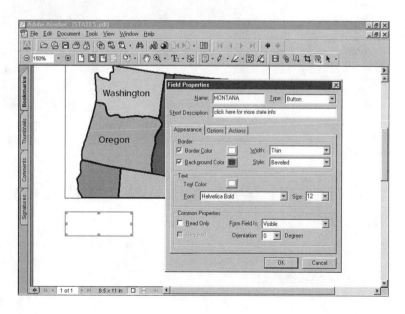

▼

▼   2. Switch to the Options tab of the Field Properties dialog box. For the Highlight
       option, choose Push; for the Layout option, choose Text Only. For the Button Face
       When option, choose Up. These options will create a button, with text on it, that
       will appear before the user clicks on it.

    3. In the Button Face Attributes section, in the Text field, type the text you want to
       appear on the button. Return to the Appearance tab and select the text options
       (color, font, and size).

    4. To add the sound action, click the Action tab.

    5. Test the button by switching to the Hand tool and clicking the button. If you want
       to make changes to the appearance or other attributes of the button, choose the
▲   Form tool and double-click the button. Make the necessary changes and click OK.

Figure 17.6 shows two examples of buttons that link to sound files. The one on the left
was created in the native application—in this case, Adobe InDesign, a page layout program. Using the Movie tool, an invisible link was created to the sound file.

The button on the right was created using the Form tool in Acrobat. Each button plays
the sound when clicked, but each was created with a different Acrobat tool.

FIGURE 17.6

Side-by-side examples of buttons used to play sounds in Acrobat. The example on the left was created in another application and the invisible link added in Acrobat. The example on the right was created in Acrobat using the Form tool.

Adding Buttons Such as Stop, Play, and Pause

When you add a movie to the PDF file, you can also add a controller that gives the user
some control over the play of the movie. Start by using the Movie tool to add a movie to
the PDF document.

In the Movie Properties dialog box, enable the Show Controller check box. When you click OK to close the dialog box and then use the Hand tool to play the movie, a controller box appears under the movie (see Figure 17.7), with buttons to play, pause and stop the movie.

FIGURE 17.7

Enable the Show Controller check box in the Movie Properties dialog box to add a controller bar under the movie, which you can use to stop, start, and replay the movie.

17

Stopping and Restarting the Movie Without a Controller

Even without the addition of a controller, the user can stop and restart the movie by using various keys.

To stop the movie altogether, press the Escape key. To pause a movie, press the Return or Enter key; use the same key to restart the movie. You can simply click the movie using the Hand tool to restart it from the beginning.

Important Considerations When Using Movies and Sounds

To play movie and sound files correctly, you must take into account certain considerations. For movies to play, you must have Apple QuickTime 5 or later installed on Macintosh or IBM-compatible computers. (IBM-compatible computers can use Microsoft Video instead of QuickTime.)

If you use MPEG files (see the section on movie and sound file formats, later in this hour), you must have QuickTime 5.0 or later installed on your computer.

To play sound files, the viewer of your PDF file must have the appropriate sound card and speaker system installed on the computer as well.

Using a Page Action to Play a Sound

Another interesting way to add a sound to a PDF file is to arrange for the sound to play automatically when the user reaches the appropriate page. You can accomplish this goal by adding a page action. Remember that a *page action* is an action that occurs when a page opens or closes; it occurs automatically, without the user having to click a button.

Task: Adding a Page Action to Your PDF File

In this task, we'll add a page action to the PDF document.

1. To add a sound to a PDF as a page action, open the PDF file to the page to which you want to add the sound. From the menu bar, choose Document, Set Page Action.

2. Add the page action in the Page Actions dialog box (see Figure 17.8), and choose whether you want the action to occur when the user goes to that page or leaves that page.

FIGURE 17.8

Add a sound as a page action by selecting options in the Page Actions dialog box.

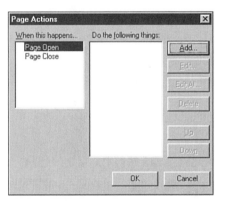

You might want a sound to play when users get to the page to welcome them to a particular part of the document or to instruct them on how to work with that page (for example, the sound file might be a recording of a voice saying, "click the photos to see a larger view").

3. Choose either the Page Open or Page Close option and click the Add button to add the action to the page. The Add and Action dialog box opens.

4. From the Type drop-down list box, choose Sound as the page action type. Click Select Sound (see Figure 17.9) to browse to find the sound file you want to add and click OK.

▼

▲

5. To test the action, go to another page (if your action was set to play when the page closes) and come back to the page (if your action was set to play when the page opens).

FIGURE 17.9

Choose Sound as the page action type and then browse to find the sound file.

17

Sound files for Macintosh computers can be any of the following formats: AIFF, Sound Mover (FSSD), QuickTime, or System 7 sound files. Sound files for IBM-compatible computers must be AIF, QuickTime, or WAV files. Whatever the original format, Acrobat will convert the sound files to QuickTime format, which means that they can be played on all computer platforms.

Saving your movie files in the QuickTime format is the best option because QuickTime files will play on all computer platforms.

QuickTime is available on the installer disks of Acrobat for both Macintosh and IBM-compatible platforms. Macintosh users most likely have QuickTime installed already because it is included with the operating system.

AVI files (Audio Video Interleave) cannot be read by Macintosh users with QuickTime 3.0 or earlier. Therefore, your best option is to convert AVI files to QuickTime before using them in Acrobat, if your audience may include Macintosh users.

Summary

In this hour, we have explored many options for using the multimedia features within Acrobat. As we have learned, adding multimedia features to a PDF document greatly increases its visual impact and gives the document options for easier navigation and interesting appeal.

By adding movies to PDF files, we learned to open a whole set of possibilities. Movies can be used to get a message across, sell a product, or relate a story. They can be used on the World Wide Web, for interactive CDs, and in a variety of other ways. Movie files are not a part of the PDF document; instead, the PDF file contains a link to the movie file. The user clicks a link to play the movie.

Workshop

To review the information we have covered in this hour, this workshop begins with a few questions on topics that might be of interest to you when adding movies and sounds to your PDF documents. After the requisite quiz, you'll find some short exercises designed to help get you up and running with multimedia in Acrobat.

Q&A

Q Are there any ways to add movies and sounds other than using the Movie or Form tool?

A Yes. You also can use the Link tool to add a movie or sound. Simply click and drag over an area with the Link tool to create the clickable area. In the Link Properties dialog box, indicate whether you want this to be a movie or sound action and browse to choose the appropriate file.

Q What software do I need to add a sound to my PDF document?

A Sounds are easily created on your computer with a microphone and a sound recording application (provided that the correct sound card and speakers are installed). There are many software options available for this purpose, or you can find a suitable substitute on the World Wide Web. Examples of sites offering such applications for free or for a fee include www.macupdate.com and www.freeware.com.

Q Can I use home movies from my video camera to add to a PDF file?

A Yes, but first these movies must be converted and compressed into an acceptable format. Use a video-editing program such as Adobe Premiere to save the file to an appropriate format. Then you can use it in your PDF file.

Q Can I add a sound to my PDF that conveys a message to others in the office when they open the document?

A Yes. The Audio Notes tool allows you to save a sound file, provided that you have a microphone and sound card installed. You can then attach the sound file to the document. The user double-clicks it with the Hand tool, just as they would any other comment, to play the sound.

Q I want a movie to play on every page in the document. Is that possible to set up without having to place it manually on each page?

A Yes. Use the Form tool to add the movie. Form fields can be copied and pasted or duplicated on each page. When you duplicate the field (using Tools, Forms, Fields, Duplicate), the link works on all pages on which the field is duplicated.

Quiz

1. Which tool is *not* used to add a sound or movie to a PDF document?

    a. Link tool

    b. Strikeout tool

    c. Movie tool

2. What movie format is best to use for movies to be viewed on Macintosh and IBM-compatible platforms?

    a. MP3

    b. TIFF

    c. QuickTime

3. A controller is added to a movie to

    a. Control the resolution of the movie when it's playing.

    b. Allow the user to switch between color and black-and-white video.

    c. Offer controls for the user to stop, play, and pause the movie.

Quiz Answers

1. **b** The Strikeout tool is not used to add multimedia; it is a graphic mark-up tool.

2. **c** QuickTime is the universal format because it is acceptable for both Macintosh and IBM-compatible computers.

3. **c** The controller gives the user a way to stop, play, and pause the movie.

17

Exercises

1. Add a movie to a PDF document with the controller option turned on; add the movie again with the option turned off. Practice using the Hand tool to stop, start, and pause the movie.

2. Add a sound or movie to a PDF using the various ways available: by using the Link tool, the Movie tool, and the Form tool. Next, add a page action that uses a sound or movie file.

3. Think of the different ways movies and sounds can add impact to your PDF file. Practice adding movie and sound files to your PDF files using the various options available in Acrobat. For instance, try creating a button with the Form tool and adding a sound action to that button.

HOUR 18

Using Acrobat for Presentations: The Full-Screen Mode

An integral part of the business world is meetings, conferences, and seminars—the process of presenting ideas and policies to others in the business community. Acrobat's full-screen mode can be a major contributor to this process, allowing you to prepare quality presentations in the manner of slideshows or overhead projections. All you have to do is select a few simple options, and the full-screen mode can work for you.

Here are some of the areas we will discuss in this hour:

- Creating presentations
- Design considerations for full-screen documents
- Setting documents to full-screen mode
- Changing full-screen preferences

Creating Presentations

Presentations in the business community are becoming more and more popular. The information conveyed in these presentations must be introduced in a eye-catching and easy-to-follow format (see Figure 18.1).

FIGURE 18.1

Eye-catching presentations are easily produced in Acrobat using full-screen mode capabilities.

More and more businesses are turning to Acrobat to allow them to easily put together presentations suitable for overhead projector or slideshow use.

Choose an application for your full-screen documents that will allow you to use color and graphics when necessary. Some good choices for this are Adobe PageMaker, QuarkXpress, Adobe Indesign, Illustrator, and Photoshop.

Although you can use word processing applications, they might not offer you the full gamut of design choices that the aforementioned applications do.

Use quality graphics with vibrant colors for the best results. Washed-out graphics projected onto a screen don't produce the most eye-catching end products.

Documents prepared in full-screen mode do not show the menu bar, toolbar, window controls, or status bar. You can choose to have the pages of your presentation advance automatically or you can control the presentation yourself by using the right-arrow key to advance through the pages.

Task: Setting a PDF Document to View in Full-Screen Mode

In this task, we will begin to study the full-screen mode. Later in this hour, we will discuss design considerations when putting together a presentation for use in full-screen mode.

1. Open the PDF document you want to display in full-screen mode.

2. From the menu bar, select File, Document Properties, Open. The Document Open Options dialog box appears as shown in Figure 18.2.

FIGURE 18.2

The Document Open Options dialog box allows you to select the Open in Full Screen Mode option.

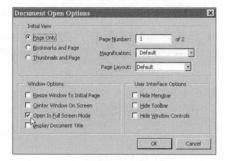

3. Enable the Open in Full Screen Mode check box.

4. Click OK.

5. Save the document and reopen it to view it in full-screen mode.

6. Press the keyboard Esc key to exit full-screen mode. This is a preference setting, which is on by default. We will discuss preferences for full-screen mode later in this hour.

▲

You don't have to check the User Interface Options when you choose Open in Full Screen Mode. Those items are automatically hidden for you. By checking these items, you will have to restore the menu bar and toolbar—either by going to the View menu or by using the F8 and F9 keyboard shortcuts.

18

Design Considerations for Full-Screen Presentations

Design is an important part of a successful presentation of any kind. It is even more important in a PDF file that you intend to display in full-screen mode.

Preparing a document or series of documents with similar color and style themes helps to tie the entire presentation together. Some designers choose to add a simple color bar or the corporate logo at the top or bottom of each page to give a look of unity to the entire presentation (as shown in Figure 18.3). Remember that less is more when it comes to design—and that rule applies here as well.

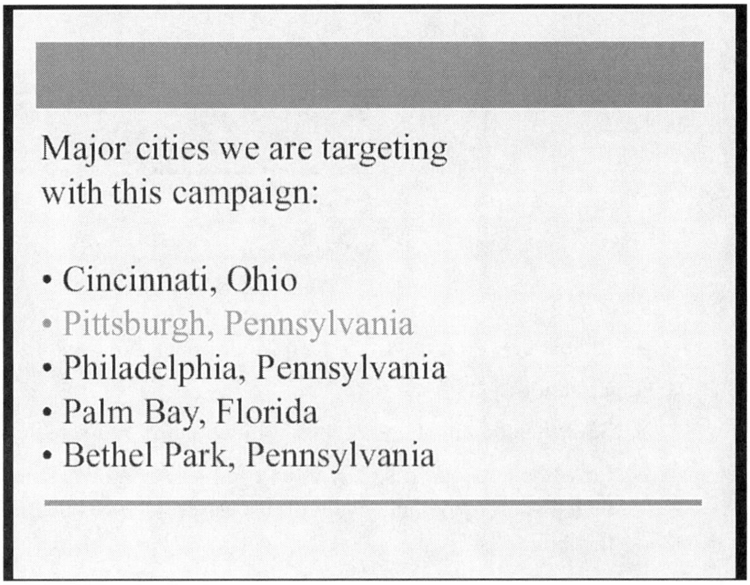

FIGURE 18.3

Documents to be displayed in full-screen mode should be clean and concise, and can support the addition of color to get the point across to the user.

> Major cities we are targeting
> with this campaign:
>
> • Cincinnati, Ohio
> • Pittsburgh, Pennsylvania
> • Philadelphia, Pennsylvania
> • Palm Bay, Florida
> • Bethel Park, Pennsylvania

Making full use of the entire screen is another tip for successful full-screen presentations. Don't waste the extra space you access in full-screen mode when the toolbars, status bar, and window controls disappear—make use of it. You might choose to enlarge the type, add a larger or more elaborate graphic, or simply frame the pages in an eye-pleasing color or design.

As in any large format presentation, calling attention to the item being discussed on that page is a good idea. For instance, in a list of bulleted items being discussed one by one on consecutive pages, highlight the text currently being talked about or change the color of the bullet. These tips help to pinpoint the information for the audience, making it easier to follow the presentation (as shown in Figure 18.4).

FIGURE 18.4
Highlighting the copy being discussed on that particular page—with color, underlining, or a bold look—gives the audience a focus point and helps them to follow the material more successfully.

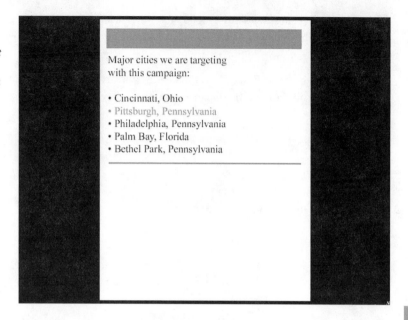

Setting Documents to Open in Full-Screen Mode

You have already learned how to set the Document Open Options so that the document will open in full-screen mode.

Macintosh users with dual monitors installed can choose which monitor the document will display on in the full-screen preferences:

- **Main:** Chooses the monitor displaying the menu bar.
- **Largest Intersection:** Chooses the monitor with largest portion of the document displayed.
- **Deepest:** Opts for the monitor with the most colors.
- **Widest:** Chooses the monitor with the greatest horizontal resolution.
- **Tallest:** Chooses the monitor with the greatest vertical resolution.
- **Largest Area:** Picks the monitor with the most pixels.

Now let's discuss some other things you can do with full-screen mode.

18

If you are using full-screen mode, you have several ways to page through the document. To view the document in full-screen mode at any time, choose View, Full Screen from the menu bar (see Figure 18.5).

Press the Enter or Return key, the PageDown key, the right-arrow key, or the down-arrow key to scroll through the document, page by page.

FIGURE 18.5

Display any PDF document in full-screen mode at any time by choosing View, Full Screen.

Press the Esc key to exit the full-screen mode (if your preferences were set that way), or use the Ctrl+L (IBM-compatible) or Command+L (Macintosh) keyboard shortcut.

Changing Full-Screen Preferences

To change the preference settings for full-screen mode, select Edit, Preferences, General to open the Preferences dialog box for the PDF document. Select Full Screen from the pane at left (see Figure 18.6).

The following sections explore the preference settings for full-screen mode.

Figure 18.6

Figure 18.6

Preference settings for full-screen mode help to control the look and performance of Acrobat.

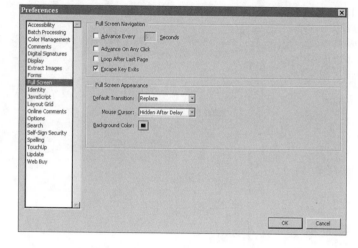

Full-Screen Navigation

The following list describes the Full-Screen navigation options, and how you can use them effectively:

- You may choose to have Acrobat automatically advance the pages. If you select this option, you can indicate the time in seconds each page is to show on the screen.

- You can also choose to advance the pages whenever you click the mouse. This option gives you more control over when the pages advance.

- Selecting the Escape Key Exits option is a good idea; this option makes it possible for you to retreat from full-screen mode if necessary. This option is selected for you by default.

- Loop After Last Page (Figure 18.7 shows the Preferences dialog box with this option turned on) allows the document to return to the beginning and continuously play.

View your document in full-screen mode at any time by pressing Ctrl+L (Macintosh users press Command+L). When you are viewing the document in full-screen mode, the menu bar and toolbar are hidden.

18

Figure **18.7**

*Loop After Last Page
allows the document to
replay when it reaches
the end, in a continu-
ous fashion.*

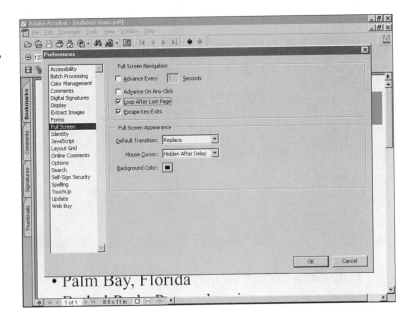

Full-Screen Appearance

This list presents the Full-Screen Appearance preference settings and describes how they
can help you control the look and action of your PDF document in full-screen mode.

- The Default Transition drop-down list (shown in Figure 18.8) gives you options for
  how the pages are displayed as one replaces the other. Dissolve causes the page to
  appear to dissolve as the new page appears. No Transition allows the new page to
  appear without any effects.

- You can control how the mouse pointer is handled during the presentation. You can
  choose for it to be visible, hidden, or hidden after a delay.

- Click the Background Color option to open the Color dialog box, which allows you
  to control the background color behind the document (see Figure 18.9). You can
  choose one of the preset colors or click the Define Custom Colors button to access
  the system color palette. (Macintosh users: instead of a preset palette, this button
  takes you directly to the system color palettes.)

FIGURE 18.8

The drop-down list that appears when you choose Default Transition. These options control the look as one page leaves and another page takes its place onscreen.

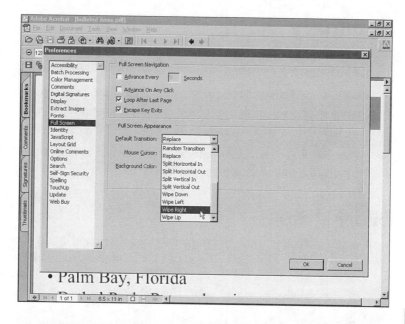

FIGURE 18.9

Click the Define Custom Colors button in the Color dialog box to create custom colors for the background of documents in full-screen mode.

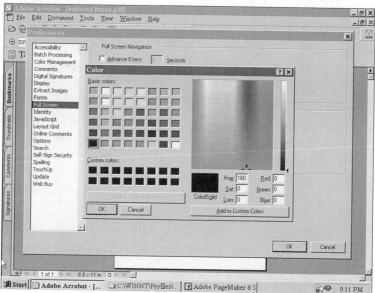

18

Summary

As we have learned in this hour, exciting presentations can be made easily using Acrobat, with full-screen mode as a leading contender for slideshow simulation.

We discussed how remembering to design the document properly in the native application will give you more control and creativity when it is opened in Acrobat and will allow you to transform the pages into an interactive, eye-catching presentation.

Now, when we create documents and view them in full-screen mode, we are more familiar with the preference settings that can control how the document looks and behaves.

Workshop

In this workshop, we'll review the information covered in this hour to reinforce your new-found knowledge. We'll begin with a short question-and-answer session on issues relating to the full-screen mode. Multiple-choice questions follow that, with a final series of short, hands-on exercises to reinforce the facts about full-screen documents.

Q&A

Q When I set up my full-screen PDF to advance, what are the parameters I have to stay within?

A The option you speak of, in the Full-Screen Preferences dialog box, can be set with a value from 1 to 32767 seconds. A good rule of thumb is to set it somewhere between 1 and 60 seconds.

Q I set my document for full-screen, but my mouse pointer is still there, and it looks dumb. Can I change that?

A Absolutely! In the Full-Screen Preferences dialog box, click the arrow next to the Mouse Cursor option and choose an option. Hiding the cursor in full-screen keeps the pointer from being in view, but it will appear again when you exit full-screen mode.

Q I have dual monitors on my system, but the document appears in full-screen mode only appear on one monitor. Am I doing something wrong?

A No. When you are running Windows 98, 2000, or Mac OS, even with dual monitors, the view appears on only one monitor. Mac users can choose Monitor to select which one the document will display on (see the tip earlier in this hour for more information on this topic).

Quiz

1. **What keyboard shortcut do you use to set a document to view in full-screen mode?**

    a. Ctrl+backspace (Macintosh users: Command+backspace).

    b. Ctrl+F+S+V (Macintosh users: Command+F+S+V).

    c. Ctrl+L (Macintosh users: Command+L).

2. **Where do you set a document to open in full-screen mode?**

    a. Open Options, under File, Document Properties.

    b. File, View, Open in Full-Screen

    c. Window, Full-Screen View, Set to Open

3. **How can you advance manually through a full-screen PDF?**

    a. Use the right-arrow and left-arrow keys.

    b. Press Shift+R or Shift+L.

    c. You cannot manually advance through a full-screen PDF.

Quiz Answers

1. **c**   The correct keyboard shortcut is Ctrl+L (Macintosh users: Command+L

2. **a**   Control the opening features with the Open Options, under File, Document Properties.

3. **a**   The right-arrow and left-arrow keys allow you to manually advance through the PDF.

18

Exercises

These exercises will give you some hands-on practice in using the full-screen mode.

1. Try some of the different default transition modes for your full-screen PDF. Examine the differences between them (for example, the Dissolve option creates a special effect as the new pages overtakes the previous one).

2. Look at the design of other PDF documents and practice viewing them in full-screen mode to decide which ones look good in this mode. Note the design features that make this so.

3. Practice using the keyboard shortcut (Ctrl+L for users of IBM-compatible computers and Command+L for Mac users) to switch a document to full-screen mode instantly.

PART VIII

Advanced Topics

Hour

Hour 19

Automating Acrobat with Batch Processing

The task of editing multiple PDF files is greatly simplified with the use of batch processing. Batch processing is a feature of several Adobe applications, including Illustrator, Photoshop, and Acrobat. The advantages of using this time-saving feature are far-reaching.

In this hour, we will cover the following topics:

- Overview of batch processing
- Using predefined batch sequences
- Editing the default sequences
- Creating your own batch sequence
- Applying a batch sequence
- Sharing batch sequences among different computers
- Useful batch processing examples

Overview of Batch Processing

Imagine being able to automate the process of performing the same function on a group of PDF documents, thus eliminating the need to work on one document at a time. This is the thinking behind the process known as batch processing.

Batch processing allows you to apply an action or series of actions to a group of PDF documents in one step. The actions used by batch processing are known as *batch sequences*, and Acrobat comes with several predefined batch sequences. This means that you can use the sequences already set up for you, or you can define your own custom batch sequences to perform functions other than those performed by the defaults.

To fully understand this unique and useful feature of Acrobat, let's begin by discussing the default, or predefined batch sequences. Later in the hour, we will apply a batch process to a series of documents. Then we will explore how to edit existing sequences and how to create your own batch sequences.

Using Predefined Batch Sequences

The predefined, or default, batch sequences that come with the installation of Acrobat are located on the menu bar under File, Batch Processing. The predefined batch sequences include Create Thumbnails, Fast Web View, Open All, Print 1st Page of All, Print All, Remove File Attachments, Save All As RTF, and Set Security to No Changes.

These basic functions are often performed on multiple PDF files, and Acrobat's batch processing allows you to perform these functions quickly and effortlessly to a group of PDF files.

Task: Batch Processing Multiple PDFs

In this task, we'll apply a batch process function to a group of PDF documents.

1. Make sure that the files you want to batch process are located in the same folder (on IBM-compatible computers, this is a necessary step).

> Be sure that the folder contains only the documents you want to batch process (you will select that folder later in the batch processing process). If you want to use only certain documents, move them to their own folder.

2. Choose File, Batch Processing, Create Thumbnails. The Run Sequence Confirmation dialog box opens, along with a message that prompts you to choose the folder you want to process. Click OK.

3. Browse to choose the folder of PDFs you want to process and click Open.

By choosing Create Thumbnails as our sequence (as shown in Figure 19.1), we are telling Acrobat to create thumbnails for all the documents we have selected within that folder. Acrobat will save and close the documents with the newly embedded thumbnails.

The collection of files you chose opens in Acrobat, and any warnings or errors will be listed in a dialog box. If you receive no warnings or errors, your collection of files was successfully opened.

FIGURE 19.1

Batch processing begins by choosing a batch sequence you want to run, or perform, on a group of PDF documents.

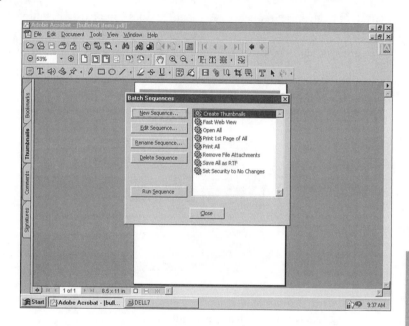

The most efficient way to organize for batch processing success is to begin by moving the PDF files you want to batch process to a separate folder (this is necessary on IBM-compatible computers; it is not necessary but recommended on Macintosh computers).

Also, creating an "output" folder for the finished PDF documents is a good idea. Of course, such a folder is not necessary if the batch sequence you are applying does not alter the original documents. But any sequence that alters the original PDF documents—that is, a sequence that creates new PDFs with the changes—should have a separate folder for the newly altered PDF files. It is easiest to create that folder from the beginning, before the sequence is applied.

When you edit the sequence, one of the options available to you is to choose the output folder. You can indicate where you want the newly changed PDFs to be stored.

Editing the Batch Sequences

Now that you have experimented with an existing batch sequence, let's delve into the realm of editing a batch sequence, that is, customizing a sequence for your specific needs. You might want to simply add to or slightly alter a predefined sequence, or you might want to create a new one altogether. We will start by editing a predefined sequence; later, we will create a new one.

Task: Editing a Batch Sequence

Using the preset sequences Acrobat provides can be useful, but being able to edit the sequences makes this feature even more functional. You have control over the entire process, and can customize the sequences to work more efficiently for you.

1. Begin to edit a batch sequence by choosing File, Batch Processing. From the Batch Sequences dialog box, choose a sequence to edit and click Edit Sequence. For this example, choose Create Thumbnails as the sequence to edit (see Figure 19.2).

FIGURE 19.2

Choose the batch sequence you want to edit and click Edit Sequence.

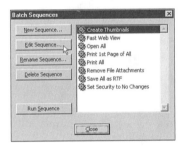

The dialog box that next appears offers you the option to select a sequence of commands from the list (see Figure 19.3).

FIGURE 19.3

The Batch Edit Sequence—Create Thumbnails dialog box.

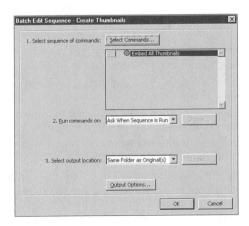

2. Click Select Commands to open the Edit Sequence dialog box (see Figure 19.4). Let's add the Print command to our sequence of commands. To do this, choose the Print command from the list on the left and click the Add button to add it to the list of commands on the right. This means that, when we execute the Create Thumbnails batch sequence, not only will all thumbnails be embedded, the documents will print as well.

Note that you can select commands from the list on the right and click the Remove button to delete them from your final list. You can also rearrange the order of the commands in the list on the left by selecting a command and clicking the Move Up and Move Down buttons.

3. Click OK to close the Edit Sequence dialog box and return to the Batch Edit Sequence—Create Thumbnails dialog box.

FIGURE 19.4

Add, remove, and rearrange commands in the batch sequence to customize the sequence.

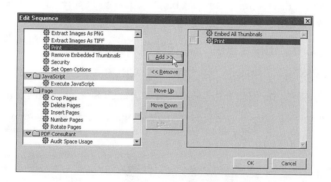

4. In the Batch Edit Sequence—Create Thumbnails dialog box, you can choose when to run the sequence and can also select the output location. Here is where you specify the folder in which you want to place the new versions of the PDF files; of course, you can also indicate that you want the new versions in the same folder as the originals.

5. Click the Output Options button to open the Output Options dialog box (see Figure 19.5). In this dialog box, you can specify whether you want the new versions of the files to overwrite the original files, you can optimize the files for Fast Web View, and so on. For this exercise, do not change any of these options. Click OK to close this dialog box and then click OK again to close the Batch Edit Sequence dialog box.

6. In the Batch Sequences dialog box, click the Run Sequence button to run your newly edited sequence. In this instance, the files will be printed after thumbnails are embedded.

19

FIGURE **19.5**

Choose how to handle newly processed files and other options from the Output Options dialog box.

Creating Your Own Batch Sequence

The process of creating your own batch sequence is very similar to that for editing a batch sequence.

Task: Creating a New Batch Sequence

In this task, we'll create a new batch sequence of our own.

1. Choose File, Batch Processing, Edit Batch Sequences from the menu bar.

2. Click the New Sequence button and type a name for the new sequence as shown in Figure 19.6. Click OK.

FIGURE **19.6**

We named our new sequence Remove Embedded Thumbnails.

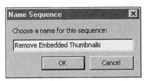

3. In the Edit Sequence dialog box that opens next, click Select Commands. Choose Remove Embedded Thumbnails from the list of possible commands on the left and click the Add button to add this command to the list on the right side of the dialog box (see Figure 19.7).

4. Click OK to finish the new sequence. Choose a new folder, if desired, from the Batch Edit Sequence dialog box that appears and click OK.

   Your new batch sequence has been saved, and you can now choose to run the sequence if you want.

To test the newly created batch sequence, choose File, Batch Processing, Remove Embedded Thumbnails. Choose the folder and files you want to process and click Select. The sequence will run. Congratulations!

FIGURE **19.7**

Adding a command in the Edit Sequence dialog box.

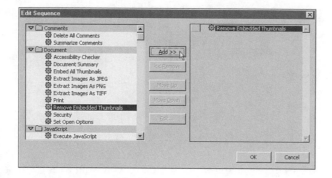

Sharing Batch Sequences Among Other Computers

After you have created custom batch sequences to perform automatic tasks that fit your particular needs, why not install those sequences on other computers in your office? Remember, the PDF workflow is most successful when everyone is working smarter and more efficiently, adding the PDF benefits to their everyday tasks.

Copying your custom batch sequences to other computers ensures that others will be able to take advantage of the speed and accuracy you have incorporated into your work environment.

Task: Copying Sequences to Other Workstations

After you create the custom batch sequences you want to copy to other computers, follow these steps for IBM-compatible computers:

1. Open this path on your hard drive: `C:\Program Files\Adobe\Acrobat 5.0\Acrobat\Sequences\ENU`. All batch sequences—predefined sequences as well as any custom sequences you have created—are stored in the `ENU` folder as shown in Figure 19.8.

2. Copy the desired custom files and paste them into the same location on the other computer. All the user of that computer has to do to access these new files is restart Acrobat.

If the workstations are connected over a network, copying between computers is a one-step process. If the computers are not networked, you will have to copy them to a disk and use that disk to put the files on the respective computers.

19

FIGURE **19.8**

Custom and default batch sequences are saved in the ENU *folder in your Acrobat program folder and can be copied to the same location on another computer.*

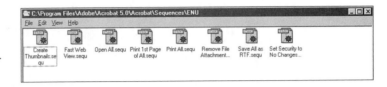

After you create the custom batch sequences you want to copy to other computers, follow these steps for Macintosh computers:

1. Open this path on your hard drive: Applications:Adobe Acrobat 5.0:Sequences:ENU. All batch sequences—predefined as well as any custom sequences you have created—are stored in the ENU folder. (Macintosh users: Go to your hard drive and open this path: Applications, Adobe Acrobat, Sequences, ENU.)

3. Copy the desired custom files and paste them into the same location on the other computer. All the user of that computer has to do to access those sequences is restart Acrobat.

Useful Batch-Processing Examples

The following list explores some scenarios beyond the obvious in which batch processing can simplify your workflow.

- If you are working with comments, you may want to set up a batch sequence to summarize your comments automatically for a group of PDF documents. Batching this process can save you a lot of time opening each document and summarizing comments manually. Use the Comments, Summarize Comments command to set up this sequence.

- Deleting comments in a batch process is another timesaver. After you have summarized all the comments in a group of PDF files, you may want to remove all the comments at once. Why not create a batch sequence that does it in one easy step? Choose the Comments, Delete All Comments command to accomplish this task.

- Running a sequence to use the Accessibility Checker on a set of documents is another way to use batch processing, when you are preparing documents for use on the Web or for visually impaired persons. (For more on accessibility, see Hour 23, "Making PDF Files Accessible for All.") Choose the Document, Accessibility Checker command.

- Rotating pages is another good example, if the orientation of the PDFs has to be altered (for example, if you want to switch from landscape to portrait orientation). Other sequence examples include removing security options and extracting images. To set up this sequence, use the Page, Rotate Pages command.

As you become more adept at processing PDF files in batches, you will undoubtedly come up with examples of how to use this time-saving feature to get the most out of Acrobat. You will also learn to customize the sequences you use to best serve your needs.

Preferences Settings for Batch Processing

As is true with the other features of the application, the preference settings give you greater control over the batch processing of multiple PDF documents. To access the preferences for batch processing, choose Edit, Preferences, General. In the Preferences dialog box, select Batch Processing from the list in the pane at left.

The options available to you in the batch processing preferences are as follows:

- **Deleting Run Confirmation Dialog.** Enable this option if you want to see a message confirming that the sequence was successfully run, or indicating that an error prevented the action from taking place.

- **Save Warnings and Errors In Log File.** If an error occurs during the running of a batch sequence, this option allows Acrobat to save a record of the errors.

- **Security Handler.** To control the use of batch sequences, enable this option. There are three choices for security handling: The default is Do Not Ask for Password, which allows anyone to use the sequence. Acrobat Standard Security uses the basic security settings, such as a password for opening the file or one for changing the file. And Acrobat Self-Sign Security specifies that only certain people, using digital signatures, can access the files. (For more information on digital signatures, see Hour 14, "Creating and Applying Digital Signatures.")

19

Summary

Batch processing is a useful tool for automating tasks within the office. The batch sequences you customize for your own specific needs can be copied to other computers so that others in the office can make use of them.

In this hour, you learned to create your own sequences as well as how to edit existing ones. The examples of different types of sequences can help you find uses for this feature in your own work environment. You also learned how to copy sequences to other workstations so that the sequences you create can be run by multiple users.

Workshop

This workshop answers some typical questions related to batch processing. Included in the review is a quiz with multiple-choice questions and a few exercises that are designed to give you hands-on experience with the material covered in this hour.

Q&A

Q Can I delete batch sequences from the list?

A Yes. To remove a batch sequence from the list, choose File, Batch Processing, Edit Batch Sequences. Select the sequence you want to take out and click the Delete Sequence button. Alternatively, you can delete the sequence from the ENU folder and restart the application.

Q Can I choose different export options for images within the PDF file and add them to my sequences?

A Yes. Exporting images using batch sequences offers the same options as choosing File, Export: JPEG, PNG, and TIFF. In addition, you can choose to export the text as RTF (Rich Text Format). These options all appear under the Document heading, under the Select Command section of the Batch Edit Sequence dialog box.

Q I am preparing my PDFs for use on the Web. Is there a batch sequence that will help me prepare them properly?

A Yes. Fast Web View is a predefined batch sequence that can help prepare your documents by doing the following:

- Removing duplicate backgrounds on pages
- Deleting unused objects on the pages
- Prepare pages for "byte-serving"

When byte-serving is enabled, pages can be downloaded from the Web, one page at a time. Instead of having to download the entire site, you can choose how many pages you want to download. (Fast Web View is covered in more detail in Hour 7, "Converting HTML to PDF with Web Capture.")

Quiz

1. **How do you edit an existing batch sequence?**

    a. Open the sequence in a script-editing program and edit the script there.

    b. Choose File, Batch Processing, Edit Batch Sequences, and make the necessary changes.

    c. You cannot edit an existing sequence.

2. Can the files you batch process be located in multiple folders?

    a. Not on IBM-compatible computers; all the files you want to process must be in the same folder.

    b. Yes, but all the folders must have the same name.

    c. No.

3. Which of the following is an advantage of batch processing?

    a. Faster execution of tasks on multiple PDF files.

    b. Turning PostScript files into PDF files in large numbers.

    c. Converting PDF files to HTML format.

Quiz Answers

1. **b**   Choose File, Batch Processing, Edit Batch Sequences, and make the necessary changes.

2. **a**   Not on IBM-compatible computers; all the files you want to process must be in the same folders. (You do not have to process every file in the folder, but it is advisable for organizational purposes to remove from the folder any files you do not want to process. Macintosh users can process files from multiple folders.)

3. **a**   Batch processing provides the advantage of faster execution of tasks on multiple PDF files.

Exercises

1. Choose File, Edit Batch Sequences to bring up the Batch Sequences dialog box. Examine the many functions available and become familiar with the dialog boxes used to edit the sequences. Doing so will help you get a clearer picture of how the batch sequences can better serve you.

2. Practice making custom sequences and copying them to another computer. Remember that you must restart Acrobat on that computer before it will recognize the new sequences.

19

Hour 20

Setting Preferences and Properties

The interface and performance of Acrobat—and the PDF files you open and modify in Acrobat—are directly affected by the preference and properties settings you make. Understanding these settings and the power they offer is key to getting the most out of Acrobat.

In this hour, we will explore the following topics:

- How to use document properties
- Benefits and use of a trapping key
- A general overview of document preferences
- Individual preference settings, such as display, batch processing, and comments
- Reasons why you would want to change your preference settings

Document Properties

Document properties are accessed from the File menu; they help control certain aspects of the PDF document. They can be quite beneficial to you in determining the look of the PDF and how it behaves.

Task: Examining Document Properties

In this task, we'll take a look at the Document Properties and how you can use them to affect your PDF document. We will begin by examining the Open Options.

1. Choose File, Document Properties, Open Options. The Document Open Options dialog box appears (see Figure 20.1).

2. From the options in the Initial View section, choose how you want your PDF to be viewed when it initially opens. Indicate what page number you want the file to open to, what magnification percentage, and whether you want bookmarks and thumbnails to show.

3. You will see additional choices in the Window Options and User Interface Options sections of the dialog box. An important option is Open in Full Screen Mode, which opens the document to the fullest boundaries of the screen, like a slideshow presentation. When this option is enabled, you will not see the pull-down menus at the top of the screen or the scrollbars to the right and bottom of the screen.

FIGURE 20.1

Control the appearance of the PDF when it opens by using the Document Open Options dialog box.

You may alter the settings on this menu at any time. Changes will take affect after you save the document and reopen it in Acrobat.

Accessing Other Document Properties

The document properties contain a lot of useful information about the PDF document, such as the creator and modification date, selected options for the opening of the PDF, and whether trapping has been applied to the document. The following sections explore the properties headings and discuss the importance of each.

Document Summary

You can learn a lot about your PDF file in the Document Summary. The summary contains information about the file's *native application* (the program that generated the file that was converted to the PDF), its creation and modification dates, and other data about the file itself. Of more interest to us here is the information you can enter about yourself, the purpose of the file, and keywords that can help in later searches.

Task: Using the Document Summary

In this task, you'll open the Document Summary dialog box for the document you currently have open and discover what information can be found—and provided—there.

1. Choose File, Document Properties, Summary. Figure 20.2 shows the Document Summary dialog box.

2. Note that the Document Summary gives information about the title, subject, author, and so on of the current document. The text you type in these fields becomes part of the file that can later be searched. You can specify a list of keywords that help categorize the content of the document to aid in a search later.

   Suppose that you are overseeing a law office and are responsible for assembling a series of PDFs that will be given to new employees in your firm. These PDFs will acquaint the new employees with the workings of the office. You will be indexing these PDFs to enable searches to occur later. By including *keywords* in each document's summary (keywords are words that pertain to the nature of the document, but may not actually be used in the text of the document), you increase the efficiency of the search function later. For example, including the words *orientation* and *new hire* in the summary will help you locate these documents faster when you search for them, but it is not necessary that these words be part of the actual text of the documents.

   Other information you can locate in the Document Summary dialog box includes:

   - **Binding:** from the drop-down list, select the location of the "spine" of the document if the document is to be printed and bound. The default location is Left Edge.

   - **Creator:** This field shows the application used to create the native document (before it was converted to PDF).

TASK

20

▼

- **Producer:** This field identifies the process by which the native document was converted into PDF (for example, using Acrobat Distiller).

- Other important data includes security settings (if any), the number of pages in the file, the file size, and the last date modified.

Use the information in the Document Summary for organizational purposes, such as helping to keep track of multiple copies of the same PDF.

▲

FIGURE 20.2

The Document Summary dialog box displays useful information about the development of the PDF document.

Document Fonts

To learn about the fonts used in the PDF document, choose File, Document Properties, Fonts. In the Document Fonts dialog box that opens, all the fonts used in the PDF are listed, along with *type* of font each is (Type 1, TrueType, and so on). You can also learn whether the fonts are embedded (see Figure 20.3).

> Regardless of whether you are using an IBM-compatible or Macintosh computer, there are two main types of fonts you should be aware of: Type 1 and TrueType.
>
> Type 1 (single-byte) fonts have two components: a screen font and a printer font. The screen font renders the look of the type onscreen; the printer font is necessary for the output device.
>
> Although both font types are used excessively in the business world, printers quite often have problems with TrueType fonts. Some service bureaus and printers flatly refuse to accept jobs that use TrueType fonts. It is best to check with your particular service bureau or printer to find out which category of fonts they accept.

There are other types of fonts in addition to TrueType and Type 1. Not all fonts work well with PDF. Here are two other font types; although they are less commonly used, they are acceptable for use with PDF:

- **Type 2:** Based on Compact Font Format (CFF), this category of font is acceptable for font embedding and substitution with PDF files.

- **Type 42**: Generated from the printer driver for TrueType fonts, this font type works well with PDF files.

FIGURE 20.3

The Document Properties, Fonts dialog box lists the fonts used in the document and whether or not they are embedded.

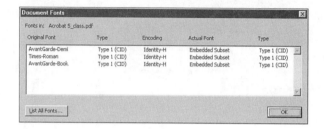

Trapping Key

Trapping is useful in high-end printing; it helps compensate for "shift" in the print process, when gaps could appear between two solid colors.

Have you ever opened a newspaper in which the color ads or comics are "fuzzy" or seem to be out of focus? This happens when shifting occurs during the printing process. Sometimes the shift can be extreme, but slight shifts can be compensated for by using trapping. Lighter shades of the colors are extended a bit beyond their natural borders, so that any gaps that appear are not as noticeable. Where the shifting would normally leave white areas that can be quite garish and noticeable, the traps provide a bit of color so that the gaps are not so obvious.

Prepress software uses trapping information when preparing the document for high-end output.

Trapping is often done in the final stages of the print process by the printer. Knowing whether the file had been trapped before sending the PDF to the printer can prevent additional trapping from being applied (and thus possibly ruining the file). To learn whether or not trapping has been applied to a particular PDF document, check for a trapping key. Open the Trapping Key dialog box by choosing File, Document Properties, Trapping Key (see Figure 20.4). Note that this is a manual setting; it is not automatic. The user of the PDF file sets this option to show that trapping has been used. Three settings can appear here:

20

- **Yes.** This option indicates that trapping has been applied to the document. The document was trapped before it was converted to PDF format.

- **No**. This option means that no trapping has been applied to the document. It is either not intended for high-end printing or trapping was mistakenly not added. If you want to apply trapping to the document, go back to the native file and add trapping before remaking the PDF file.

- **Unknown**. This option means that Acrobat is unsure about whether trapping has been applied to the PDF document.

FIGURE 20.4

Use the Trapping Key dialog box to let the user know whether trapping was applied to the native file before it was converted to PDF format.

Embedded Data Objects

As you have learned in previous hours, you can embed files such as sounds, scripts, and so on in the PDF. When you embed a file, you don't have to include it separately with the PDF when you distribute the PDF. You can see a list of the files contained inside the PDF file, also called Embedded Data Objects, in the Document Properties.

Task: Viewing Embedded Data Objects

To view the list of Embedded Data Objects for the currently open PDF file, follow these steps:

1. Choose File, Document Properties, Embedded Data Objects. Figure 20.5 shows the dialog box that opens. You can add or delete objects using this dialog box, so let's add one.

2. Click the Import button and browse to find the file you want to embed in your PDF document. After locating the file, click Open. Acrobat prompts you to enter a name for the object. By default, the filename appears in the entry box.

3. If you want to launch the embedded file, select it from the Embedded Data Objects list and click Open. You will receive a message concerning the possibility of catching viruses by opening embedded files; click OK to open the file.

4. Now we will delete it from the list by selecting the file and choosing Delete. Note that we are deleting the file as part of this exercise; you would not typically do this to a PDF file.

FIGURE 20.5
The Embedded Data Objects dialog box.

Associated Index

The Associated Index document property allows you to associate an index with the PDF file. When the index name is added to the file, that index name is included in the list of available indexes when the PDF file is opened and a search is begun. Remember that indexes are part of the Catalog feature of Acrobat. For a review of the catalog and indexes, see Hour 21, "Searching Multiple PDF Files."

The Associated Index feature can save you some time when you're preparing for a search because you will not have to browse for the index you want to search after you choose the Search icon in Acrobat. It is not necessary to use the Associated Index feature to search a PDF, however. You can still browse for the index manually if the document does not have an associated index.

If you want to change the associated index, you can do so in the Select Index dialog box (see Figure 20.6). To get to this dialog box, choose File, Document Properties, Associated Index. Simply browse to choose another index, and click Open.

FIGURE 20.6
The Select Index dialog box allows you to choose an index with which this PDF file will be associated.

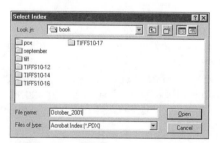

20

Document Meta Data

Information relating to the structure and makeup of the PDF document is embedded within the document as XML (Extensible Markup Language) data. This information includes, but is not limited to, the creation date, author, title, subject, and description.

The XML content of the PDF file can be extracted to HTML, XML, or some other structured type of document. Companies such as Iceni, Televisual, and Texterity will, for a fee, analyze the page's heuristics and build structured data from the PDF file. Should you want to build a custom application that extracts content from PDF files, refer to the Acrobat Core API Overview (`http://partners.adobe.com/asn/developer/acrosdk/docs.html`).

Although elements of the document are written as XML, Adobe PDF has many advantages over XML at this time. PDF is universally viewable and printable across the vast majority of hardware and software systems. XML is working on becoming as platform independent as PDF.

For business documents—especially transactional documents that will eventually run the gamut of e-Commerce—security is still a major concern. PDF maintains a strong advantage over XML because it has always had basic security that controls the user's ability to copy, print, or extract content or change comments or form fields.

If you are interested in learning more about XML, we suggest the following book: *Sams Teach Yourself XML in 24 Hours, Second Edition*, by Charles Ashbacher. Also look for information on this subject, including the latest plug-ins for Acrobat, on our Web site at `AcrobatIn24.com`.

To view the source code, click View Source. If you are familiar with XML, you can alter the code in the text window Acrobat displays it in, or you can copy and paste it into an XML editor.

Unless you are familiar with XML or have a specific reason to edit your document meta data, this is an area you most likely will not need to visit.

> You might notice that the information under Document Metadata is identical to that in the Document Summary dialog box. Any changes you make to the Document Summary will be updated and reflected in the Document Metadata code.
>
> If you want to learn more about the specific document, it is best to view the Document Summary dialog box instead of messing with the XML code. The Document Summary dialog box presents this information in a more readable format.

Base URL

If your PDF file is to be used on the World Wide Web, enter the complete URL in the Base URL section. This feature allows easier organization of Web links. Other pages that link to this one can be managed much easier (see Hour 7, "Converting HTML to PDF with Web Capture," for more information on Web links). In other words, if the URL to another site changes, you can edit the base URL and not have to edit each individual Web link that refers to that site. (If a link already contains a complete URL address, the base URL will not be implemented.)

Working with Document Preferences

The Preferences dialog box contains some important settings that affect the look of your PDF file and the performance of Acrobat itself. In the following sections, we'll explore the Preferences dialog box and some suggested settings.

Task: Accessing Preferences

To access the document preferences, follow these steps:

1. Choose Edit, Preferences, General to open the Preferences dialog box. The navigation pane on the left of the Preferences dialog box contains the major categories you can access.

2. Click the names of the different categories and observe the settings and features for each category. For example, click the Identity tab in the pane at the left to open the preferences for the computer identity. Your default e-mail address, the computer name, and other related information is listed here.

3. Select the Comments tab. The changes you make on this tab affect the look and behavior of comments within the document.

4. Go to the Layout Grid tab next. When you use the layout grid to set up forms, you will find these settings helpful in controlling the size of the squares within the grid and for changing the grid line color.

As you can see, each category deals with another aspect of Acrobat. After you have viewed several categories, let's begin a more in-depth look at each category.

Accessibility

Users with vision- or motion-related handicaps may require certain settings to make documents as readable as possible. This is known as "accessibility." The Accessibility section of the Preferences dialog box allows the creator of the PDF to control certain visual aspects for this purpose.

The creator of the PDF file can set color schemes but, more importantly, can prepare the document for the visually handicapped person. Readers translate the PDF content to a format that's easier for visually impaired users to read. On the Content Delivery section of the Accessibility page of the Preferences dialog box, you can control the number of pages delivered to the screen reader (see Figure 20.7).

Accessibility is explored in much greater detail in Hour 23, "Making PDF Files Accessible for All."

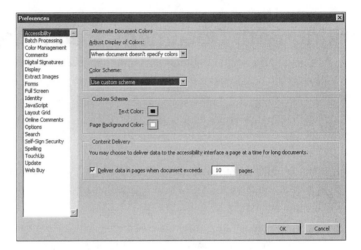

Batch Processing

Adobe products use batch processing to automate and speed up the performance of the same or similar functions. Photoshop and Illustrator are two Adobe applications that make use of batch processing; Acrobat is a third.

Acrobat's batch processing options, available by choosing File, Batch Processing, have a few settings to customize the way it handles the tasks at hand. If the Preferences dialog box is already open, you can switch to that page by selecting Batch Processing in the categories list on the left side of the dialog box.

These features are available under the Batch Processing section, and include Security Handler, which determines whether or not a password is necessary to complete the function, and also a selection for handling errors.

Color Management

When you spend a great deal of time putting together a project that will be printed, you want the color of the printed piece to be consistent with the original document. This is the concept behind color management. Even if your documents will appear online, it is important that the color be consistent with your original intent.

Color management is a main concern for graphics professionals, and Acrobat offers features to give greater control over it. On the Color Management page of the Preferences dialog box, you can choose which, if any, color settings to apply to the PDF file (see Figure 20.8).

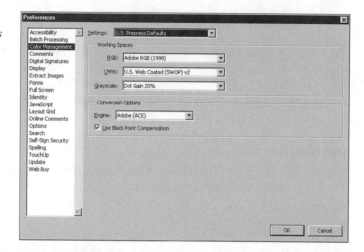

From the Settings drop-down list, you can choose from the following options:

- **U.S. Prepress Defaults**: Color management appropriate for common press conditions within the United States.

- **Europe Prepress Defaults**: Color management appropriate for European common press conditions.

- **Japan Prepress Defaults**: Color management appropriate for Japanese common press conditions.

- **Web Graphics Defaults**: Color management for documents to be distributed on the World Wide Web.

- **ColorSync Workflow**: (Macintosh only) Uses ColorSync CMS profiles chosen in the ColorSync control panel. Not available for Windows systems.

- **Emulate Photoshop 4**: Uses color workflow options of Macintosh Photoshop 4 and earlier.

- **Photoshop 5 Default Spaces**: Uses Photoshop 5 default color settings.

20

The settings you choose apply to PDF files that were not previously color managed. Acrobat uses the color settings file to extract profiles and color management system information to convert only those PDF files to which no previous color management was applied.

Unless you are working with critical color issues or using different output devices, you probably don't have to worry about color management. Most business environments are not color-critical. However, graphics personnel (printers, designers, service bureaus, and so on)do need to concern themselves with it.

Comments

The settings for comments allow you to change the font and text size for the data entered in the comments fields. Other options include automatic pop-up of comments, displaying comment sequence numbers, and always using the identity of the computer for the author name (see Figure 20.9).

Selecting the Always Use Identity for Author option causes Acrobat to use the given name of the computer as the author for all comments made to the current PDF file, but they can be easily changed in the Properties dialog box for the comments.

For example, if your computer's name is John Jones, and you select the Always Use Identity for Author option, the name that appears in the comment text boxes will be John Jones. This is a real timesaver if you are the only one who uses that computer. If you share a computer with others, don't choose this option; change the author name by selecting the comment and choosing Edit, Properties. Learn more about comments and PDFs in Hour 13, "Adding Comments and Annotations."

Digital Signatures

Signature handlers allow certain attributes for digital signatures to change, such as the data stored in the digital signature, its method of verification, and so on. Acrobat's default digital signature handler is a plug-in that comes with Acrobat. Third-party plug-ins offer additional handlers and can be downloaded from Adobe's Web site.

Digital signatures are covered in greater depth in Hour 14, "Creating and Applying Digital Signatures."

To access the settings available for digital signatures, open the Preferences dialog box and select Digital Signatures from the category list of the left side of the dialog box (see Figure 20.10).

FIGURE 20.9

Use the computer's name as the comments author, if you are the only user on the computer. Otherwise, each author would want to add his or her own author name.

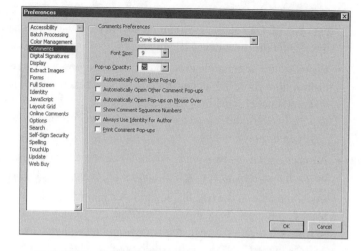

FIGURE 20.10

Use the Digital Signature page of the Preferences dialog box to control how the signature hander uses this security information.

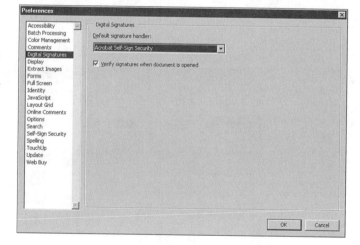

Display

There are several options available on the Display page of the Preferences dialog box:

- **Default Page Layout:** Choose an option to control the page layout for the opening of the document. Choices include displaying one page at a time, continuous side-by-side scrolling, or continuous one-on-top-of-the-next scrolling.

- **Page Units**: Choose an increment of measure here that will be used in the status bar.

- **Use Greek Text Below**: When type becomes smaller than the number of pixels you specify here, it will appear "greeked." This means that a series of gray lines will appear in place of the small text.

20

- **Transparency Grid**: Displaying the transparency grid puts a grid behind transparent objects. This option is useful for identifying when transparency is used throughout the document.

- Choosing zoom magnification and smooth text options are two more ways you can control how your PDF document will appear. Smoothing works on the edges of text and monochrome images to minimize the contrast between the text or image and the background. Good for larger text sizes, this option helps improve the onscreen display.

- Another option worth nothing is CoolType, a technology used by Adobe to offer better display of text for laptops and LCD screens (see Figure 20.11).

  CoolType adjusts the text display to work optimally with your monitor. For best results, you must also calibrate CoolType by clicking Configure CoolType and picking the best-looking text sample from the list by following the two-step process in the CoolType Setup dialog box.

You can change these settings at any time; they offer some helpful features for the display of the document.

FIGURE 20.11

CoolType Technology, employed by Adobe Systems for more accurate text display on laptops and LCD screens, is an option on the Display page of the Preferences dialog box.

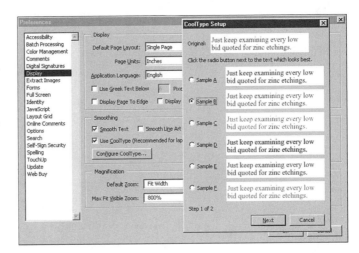

Extract Images

Acrobat Version 5 offers a new feature that allows you to extract images from a PDF file and save them in various formats. To extract the images, open the Preferences dialog box to the Extract Images page by choosing File, Export, Extract Images As (see Figure 20.12). The Preferences dialog box settings help you control how large the images must be before they will be considered in the extraction process.

If you do not have a copy of the original images, and the only copy you have is within the PDF file, extracting images is very useful because it allows you to get a digital copy of the image. The Extract Images preference settings allow you to control how small the images must be before they are ignored by the Extract Image command.

FIGURE 20.12

Use the Extract Images page of the Preferences dialog box to control how small graphics must be before they are ignored by the Extract Image command.

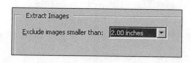

Forms

A few options for the forms feature in Acrobat exist and include highlighting the form fields, choosing the highlight color, and automatically calculating the field values (see Figure 20.13).

- **Auto Calculate Field Values:** When a form is set up to perform calculations between multiple fields, this option tells Acrobat to perform the calculation automatically.

- **Show Focus Rectangle**: Indicates the field in focus.

- **Highlight Form Fields:** With this option turned on, form fields are highlighted when selected.

FIGURE 20.13

Forms preferences include automatically calculating the field values and choosing a highlight color for the form fields.

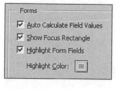

20

Full Screen

To create full-screen presentations, such as those that resemble a slide show, use the Full Screen page of the Preferences dialog box to select options. You can determine whether the cursor is visible, specify the background color, decide how often to advance through the pages, and so on (see Figure 20.14). These options allow you greater control over the performance of the full-screen presentation.

The default transition options allow you to control the look of a page in full-screen mode when the new page is replacing it. For example, the Dissolve option gives the look of the first page dissolving as the new page replaces it.

For more information on full-screen mode and the default transition options, see Hour 18, "Using Acrobat for Presentations: The Full-Screen Mode."

FIGURE 20.14

Full-screen view gives you a wonderful opportunity to create exciting slide shows and professional presentations. Transitions allow you to control the look of one page being replaced by another in full-screen mode.

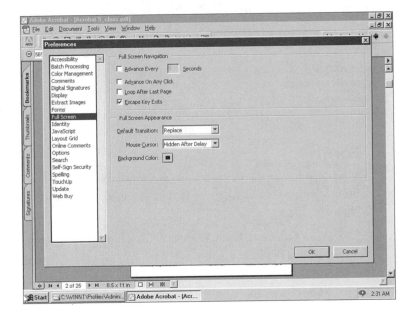

Identity

The login name of the user and important information such as e-mail address and company name, are entered on the Identity page of the Preferences dialog box (see Figure 20.15). The information from this page is used with digital signatures and comments.

When you select Always Use Identity for Author in the Comments preferences, the information you enter here in the Identity page is the name used as the comment author.

When you create a new user profile for digital signatures, the identity information is already added to the profile for you (you can always alter it, if you want).

FIGURE 20.15

The identity of the computer user is entered on the Identity page of the Preferences dialog box and will appear in conjunction with digital signatures and comments in Acrobat.

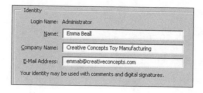

JavaScript

JavaScript is used in certain areas such as particular sections of the Form tool. If you choose Enable Acrobat JavaScript, Acrobat will write simple scripts for you, such as actions and form calculations.

FIGURE 20.16

Enable Acrobat JavaScript in the Preferences dialog box to allow Acrobat to write the code for actions and for simple calculations in form fields.

Layout Grid

Creating uniform and consistent forms is easier when the layout grid is turned on (choose View, Grid to turn on the grid).

You can control the size of the grid squares and the color of the grid lines among other things on the Layout Grid page of the Preferences dialog box (see Figure 20.17).

20

FIGURE 20.17

Layout grid options are set on this page of the Preferences dialog box and give the user more control over the creation of forms.

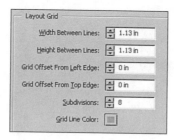

Some of the layout grid settings include

- **Width Between Lines**: Sets width between major grid lines.
- **Height Between Lines**: Sets height between major grid lines.
- **Grid Offset from Left Edge:** Offsets the grid a specified amount from the left.
- **Grid Offset from Top Edge:** Offsets the grid a specified amount from the top.
- **Subdivisions**: Use this option to add subdividing lines on the grid.
- **Grid Line Color:** Choose a color for the grid lines.

Online Comments

Online comments are an exciting feature of Acrobat that allows you to share comments with others on a server in a secure manner. On the Online Comments page of the Preferences dialog box, you can choose the type of server for the online comments (see Figure 20.18).

See the section on Online Comments in Hour 24, "Printing with Acrobat," for more on this subject.

FIGURE 20.18

Use the Online Comments page of the Preferences dialog box to provide information about the server you're using to exchange online comments.

Options

The Options page of the Preferences dialog box offers many choices for display and Web browser settings. Miscellaneous options include the use of logical page numbers, saving as optimized for Fast Web View, and opening cross-document links in the same window (see Figure 20.19).

The following list shows some of the key settings in this section:

- **Display PDF in Browser**: Uses your default browser to display any open PDF files from the World Wide Web.
- **Check Browser Settings**: Every time you open Acrobat, it will check your browser for compatibility.

FIGURE 20.19

FIGURE 20.19

Web browser settings and certain startup functions are set in the Options page of the Preferences dialog box.

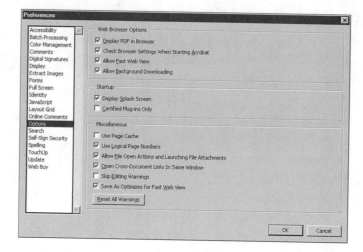

- **Allow Fast Web View**: When Web PDFs are open, Acrobat displays them one page at a time. If you disable this option, Acrobat will not display the PDF until the entire PDF file is downloaded.

- **Allow Background Downloading:** The rest of the Web-based PDF continues to download after the first page is displayed. This option works with Netscape or Netscape-compatible browsers. If this option is disabled, only the page you requested is downloaded; the others can be downloaded later.

- **Display Splash Screen**: The Acrobat splash screen will show as the program loads.

- **Certified Plug-Ins Only**: Only Adobe-certified third-party plug-ins will load when the program launches.

- **Use Page Cache**: Prepares the next page by storing it in the buffer for faster viewing.

- **Use Logical Page Numbers**: Works with the Document, Number Pages command to reorder pages in a logical fashion.

- **Allow File Open Actions and Launching File Attachments**: Flashes a warning when you open attached files and lets you cancel the open operation if you want.

- **Open Cross-Document Links in Same Window:** Opens links in the same PDF in the current window to cut down on the number of open windows.

20

Search

Acrobat Catalog's search capabilities are enhanced by settings on the Search page of the Preferences dialog box (see Figure 20.20). Sorting options for the PDF files located in the search and viewing options are just a few of the choices available here. Here are the other options:

- **Include in Query**: Here you tell Acrobat which things to include in a search, such as Document Information.

- **Results**: Allows you to choose how to show results, including how many to display at once.

- **Display**: When viewing search results, this option controls how the next item should be highlighted.

- **View Dialog Options**: Choose whether to display the dialog box during the search.

FIGURE 20.20

Specify some search options used by the Catalog on the Search page of the Preferences dialog box.

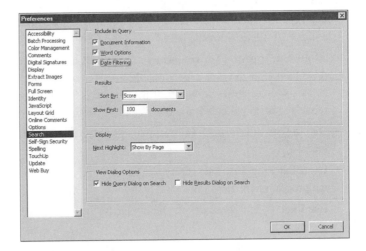

Self-Sign Security

Security for self-signing allows two options: the use or non-use of expiration dates—that is, when a digital signature is out of date, should it still be verified? The second option is the use of PKCS#7 signatures—a setting offering more capability with digital signatures (see Figure 20.21). This option increases the signature's ability to work with other digital signature solutions. Learn more about digital signatures in Hour 14, "Creating and Applying Digital Signatures."

FIGURE 20.21
The Digital Signatures options.

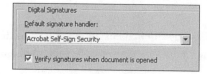

Spelling

Optional dictionaries for spelling are listed on the Spelling page of the Preferences dialog box (see Figure 20.22). Available dictionaries are listed in the pane at the left, and currently accessible ones are listed on the right. This is also where you can enable the Underline Misspelled Words check box and select an underline color.

FIGURE 20.22
Specify which dictionaries you want to use to spell check your PDF files on the Spelling page of the Preferences dialog box.

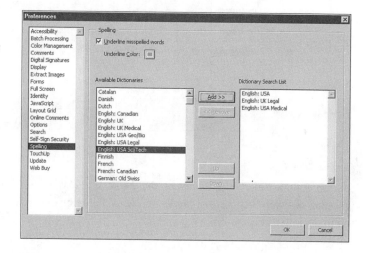

TouchUp

Set your preferences for the TouchUp tool on the TouchUp page of the Preferences dialog box, for use when you select a graphic with the tool (see Figure 20.23).

Choose an Image Editor to use for editing the graphic to set that editor as the default.

20

FIGURE 20.23
Use the TouchUp page of the Preferences dialog box to specify which image editor you want to use when you select graphics with the TouchUp tool.

Update

Acrobat can be set to look for program updates automatically, if this feature is enabled (see Figure 20.24). As updates are made available, Acrobat will alert you to the update being available.

FIGURE 20.24

Choose to have Acrobat automatically alert you when program updates become available.

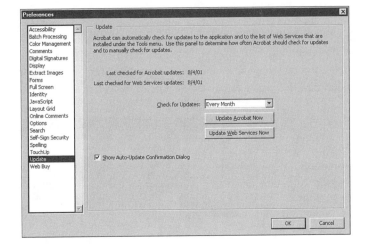

Web Buy

You can purchase electronic books on the World Wide Web; enabling the Web Buy option on the Web Buy page of the Preferences dialog box submits the required information to do so (see Figure 20.25).

The Web Buy feature allows you to purchase and download PDF files that have been locked to protect the copyrights of authors and publishers. This security is called Adobe Secure PDF technology, and Web Buy enables you to unlock these files for reading and searching purposes.

When you begin this process, Acrobat displays a series of pop-up pages that walk you through the process easily.

Save the document to a removable media, such as a Zip disk or Jaz drive if you want to use the document on other computers (it becomes portable). Saving it to a local computer locks it to that computer; the document cannot be copied.

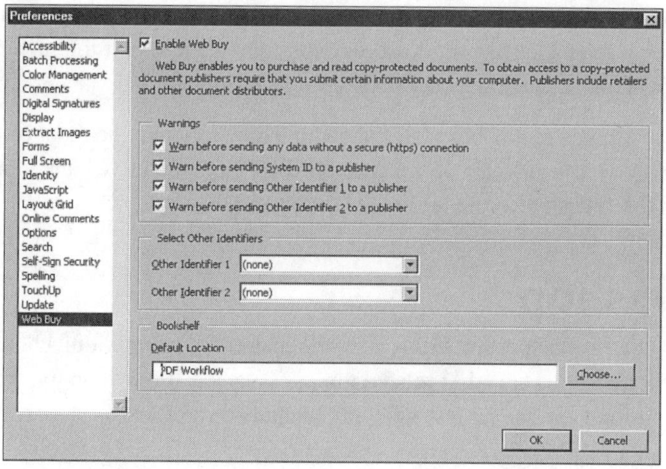

FIGURE 20.25

Web Buy allows you to purchase and download PDF files from the World Wide Web.

Setting Table/Formatted Text Preferences

Choose Edit, Preferences, Table/Formatted Text to change the settings for how formatted text is handled within Acrobat. From the Table/Formatted Text Preferences dialog box that opens, choose a default text layout, the document language, and color options for table and text. Note that this option is not available for Macintosh users.

Web Capture Preferences

The Web Capture Preferences dialog box allows you to set options for capturing Web pages as PDFs. Options include showing bookmarks, skipping secured pages, and choosing the program you want to use to open Web links. See Hour 7, "Converting HTML to PDF with Web Capture," for details.

Internet Settings

Use this important dialog box to configure your Internet and proxy settings before accessing the World Wide Web. For more information on these settings, see Hour 7.

Summary

As we have learned in this hour, creating a document and converting it to PDF is only the first step; setting options and preferences gives you total control over the document, its appearance, and the performance of Acrobat.

20

We discussed how setting a document to appear in Full-Screen mode, for instance, creates a dramatic, focused look, but you may want to exit the mode, so setting up the Escape key to allow you to exit from Full-Screen mode is a good preference choice.

Our studies in this hour have shown us how to make the most of the features in Acrobat and how to get total control over our PDF documents, which allows us to use the features to the fullest.

Workshop

In this workshop, we will review the material covered in this hour. We'll begin with a few questions covering related topics. Then we'll move on to some multiple-choice questions and end the review with a few hands-on exercises.

Q&A

Q I want to enable my PDF for byte-serving on the World Wide Web. What do I do to prepare it?

A Save As Optimized for Fast Web View is the preference setting you want to use. It restructures the PDF for page-at-a-time downloading (also referred to as *byte-serving*).

Q My layout grid is covered up by my document's background, which is the same color. Can I alter the colors of the grid lines?

A Yes. Open the general Preferences dialog box and click the Layout Grid category in the pane at left. You can choose the color of the grid lines, which is useful for items of the same color on your page, when the lines are not prominent enough. You can also lighten the grid lines so that they are not distracting when you are setting up the form.

Q Can I change options for exporting the text as Rich Text Format?

A Yes. Choose Edit, Preferences, Table/Formatted Text to open the dialog box and click the RTF Export tab.

Quiz

1. **Where do you set a document to open in Full-Screen mode?**

   a. Choose Document Properties, Summary.

   b. Choose Document Properties, Open.

   c. Choose Document Properties, Screen Mode Options.

2. **How can you set your document to use your computer's name as the author for comments?**

   a. Choose File, Options, Comments.

   b. Edit, Preferences, General, and click on the Comments tab.

   c. You cannot use your computer's name as the author of comments.

3. **Access the color settings by choosing**

   a. Edit, Color Settings

   b. File, Document Properties, Color Settings

   c. Edit, Preferences, General, and click the Color Management tab

Quiz Answers

1. **b** Choose Document Properties, Open.

2. **b** Set your comment preferences by choosing Edit, Preferences, General and clicking the Comments tab.

3. **c** Change your color settings by choosing Edit, Preferences, General and clicking the Color Management tab.

Exercises

These short exercises reinforce what you learned in this hour.

1. Experiment with different settings available when you choose the Document Properties, Open. Become accustomed to the look of the Thumbnails or Bookmarks palettes being open when the document is opened. Think of different ways to use these features to get the most out of your PDF files.

2. Change the opacity of your comments and experiment with different settings. Set the notes to pop up automatically; change the type settings for your notes.

20

HOUR 21

Searching Multiple PDF Files

Because the use of PDF files has grown tremendously in recent years, with many offices saving all their documents as PDF files, Adobe came up with a way to organize the multitudes of PDF documents and to retrieve them in an orderly fashion.

Acrobat Catalog gives you the ability to organize your PDF documents in a "library" that you can search for words or phrases within the PDF documents.

After you have created the index, or library, of PDFs, you can add or delete folders and rebuild the index at any time. These searchable indexes can be stored on network servers, CDs, and individual workstations. You can create a centralized searchable index for each related group of PDF files and store it on a computer accessible to all users who need to search the index. Indexes can also be distributed with PDF files to make them easier to search. While these index files do not allow you to search the contents of PDF files via the Internet or intranet, there are solutions available for this purpose. We discuss them toward the end of this hour.

In this hour, you will learn

- Why you should index your PDF documents
- How to build a searchable index
- How to search using the Catalog
- The difference between finding and searching
- How to refine a search
- How to purge and rebuild indexes

Why Index Your PDF Documents?

Imagine a large number of PDF documents, all pertaining to a particular subject. Also imagine that you will have to access these documents in the future. By organizing the files into a folder, and using Acrobat Catalog to assemble a directory of the files, you will be able to search all the files for a word or phrase. Acrobat will automatically categorize all the files that contain that word or phrase by order of relevance.

> When you search, you look for a word or phrase in a group of PDF documents. Access the Find feature by selecting the Find tool on the toolbar to look within the current PDF document. The Find feature is covered later in this hour.

For example, all your customer contracts are stored in a single location, perhaps organized in folders by month. You can run the Catalog for each folder, creating an index of each PDF in the folder. Then you could search by job number, customer name, or other keywords to locate specific documents. The documents could be categorized by month, of course, or by year or any other method of your choice.

Building a Searchable Index

When you create an index with Acrobat Catalog, you can select word options to facilitate the search. Enable any of the five search options by checking their accompanying box:

- **Word Stemming**: To find a variety of words with the same "root" word, select this option. For example, to find all words beginning with *back* (*backward*, *backwards*, *backwoods*, and so on), search for the word *back* and turn on the Word Stemming option.

- **Sounds Like:** Not entirely reliable, this option attempts to find words that have similar sound qualities.

- **Thesaurus**: Enable this option to search for words with meanings similar to the original word. Search for the word *want*, and Catalog will find words with similar meanings such as *desire*, *need*, or *crave*.

- **Match Case:** This option limits the search to only exact matches involving letter case. For example, if you search for *Song* with this option selected, Catalog finds only *Song* and not *song* or *SONG*.

- **Proximity:** Finds words within three pages of each other. For example, use this option and search for *choice* and *selection*, and Catalog finds instances where these two words are used within that three-page boundary; Catalog ignores instances that are not within three pages.

Let's begin by creating an index using Acrobat Catalog. Before you start the next task, create a folder that contains all the PDFs you want to appear in the index.

Task: Building an Index

Creating the index is the first step to using Acrobat Catalog. in this task, we will specify the PDF documents to include in the index and select word options to efficiently narrow our searches later. We will create the index and then learn how to use it to perform a search.

1. Make sure that the PDFs you want to categorize are all located together in a single folder.

2. Launch Acrobat and choose Tools, Catalog. The Adobe Catalog dialog box pops up (see Figure 21.1).

FIGURE 21.1

Choose Tools, Catalog to open the Adobe Catalog dialog box to begin creating your index.

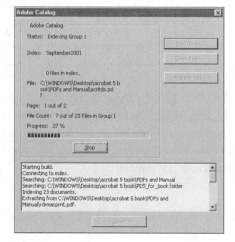

21

3. Click the New Index button. The New Index Definition dialog box opens (see Figure 21.2). In the Index Title field, type the filename for your index. For this example, we are naming the index "September2001."

FIGURE **21.2**

Use the New Index Definition dialog box to name your index.

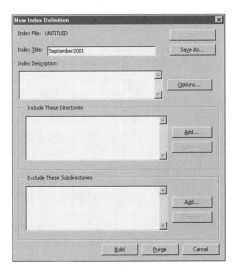

4. Click the Options button to open the Options dialog box. Here you can specify words you do *not* want to include in the index, and choose options such as Match Case and so on. When you have made your selections, click OK to return to the New Index Definition dialog box. As mentioned earlier, the Match Case option narrows your search by finding only those instances where the word or words are capitalized exactly as you type them.

> Excluding words that appear numerous times in every document, such as your company name, will refine and streamline the index.

5. Click the Add button in the Include These Directories section of the dialog box. In the dialog box that opens, you can select the folder or folders you want to include in the index. In this example, we are using a folder called September. Indicate any folders or subfolders that have been previously indexed and that you would like to delete in the Exclude These Subdirectories list. Note that this action does not delete the PDF files from your hard drive; it eliminates them from being included in the new index.

6. When you have chosen all the folders to be included and excluded from the index, click the Build button to create the index. A dialog box appears to prompt you to save the index. For best results, save this index file in the original folder (the folder containing the PDF files you just indexed).

7. When you click Save, Catalog begins building your index. It searches each document and categorizes each word in each document. A progress bar charts the process as the index is being built. When it is complete, the message at the bottom of the window (you may have to scroll to view it) is `Index Build Successful`.

8. Click the Close button.

> For more accurate and efficient searches using the indexes you create in Acrobat Catalog, prepare your documents first. Organize the PDF files into a folder, as mentioned earlier.
>
> Name the PDF files properly, with correct extensions and appropriate naming conventions. On IBM-compatible computers, files must have the .pdf extension. In addition, filenames should not use spaces, hyphens, slashes (/), or other special characters, which may create problems on IBM-compatible computers.
>
> Fill out the Document Summary sheet for each PDF document (access this sheet by choosing File, Document Properties, Summary) before creating the index. Filling in the title, keywords, and so on helps refine the index and makes searching go more smoothly. Figure 21.3 shows a Document Summary sheet for a PDF file.

FIGURE 21.3

To make the index work more efficiently, use the Document Summary sheet (accessed by selecting File, Document Properties, Summary) to add keywords and so on.

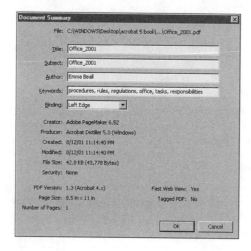

21

Searching Using the Catalog

After you create an index, you can use it to search for specific words or phrases within a group of PDF files.

Task: Using the Search feature in Acrobat

To use the index you just created, you must start by launching Acrobat. You can search with or without a file open.

1. In Acrobat, click the Search icon in the toolbar (see Figure 21.4). You can also access the search command by selecting Edit, Search, Query from the menu commands.

FIGURE 21.4

Use the Search tool on the toolbar to begin the search.

2. In the Adobe Acrobat Search dialog box that opens, click the Indexes button. The Index Selection dialog box opens, listing all the indexes that Acrobat will be searching. If there are any indexes from a previous search, highlight them and click Remove. Otherwise, click the Add button and browse to find the index you just created. When you have added all the indexes you want to use for this search, click OK. Figure 21.5 shows the Index Selection dialog box with the proper index selected for our search.

Removing a previous search index from the Index Selection dialog box is useful if you will not be using that index again. If the index will be used in the future, you may decide to simply deselect it rather than remove it in this search.

Consider the Acrobat Online Guides. They are online help files—a useful feature of Acrobat for looking up specific subjects pertaining to the program. Keeping this index in your Index Selection dialog box (that is, deselecting it rather than removing it) makes it easier to select it the next time you need to use it.

You can use multiple indexes in a search. Suppose that you are searching your archived PDFs for a particular job from 1999. If you have an index for each month in 1999, you can add all the indexes to your search and search them all at once instead of searching them individually.

▼

▼ **FIGURE 21.5**

Select the indexes you want to search and deselect any indexes you do not want to search. Click OK to begin the search.

3. In the Adobe Acrobat Search dialog box, type the word, words, or phrases you want to look for. Select any of the search-refinement options at the bottom of the dialog box, if desired.

4. Click Search. Acrobat searches through every document in the indexes you chose, and brings up a list of documents that contain the specified word or phrase.

5. Acrobat lists the documents by order of relevance, beginning with the document in which the word or phrase is used most often (see Figure 21.6).

FIGURE 21.6

The items located during the search are listed in order of relevance, beginning with the most relevant.

6. Select a document in the result list and click the Info button to view the Document Info dialog box for that document. Figure 21.7 shows the Document Info dialog box for a PDF named final_ad2.pdf. When you're done viewing this information, click OK to close the Document Info dialog box.

   Note that the entry box at the bottom of the window shows the full path name for

▼ the selected PDF document.

21

7. Back in the Search Results dialog box, select a PDF in the list and click View to open that PDF file in Acrobat. When the file opens, Acrobat highlights the specified word or phrase within the document, making it easy to see where the search phrase is used.

FIGURE 21.7

View the Document Info sheet for a selected PDF document by clicking the Info button in the Search Results dialog box.

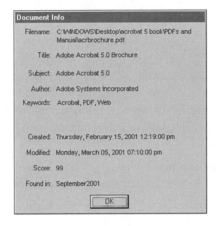

 You can also access Acrobat's Search features by choosing Edit, Search from the menu bar.

Choose the Select Indexes command to pick the indexes you want to use; choose the Query command to find a word or phrase in the indexes you have already selected.

Choose the Results command to view results from the last search.

Finding Versus Searching

It is important to understand the difference between the Find command and the Search command in Acrobat. Let's explore the difference between the two commands.

Use the Find command to search the open document for a particular word or phrase. When you click the Find tool on the toolbar, Acrobat opens the Find dialog box shown in Figure 21.8. Type the word or phrase you want to find in the current document.

Options for the Find command include:

- **Match Whole Word Only**: Finds only the exact word, not any elaborations of it. Acrobat returns only individual words, not words contained in other words—as *the* is contained in *together.*

- **Match Case**: Finds words only with exact case match.
- **Find Backwards**: Looks for the word or phrase from the current view, backwards through the document.
- **Ignore Asian Character Width**: For Asian language versions of Acrobat, used to control the searching for full or half-width Kana characters.

The Find command allows you to look for words only within the current document. To look for the word or phrase in a group of documents, you use the Search feature— assuming that you have already created an index that includes the documents you want to search. Refer to "Searching Using the Catalog," earlier in this hour, for details on using the Search command.

FIGURE 21.8

Choose the Find tool from the toolbar to look for a word or phrase within the current document.

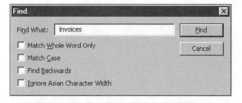

If you want a certain index always associated with a PDF file, you can attach an index to the PDF document. This will cause the index you specify to be used whenever someone uses the search command in the document. Select File, Document Properties, Associated Index. Then select the index file to attach to the PDF file. Note that both the index file and the PDF file will need to be accessible to anyone who needs to search the index. This is a useful way to attach an index to a PDF file if you are distributing a group of PDF files on a CD-ROM.

Refining a Search

You can do several things to improve the efficiency of your search. The following sections talk about the preference settings you can make to help refine the search along with several other options you might want to consider.

Search Preferences

Choose Edit, Preferences, General to open the Preferences dialog box. Click the Search category in the pane at the left of the dialog box to open the Search sheet (see Figure 21.9).

21

Macintosh users should note that Search is not part of the General Preferences on the Mac. Instead, you must choose Edit, Preferences, Search.

Search preferences and Catalog preferences are different. Search preferences affect how searches are handled within Acrobat. Catalog preferences affect the building of an index within Acrobat Catalog itself.

FIGURE 21.9

Specify your searching preferences on the Search sheet in the Preferences dialog box.

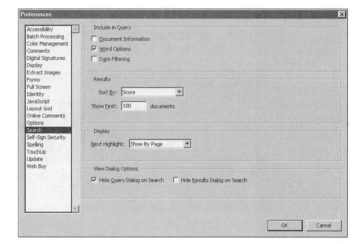

You can use the following options in the Search sheet of the Preferences dialog box to refine your searches:

- To include certain information in the search results—such as document summary information or dates—enable the appropriate check boxes at the top of the dialog box, in the Include in Query section.

- Enabling the Document Info or Date Filtering check box adds fields to the Adobe Acrobat Search dialog box where you can specify the document info to search for, or the creation and modification dates of the PDF files.

- You can control how the search results are displayed by specifying options in the Results section. You can specify how many results are displayed and how they are categorized.

- In the Display area of the preferences sheet, you can control how the highlighted results on the page are shown. The Next Highlight field lists options that control how the results are displayed when you click the View button in the Search Results dialog box.

- The Hide Query Dialog option hides the dialog box when a search is being performed.
- The Hide Results Dialog on Search option hides the dialog box when you are viewing search results.

Enable the desired options and click OK to close the Preferences dialog box.

Other Considerations for Refining a Search

To further refine your search, you can work with the Search Results dialog box and perform an additional search on those results, to pinpoint a particular category even further.

In addition, you can use the Word Assistant to build a list of search words. When you choose options such as Word Stemming, Sounds Like, or Thesaurus, Word Assistant establishes whether those options would be useful in this particular search. For example, if the list of suggested words is too long, you can edit the list and copy and paste it from Word Assistant to the Search dialog box.

Task: Refining the Search Using the Search Results

In this task, we will start with a search we've already performed, view the search results, and refine the search further.

1. After you have performed a search, you can display the Acrobat Catalog Search window again by choosing Edit, Search, Query. In the Acrobat Catalog Search dialog box that opens, you can choose to edit or replace the query that produced the initial results.

2. If your initial search used a string of words or a phrase, you might want to use Word Assistant to further simplify the search. To use the Word Assistant, choose Edit, Search, Word Assistant. The Word Assistant dialog box opens, as shown in Figure 21.10.

FIGURE 21.10

Use the Word Assistant to further refine a search.

21

3. To further refine our search, we will use Word Assistant to find words similar in meaning to *vacation*. To accomplish this, type a word in the Word field. In the Assist section, choose Thesaurus, and click the Lookup button. Word Assistant displays a list of words with similar meaning to the word you typed. You can copy and paste these words into your search to help refine the search process.

> When you're searching for multiple words, separate the words in your search with commas. If the words are not separated with commas, Catalog attempts to search for the word string in its entirety.

4. Double-click one of the new words in Word Assistant to make that word appear in the Word text box. As mentioned earlier, Word Assistant is useful as a helper for refining a search; the new word or words can be added to the search by copying and pasting, or double-clicking to add the words.

Task: Using Acrobat's Refine Search Feature

In addition to changing the search parameters as described in the preceding task, you can choose Refine to edit an existing search.

1. Choose Edit, Search, Results to display the Search Results window. Select and show the results of a previous search.

2. Choose Edit, Search, Query to open the Search dialog box. Edit or replace the query that produced the first list.

3. Press the Ctrl key (on IBM-compatible machines) or the Option key (on Macs). The button labeled Search changes to Refine. Click Refine to perform a search that will result in a subset of the previous list and match the new query.

Purging and Rebuilding Indexes

Rebuilding an index is necessary if you want to add new files to the index, or if you have deleted or moved files from the original folder and don't have to include them in the index.

However, simply rebuilding an index does not remove the original documents from the index entirely. The names of the documents will still remain, but will be indicated as invalid, meaning they will not be included in the search.

Extra documents can greatly increase search time—even if they are marked as "invalid"—and can use extra disk space. To avoid this situation, it is a good idea to purge the index before rebuilding it.

Purging an index streamlines the index, especially if you have added and removed multiple files over time. The actual PDF files are not removed; they are only marked as being invalid for the search. Purging the index lets you start with a clean slate so that you create the index using only the requested files. The "clean" index speeds search times.

Task: Purging and Rebuilding an Index

In this task, we will purge an index and then rebuild it using Acrobat Catalog.

1. Close all open documents. Still in Acrobat, choose Tools, Catalog. The Adobe Catalog dialog box opens.

2. Click the Open Index button. In the Select Index File dialog box that opens, locate the index that you want to purge and rebuild. Click the Open button to display the Index Definition dialog box (see Figure 21.11).

FIGURE 21.11

Open the index file you want to purge and click the Purge button in the Index Definition dialog box.

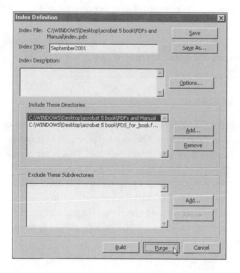

3. Click the Purge button at the bottom of the dialog box. A message appears to alert you to the amount of time it will take to purge (see Figure 21.12). Click OK to purge the index.

4. After you purge the original index, open it and click Build to build a new index.

   If you want to change search preferences or Catalog preferences, as described earlier in this hour, do so before you build the new index.

21

FIGURE 21.12

To purge an index, open it and click the Purge button. After the index has been purged, you can create a new one by choosing Build.

When purging an index, you may notice that it takes a very long time. Here is why:

Under the Catalog preferences, you can change the Delay Before Purge setting to a shorter time. The default is 905 seconds, or approximately 15 minutes. Adobe recommends that you do not change this setting, in case others are using the index. You'll want to give them ample warning that the index will be purged.

You might want to change this setting to a shorter time, especially if you're using a standalone computer and no other users could possibly interact with the index.

To access the Catalog preferences, choose Tools, Catalog; in the dialog box that appears, choose Preferences.

If you will be placing many PDF files on your intranet or Internet site, they can be made searchable. This does not involve using Acrobat catalog. Instead you need to use the PDF iFilter. This filter is available free from the Adobe web site and it allows Microsoft's Indexing Service to index PDF files and all other content on an Internet or intranet site. Indexing Service is a Microsoft Windows 2000 service for file systems and Web servers and is not part of Adobe Acrobat. At the time of publication, this was the most widely used method for making a large group of PDF files searchable through a web browser interface.

Summary

As we have learned in this hour, you can improve your efficiency in working with multiple PDF documents using Acrobat's Catalog feature.

We discussed how to improve your search results and decrease your search time by planning ahead. Adding document info, such as keywords, and naming the files correctly is a great way to start.

In addition, we built an index, performed a search, and rebuilt the index with Catalog, learning ways to refine our searches and build a more efficient index. Organize the PDF files into a single folder and save the index in that folder for best results.

Plan how to best use the Catalog feature for your own particular situation and be consistent to increase your searching efficiency. For instance, when naming files and when searching with Catalog, choose job numbers, dates, or customer names, depending on your specific situation, and keep the searching results consistent.

Workshop

In this workshop, we will review the material covered in this hour. The questions and answers cover issues related to Catalog and the searching of PDF documents. The multiple-choice questions and the series of hands-on exercises will recap what you learned in this hour.

Q&A

Q What are Boolean characters?

A Boolean characters are added to refine your search. Booleans include and, or, and not. For example, if your search involves looking for the word Cincinnati and you want to include a common misspelling such as Cincinatti, you can use the Boolean and or or to include documents that have this alternative spelling in your search results.

Q How do I copy my index to a network server?

A Save the original index in the folder of indexed PDF documents and copy the entire folder to the network server. As long as the documents are properly named, and all contents remain unchanged, the index will work. Rebuild, or purge and rebuild, the index if the contents of the folder change.

Q Can I spell check my document using Catalog?

A No. Spell checking within Acrobat applies only to comments and form fields. You must spell check the document in the native application, before converting it to PDF.

Quiz

1. Word Assistant is useful for

    a. Finding spelling errors in a PDF document.

    b. Giving other word options to refine a search.

    c. Helping you rephrase some text and change it in Acrobat.

21

2. **Finding and searching differ because**

    a. Finding works on all open documents; searching does not.

    b. Finding works on the current document; searching uses an index or indexes you select.

    c. Finding locates single words; searching is used for phrases only.

3. **Indexes are useful for**

    a. The Internet.

    b. Network servers.

    c. Local computers and network servers.

Quiz Answers

1. **b** Word Assistant is used to give other word options to refine a search.

2. **b** The Find feature allows you to look through the current document; the Search feature conducts a query of multiple PDF documents and involves the use of an index.

3. **c** Catalog is used on local computers and network servers.

Exercises

These simple, hands-on exercises will reinforce the knowledge you gained in this hour and prepare you to move on to the next topic.

1. Practice refining your searches with word options such as change case and word stemming. Become familiar with how these options can change the results of your search.

2. Choose to view a document after you display the search results. Notice how the selected word or phrase is highlighted. Practice changing these display preferences using the Preferences dialog box, and see how the view options change accordingly.

Hour 22

Designing PDF Documents

Designing a document that will be converted to PDF format requires a bit of forethought before you actually dive in and create it. In this hour, we will discuss some guidelines you can follow to assist you in the creation of such documents. We'll also offer tips for successful PDF files—documents that are easy to read, successful in their approach, and appealing at the same time.

In this hour, we will cover the following topics:

- Paper versus digital; taking into consideration the final purpose of the document
- Screen sizes and resolution
- Typeface considerations
- Graphics resolution
- Color space

Paper Versus Digital

Digital documents (the kind created in programs such as Microsoft Word, Adobe Illustrator, and QuarkXpress) can all be converted to PDF documents—but why would you want to? The answer is a multifaceted one. PDF documents are smaller and can be easily e-mailed; documents created by these native programs can be too large to e-mail, especially with placed graphics.

You can also turn PDF documents into interactive forms easily, using the Form tool in Acrobat. By considering what you want the form to do when you create the original document, you determine the final look of the form. For example, you can add buttons to the document in Acrobat and assign actions such as "print" or "submit," but the options you have to affect the appearance of the buttons created in Acrobat are limited. One solution is to add the buttons to the original document, before you convert the file to PDF. Using a graphic or some eye-catching type, you create the look of the button in the native program, and add the interactive feature (the action) in Acrobat.

PDF files can be used for high-end printing, too. Instead of gathering all the linked graphic files and fonts to send to the printer, you can convert the document to PDF using the proper settings, and you will have a self-contained printer file, complete with color management information and embedded fonts. The PDF is ready to send to the printer for high-quality output.

Knowing the final purpose of your PDF document—*before* you create it—gives you more control over the final PDF. Some basic design rules can apply to both types of PDF documents, but there are differences as well.

We have already explored the different settings you can choose when creating the PDF, depending on the use of the final document. For example, in a text-based PDF that you will e-mail to a colleague to look over, keeping the file size small is of extreme importance, more so than the quality of the graphics. However, if you are preparing a PDF document for high-end printing, and the document will not be e-mailed but rather sent to a printer on a CD, then quality is the main concern and file size is of little importance.

Therefore, the first design concept you must understand is knowing what the basic use of your PDF document is. Then you can prepare the file accordingly.

Considering Graphics

Imagine that you are preparing a simple text document for interoffice use. Because the document is to be used for interoffice distribution, it will most likely be e-mailed. Because the document should be kept at a relatively small file size for e-mail, you will want to limit the number of graphics to perhaps a company logo (see Figure 22.1). You might also want to use graphics saved at low resolution, which would not dramatically increase the file size, so that the document can be easily e-mailed.

FIGURE 22.1

PDFs intended for e-mail should have a smaller file size; you can use limited numbers of low-resolution graphics—or eliminate the graphics—in this type of PDF.

Now let's discuss the preparation of PDFs *with* graphics. If you intend to print the document, and the document contains graphics, the file must be converted to PDF in a manner that gives adequate graphics quality for output to a desktop printer or to a high-end output device.

Screen Sizes and Resolution

Documents to be viewed online or onscreen require a different set of guidelines than documents to be printed or e-mailed. You can increase the readability of the document if you take into consideration the size of the monitor your document will be viewed on. If you prepare your files for use on a smaller monitor, your documents can be viewed properly on small *and* large screens.

A good rule of thumb is to prepare the document for use on a 14-inch monitor. Doing so allows the user to view the document at 100% so that they don't have to scale it down to see the full width. Good design makes it acceptable for users to scroll vertically to view the remainder of the document, but most experts do not recommend horizontal scrolling. Scrolling across the document is annoying because you must constantly scroll back and forth to read the document.

Depending on the resolution of the user's monitor, the document you prepare for use on a 14-inch screen will appear larger or smaller than your optimized document. Creating the PDF document with your monitor resolution set at 640×480 will give a good end result if the intended audience is using 13- or 14-inch monitors. A resolution of 800×600 is a better choice if the intended audience will use 15- or 18-inch monitors. Note that monitor resolution is measured in *pixels*, which are the tiny squares that make up your screen. Use the Windows Display Properties dialog box to change the resolution of your monitor (see Figure 22.2). On a Macintosh computer, click the Apple icon and choose Control Panel, Monitor.

FIGURE 22.2

Change your monitor resolution by clicking the Start button and selecting Settings, Control Panel, Display on an IBM-compatible computer.

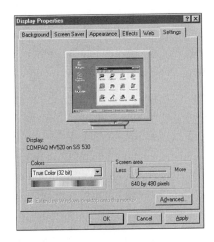

Typeface Considerations

Choosing an appropriate type style—or font—is another critical factor in determining whether your document can be easily read. Using sans serif typefaces for smaller type is an recommended. (Serifs are the "tails" on the downstrokes of the letters that can make type difficult to read at smaller sizes.) If a serif type is your only option, then increasing the letter spacing a bit can help make the document more readable in its final form.

Examples of sans serif type are Arial, Helvetica, Futura, Eras, and Impact. As you can see in Figure 22.3, sans serif typefaces have cleaner lines and are less complicated than serif typefaces.

Serif typefaces include Times Roman, Century, Palatino, and Courier. These fonts are more traditional looking, but should be avoided if they are to be used at very small sizes to increase readability. Figure 22.4 shows several serif typefaces at various sizes.

22

FIGURE 22.3

Sans serif fonts are legible even at small sizes.

FIGURE 22.4

Serif fonts have "tails" on the downstrokes of the letters that make these fonts difficult to read at small sizes.

You can achieve interesting designs when preparing type documents by varying the use of serif and sans serif types. Using sans serif for the body copy and serif for the headlines can create a pleasing effect (see Figure 22.5). The body copy will be readable, and the different look for the headlines can make them stand out more and give the final document style.

Avoid certain typefaces and type sizes if the PDF document is to be printed on a desktop-style printer. Depending on the quality of the printer and its output, the letters may "fill in," making the words illegible. Choosing a sans serif typeface or increasing the letter spacing are two ways to help avoid this readability dilemma.

Figure 22.5

Use a pleasing combination of serif and sans serif fonts in a document.

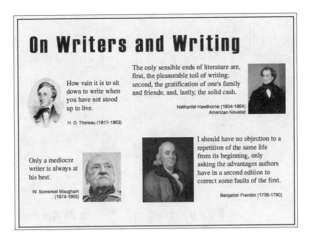

If you are creating text-intensive documents, the spacing between lines—often
New Term referred to as line spacing or *leading*—is critical in keeping legibility high.
Although designers usually prefer a tighter leading (that is, less space between lines),
tight leading does not make a document very readable. If you want your document to be
read, provide ample line spacing for the body text to make it appealing but still allow the
user to read the text easily.

The target audience should be a consideration when you are putting the document
together. Who will read your file affects decisions you make concerning the design of the
final PDF file. For example, visually impaired or elderly persons require even more leading between lines, or even larger type sizes, so keep this in mind when creating your document. Figure 22.6 shows a document designed for people with vision impairments.

Figure 22.6

This document has been designed for people who have difficulty seeing; it uses larger font sizes and increases the leading in large blocks of text.

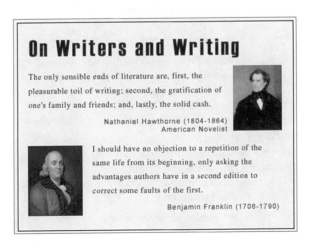

22

Here are some other considerations for type in PDF documents:

- Using underlined type for online documents is not a good idea because the type will look like a link. This can be confusing to your readers, so eliminate underlined type altogether. You can draw attention to the text in other ways, such as with quotation marks, all capital letters, bold text, and so on.

- Using underlined text *is* acceptable, however, in documents that will *not* be used online. In a printed document, underlined text will not be mistaken as a link. The exceptions to this rule, however, are instances in which it is grammatically correct to underline text, such as book titles, entries in bibliographies, and so on. Of course, there might be cases in which underlined text in a PDF document is intended to be used as an actual link to another page in the file.

- Make your text-intensive documents appear more interesting by adding white space when you can. You can provide white space easily by putting an extra paragraph return or two between topics.

- Use boldface type for emphasis, but don't overuse it. As with any design, too much of a good thing can be monotonous. Perhaps you'll choose to emphasize headlines or important words in the text with bold, but don't overdo it.

- The beginning of a new paragraph can be noted in several ways. The two most common methods are using extra space between paragraphs and indenting the first line of a paragraph. The more eye-pleasing of the two is the extra space between paragraphs. This "break" allows the copy to continue to flow, but does not bog down the viewer's eye, especially with documents containing lots of text (see Figure 22.7).

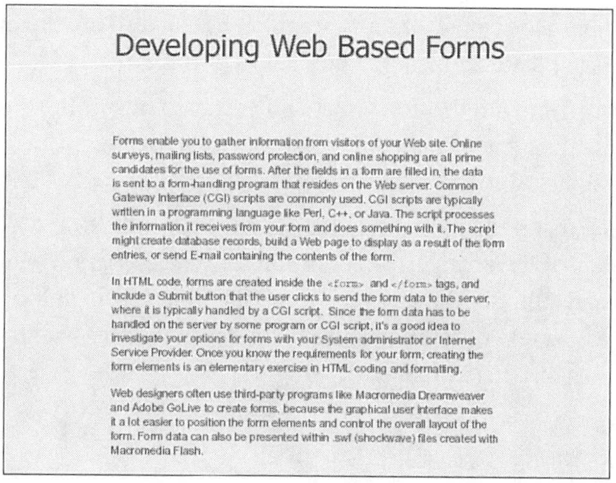

FIGURE 22.7
Documents containing large amounts of text need a break between paragraphs to aid readability and keep the design interesting. To do this, add extra space between paragraphs as shown here or indent the first line of the paragraph.

Developing Web Based Forms

Forms enable you to gather information from visitors of your Web site. Online surveys, mailing lists, password protection, and online shopping are all prime candidates for the use of forms. After the fields in a form are filled in, the data is sent to a form-handling program that resides on the Web server. Common Gateway Interface (CGI) scripts are commonly used. CGI scripts are typically written in a programming language like Perl, C++, or Java. The script processes the information it receives from your form and does something with it. The script might create database records, build a Web page to display as a result of the form entries, or send E-mail containing the contents of the form.

In HTML code, forms are created inside the `<form>` and `</form>` tags, and include a Submit button that the user clicks to send the form data to the server, where it is typically handled by a CGI script. Since the form data has to be handled on the server by some program or CGI script, it's a good idea to investigate your options for forms with your System administrator or Internet Service Provider. Once you know the requirements for your form, creating the form elements is an elementary exercise in HTML coding and formatting.

Web designers often use third-party programs like Macromedia Dreamweaver and Adobe GoLive to create forms, because the graphical user interface makes it a lot easier to position the form elements and control the overall layout of the form. Form data can also be presented within .swf (shockwave) files created with Macromedia Flash.

Breaking a single, wide column into multiple columns prevents the viewer's eye from having to scan the entire width of the document, which sometimes can be difficult to do. Printed documents usually adhere to the 65–70 character-wide rule; a good rule of thumb for online documents is 580 pixels, the width of a 14-inch monitor, accounting for scrollbars.

▼ TASK

Task: Comparing Typefaces

To help you become more familiar with the different looks you can achieve with type, this task explores some different typefaces, including serif and sans serif type.

1. Launch the authoring application with which you plan to create the document and type some text on the page. Experiment with serif and sans serif typefaces so that you are comfortable with the differences between them.

   Remember that serif type has little "tails" or "hooks" on the letters; sans serif type does not. Become familiar with the fonts on your computer and which ones look good when used together.

Generally, it is not a good idea to mix sans serif type with serif type in the body text. One exception to that rule is to use a serif font for body text and a sans serif font for the headlines. That is a common technique that results in a modern, clean look.

2. Vary the size of the type and print the document on your printer. Examine the final document to see which fonts are more readable. This exercise will help you in preparing the document for its final PDF format.

3. Experiment with the horizontal and vertical scale of the type to get a feel for the way scaling can change the look of the text. Scaling over 100% expands the type; scaling below 100% condenses it.

4. Notice that line spacing can vary greatly depending on whether the type is in all capitals or lowercase, in a script font or block letters. You can increase or decrease the readability of the text by altering the line spacing: Too much line spacing makes the text difficult to follow, whereas too little spacing causes the tops and bottoms of letters to touch.

Graphic Resolution

The artwork and photographs used in your document must be saved properly to produce the final output you desire. Graphics used in high-end printing should be of a higher quality than graphics used for online documents.

NEW TERM If you are preparing your document for online use, save the graphics at 72*dpi*. This means 72 *dots per inch*, a term used by graphics professionals to determine the quality of a graphics. The higher the dpi—the more dots per inch—the better the quality of the graphics and the larger the file size.

Graphics saved at 72dpi are used for online viewing or for a document that will simply be viewed on a computer monitor. Because computer monitors have a resolution of 72dpi, the graphics will appear crisp and clear.

If you are preparing the document for high-end printing, 72dpi graphics are *not* acceptable; graphics at that resolution will appear jagged or bitmapped when printed. Therefore, you must save graphics intended for printing at higher resolutions, such as 300dpi for photographs or continuous-tone images, and 1,200dpi for line art or graphics that contain solid areas of black and white (see Figure 22.8).

FIGURE 22.8
Different image types.

If you are scanning artwork to be used in your PDF document, take input resolution into consideration when scanning. You can always lower the resolution of a graphic in an image-editing program such as Adobe Photoshop, but you cannot increase the resolution after the graphic has been scanned. Increasing the resolution artificially will produce a blurred image.

Color Space

Color space is a term used to define the way colors are handled within the image. The two main color spaces we deal with when working with PDF documents are RGB (Red, Green, Blue) and CMYK (Cyan, Magenta, Yellow, Black). RGB is for documents used on the World Wide Web, and CMYK is for printed documents. When adding graphics to your PDF, keep the final purpose of the document in mind. If the document is to be used for high-end printing, you must save the graphics in the CMYK color space for proper color separations to occur. The four color inks (CMYK) employed in process printing are used in differing combinations to produce full-color photos and artwork in high-end printing.

If you are planning to send your document to a printer, and you do not save the graphics in the CMYK color space, the graphics will not properly separate in the final output (check with your printer for further details on CMYK).

If you are using the final PDF file for desktop or laser printer output only, the graphics can be saved as either CMYK or RGB. Check the user guide that came with your printer to find out which color space will produce better quality on your particular printer.

Documents being used on the World Wide Web must have color graphics saved in the RGB (Red, Green, Blue) color space. Graphics that are not saved in the RGB color space will not appear properly when the document is viewed in an Internet browser. The images will drop off the PDF entirely, will appear distorted, or will appear with lines or stripes.

Graphics saved as RGB have more colors available than those saved as CMYK. The RGB color space has 16.7 million colors available, so your graphics have access to all those colors, enabling them to appear brighter and more colorful than the same graphics saved in the CMYK color space. The CMYK color space has only several thousand colors.

Because not every color can be reproduced in CMYK, that color space is more "limiting" than RGB. This is just a limitation of high-end color printing. If the color graphics have been properly color corrected, the final output will look good, regardless of the limits of CMYK.

If your graphics are saved in the improper color space for your PDF's final destination, you can easily switch them to another color space in your image editing application.

- **Photoshop:** Open the graphic, choose Image, Mode, and select the color space you need. Resave the document and close it.

22

- **Illustrator (Version 9+):** Choose File, Document Color Mode and change the color space.
- **Illustrator (Versions before 9):** Open the Swatches palette; from the drop-down menu on the right side of the palette, choose to view your colors as a list. This option shows each swatch with either a CMYK icon or an RGB icon. Double-click the color name you want to change and choose the new color space.

Summary

As we have discussed in this hour, taking into consideration the end use of your PDF document is an important part of the design process. Knowing whether the PDF will be used online or for high-end printing determines the quality of graphics and the basic design of the document.

We learned about color spaces—RGB and CMYK in particular—and when to use each: CMYK is for printing purposes, while RGB is the color space used for the World Wide Web.

We explored the many facets of adding type to our PDF documents, and how the choices we make for type style and line spacing can greatly affect readability.

Because you have more control over online PDFs than you do over HTML documents, you can design the document exactly as you want it to appear. Prepare the document to get your message across to the viewer, but also make it eye catching and easy to read. Use the powerful features of Acrobat to make the document more user friendly, but start with a good design. Even the power of Acrobat's tools cannot correct a poorly designed document, so do your homework and prepare the document correctly. Doing so ensures a successful end product: A PDF that can be easily read and that is pleasing to the eye.

Workshop

In this workshop, we'll address some questions that cover issues related to this hour's topics. After the multiple-choice quiz, we'll finish up with some hand-on exercises designed to reinforce what you learned this hour.

Q&A

Q Can I change the typeface in a PDF document?

A You can change the typeface in a PDF document by using Acrobat's Text Attributes palette—but only one line of text at a time. Therefore, it is better to determine what type styles to use when you create the native document. Acrobat will display the document using exactly the same type styles you used to create the original document, whether the PDF is used online or printed.

Q How can I determine whether the document was saved with text editing capabilities?

A All PDFs have editable text, regardless of whether the fonts were embedded. To change the type extensively (for example, to change wording), the fonts must be embedded. To determine whether the fonts were embedded, open the PDF and choose File, Document Properties, Fonts. This command displays all the fonts used in the PDF document, the type of font (True Type, Type 1, and so on), and whether the font was embedded in the PDF.

Q What if I am preparing a document for print *and* for the Web?

A The graphics you save for the Web version of the document should be in RGB, but you can alter your Distiller settings to handle the job properly for the Web (see Hour 24, "Printing with Acrobat").

Quiz

1. **Can graphics be altered from CMYK to RGB in Acrobat?**

    a. Yes. Acrobat can switch the color spaces for graphics.

    b. No. They cannot be altered from within Acrobat.

    c. After a graphic has been saved in a certain color space, it cannot be altered at all.

2. **The term *dpi* refers to**

    a. *Dots per inch*, a term that refers to the resolution of a graphic or that is used to describe the monitor resolution of your computer.

    b. *Data prepared for Internet use*, a term used for PDFs that will be used on the World Wide Web.

    c. *Data per inch*, a term used to describe the size of text in a PDF document.

3. You can make your PDF document generally more readable for online use by

    a. Using as many different type styles as possible.

    b. Underlining text to add emphasis.

    c. Using sans serif type for body text and adding extra space between paragraphs.

22

Quiz Answers

1. **b**   No. The graphic cannot be altered from within Acrobat. Return to your image-editing program and switch color spaces there.

2. **a**   The term *dpi* (dots per inch) refers to resolution.

3. **c**   Using sans serif type for body text and adding extra space between paragraphs makes online viewing easier.

Exercises

These short exercises reiterate what was covered in this hour. Reinforce what you learned in this hour by performing these hands-on exercises.

1. Prepare a document that uses continuous-tone graphics, such as photographs. Save the document as a low-resolution PDF and again as a high-resolution PDF. Compare the file size and quality of the graphics in the two documents.

2. Experiment with different letter spacing and line spacing options in the native application. Save different versions of the original document as PDFs to see how readable they are at different screen magnifications.

3. View pages on the World Wide Web and take notes on which ones are easy to read and which are not. Create some pages in your native application and prepare them as though they are being used on the World Wide Web. Convert them to PDF and examine them for readability at different view magnifications. The knowledge you gain will be useful when you are preparing PDFs for use on the Web.

HOUR 23

Making PDF Files Accessible for All

What exactly is accessibility? Why would I want to make my PDF documents accessible? How can I tell whether a PDF document has been made accessible before I receive it? These questions—and more—will be answered in this hour, as we delve into the creation and editing of accessible PDF files.

One of the primary reasons PDF files have become so popular is that they are universally accepted. But when we post things to the Web, we should not forget about visually impaired Internet users. All federal agencies in the United States are now making their PDF files accessible for visually impaired users, as are most state agencies and large corporations.

Federal agencies are actually required to make all PDF documents on their Web sites "accessible" to the general public—that is, so that the files can be read by all, including those persons who are visually or motion impaired. Visually or motion impaired persons are able to read the data in PDF documents using an assisting device called a *screen reader*. Screen readers are made by manufacturers such as GW Micro (`gwmicro.com`) and Freedom Scientific (`freedomscientific.com`) and are currently available for IBM-compatible systems only.

If the document is prepared with the proper accessibility features in place, the screen reader converts the data into a readable format.

In this hour, we will become familiar with the following topics:

- Accessibility features
- Creating tagged PDF files for screen-reader conversion
- Using the Accessibility Checker
- Editing the logical structure tree
- Using the Make Accessible plug-in for Windows users

Accessibility Features

A statutory section of the Rehabilitation Act of 1973, Section 508, was greatly strengthened by Congress in 1998. Section 508 states that "federal agencies are required to make their electronic and information technology accessible to people with disabilities" (for more information on the Rehabilitation Act, and Section 508, go to `http://www.section508.gov`).

NEW TERM In this, the electronic age, technology—including any equipment or interconnected system used to share information online—is known as *Electronic and Information Technology*, or simply EIT.

EIT includes, but is not limited to, the following elements:

- World Wide Web sites
- Telecommunication products such as telephones
- Information kiosks
- Office equipment such as fax machines
- Multimedia such as video

Documents to be used on the World Wide Web, whether they are in HTML or PDF format, need more than additional details to be truly accessible. There are lots of visual clues that help sighted persons decipher and navigate a document. Examples of these kinds of clues are extra paragraph spacing, bold headlines, indented quotations, and so on. These clues help the reader determine the importance of the data, the order in which to read the data, and so on.

Unfortunately, screen-reading software cannot depend on such visual clues. Because it interprets the text in a non-visual format, the software relies on the underlying structure of the document to be able to interpret the page. The document must have hidden clues for the screen reader to tell it the order to read things and how to present the text in a logical manner. Other examples of hidden clues might be text descriptions in place of the original graphics, and the handling of links to other pages. This underlying information is referred to as the *logical structure tree* of the document.

In addition to creating the structured PDF, you can alter Acrobat settings to make the PDF document accessible to screen readers, thus enabling the visually impaired to get the necessary information from your documents.

23

Successfully preparing accessible documents relies on two important factors:

- The original documents to be structured must contain information about how text flows from page to page.
- Publishing tools, such as Acrobat 5.0, which can keep and encode the content and structure of the document to use in conjunction with screen readers.

For advanced Acrobat users, more information on extensive editing of the logical structure tree can be obtained in the technical note TN 5406 included with the Acrobat 5.0 Software Development Kit.

Tagged PDF Documents

PDF documents are a large part of the accessibility equation. One way to begin creating an accessible PDF is to create a "tagged" PDF. Tagged PDFs contain structural data that keeps the text in a logical reading order. Tagged PDFs also assist in the translation of the data to a universal format called Unicode. This format works with text, regardless of the original font, and handles special characters (hyphens, copyright symbols, and so on) so that the text can be read by the screen reader.

Tagged PDF files also offer an easy transition from PDF to other file formats such as RTF (Rich Text Format) while maintaining basic formatting and structure. Tagged PDFs also allow easy conversion to other devices, such as eBook readers, and make it possible for screen readers to be used by visually impaired persons

Currently, the major screen reading software programs are available for IBM-compatible computers only.

In addition to using tagged PDFs to make your documents accessible, you can use the Make Accessible plug-in to convert any new or existing PDF document to an accessible one. Later in this hour, we will learn more about the Make Accessible plug-in.

> Because things on the World Wide Web are constantly being updated and improved, it is a good idea to keep on top of what is new in accessibility. The World Wide Web Consortium, an organization that oversees usage and guidelines for the World Wide Web, has a Web site you can go to for the latest news in accessibility: http://www.w3.org/WAI/.

Preparing Tagged PDF Documents

Currently, applications that can create tagged PDF documents include:

- Microsoft Office 2000
- Adobe PageMaker 7.0

Tagged PDF documents are then brought into Acrobat 5 to further enhance their accessibility, as you will learn in this hour.

In addition to the basic components of PDF documents, tagged PDFs have important information beyond what is visible in the document. Tagged PDF files contain a logical structure "tree" that defines the basic makeup of the document. This tree includes particular codes that define word spaces, hard and soft hyphens, space between sections, lists, tables, and so on. This invisible information is used when the document is converted to RTF or when the document is used with screen readers.

Tagged PDF documents have been "optimized" for accessibility, which means they can be read by screen readers easily with reliable results.

> When converting Web pages to PDF format, Acrobat allows you to create tagged PDF files automatically. Alternatively, you can create tagged PDF files using PDFMaker 5.0, which works in conjunction with Microsoft Office 2000 for IBM-compatible computers. PDFMaker is covered in Hour 4, "Creating PDF Files from Your Electronic Documents."
>
> You can also create structured PDFs from Adobe Framemaker 6.0. Structured PDF files are similar to tagged PDF files, but they lack information about line breaks, special character information, and character-spacing information. Simply use the Save As command in Framemaker, or create a PS file and convert it to PDF using Acrobat Distiller.

Other programs also allow the easy creation of structured and tagged PDFs. Check the documentation that comes with the software to see whether the application you are using allows the creation of structured PDF files.

Task: Creating Tagged PDF Documents from Microsoft Office 2000

(*IBM-compatible only*) To create a tagged PDF document from a Microsoft Office 2000 product, follow these steps:

23

1. In the Microsoft Office 2000 application, choose Acrobat, Change Conversion Settings from the menu bar (see Figure 23.1).

2. In the Acrobat PDFMaker dialog box that appears, click the Office tab and make sure that the Embed Tags in PDF check box and "Page Labels" are enabled (see Figure 23.2). Click OK to close the dialog box.

3. Now you can create the PDF from within the Microsoft Office 2000 application by clicking the Convert to Adobe PDF icon on the application toolbar or by choosing Acrobat, Convert to Adobe PDF on the menu bar.

▲

> Before you create the tagged PDF, open your Bookmarks palette and select the styles for which you want to create Adobe PDF bookmarks.

FIGURE 23.1

To begin setting up a tagged PDF document, choose Acrobat, Change Conversion Settings from within a Microsoft Office 2000 application.

> Because of the vast number of Office users, Adobe has integrated features to help Acrobat and Microsoft Office work together.
>
> Enable your Microsoft application to convert files directly to PDF by first installing the Microsoft applications and then installing Acrobat. If necessary, uninstall Acrobat and reinstall it after you load Microsoft Office.

FIGURE 23.2

*Make sure that the
Embed Tags in PDF
option is enabled in
the Office tab of the
Acrobat PDFMaker
dialog box.*

Structured PDF Documents from Adobe Framemaker

Structured PDFs can be created from Framemaker 6 on both Macintosh and IBM-compatible platforms. These PDF files have almost all the same attributes as tagged PDF files, but they do not include information about line breaks, special characters, or character spacing. All these items can be added using Acrobat and the TouchUp command, discussed later in this hour.

Here are some things to keep in mind when converting Framemaker documents to structured PDF documents:

- To create structured PDFs from within Framemaker, you must begin by adding paragraph styles to the logical structure within the PDF document. Paragraph styles enable Acrobat to create a logical structure from a Framemaker document.

- To create tables, use the Table Designer. Simply attaching tables to your Framemaker document will not make them accessible to screen readers (see the tip following this list for more about tables in Framemaker).

- Figures for graphics must be created within Framemaker (not imported with the graphic) and have a paragraph style applied to them. Alternate text tags will be added later in Acrobat using the Tags palette.

- Enable the ability to create the logical structure tree by turning on this feature in Framemaker. This feature is available only in version 6.0. From within Framemaker, select Format, Document, PDF Setup, Structure and then enable the Generate Logical Structure check box. All paragraph styles are then included in the structure.

- To create PDF bookmarks from your Framemaker document, select Format, Document, PDF Setup, Bookmarks. Be sure that the Generate PDF Bookmarks check box is enabled. You can then determine which paragraph styles you want to include as bookmarks. Generally, you don't include every style (for instance, you might include the Subhead style but not the Photo Caption style).

Tables attached to Framemaker documents can be converted if the Make Accessible plug-in is installed on the computer before the table is attached. Download the plug-in free of charge from Adobe's Web site at www.adobe. com/support/downloads/main.html.

23

Task: Creating Structured PDF Documents from Adobe Framemaker

TASK

In this task, we will create a structured PDF using Framemaker 6.0.

1. Be sure that a PostScript printer is installed for your IBM-compatible or Macintosh computer.

2. Set up Distiller's job options for the settings you want to use in this PDF. Framemaker converts the document to PDF using the currently selected Distiller job options.

3. Open the document you want to convert. It will be saved as a single PDF document. Also open any linked Framemaker documents and test all links to be sure that they work.

4. From the original Framemaker document, choose File, Save As (or Save Book As, if you are using a Framemaker book) and choose the PDF option from the pop-up menu.

   Macintosh users: If necessary, add a .pdf extension. IBM-compatible users: The .pdf extension should already be present. Browse to choose the location to which you want to save the document and click Save.

5. The PDF Setup dialog box appears. If you have already set up Distiller the way you want it, you should not have to change anything here. Click Set; the PDF file will be created using the job options you specified.

Reflowing Tagged PDF Documents

A PDF document can be reflowed to make it easier to read. You can reflow the document right within Acrobat or you can reflow it if you are viewing the document on another device such as an eBook reader or a handheld computer. Reflowing temporarily changes the view of the document to show only a portion of each page at a time. When you click the Reflow button or choose View, Reflow, the document contents are reflowed to fill the width of your Acrobat window. If you resize the window, the text "reflows," meaning that line breaks change to fit the width of the window.

The Reflow option is available in both Acrobat and the free Acrobat Reader so that users can reflow text to fit their screens. This feature is used to increase readability so that the user of the document is not limited by the document's original line breaks.

In Acrobat, when you're authoring the document, you can use the Reflow option to see how the text fits, breaks, and is ordered within a particular screen dimension. The Reflow view is not saved with the Acrobat file; Acrobat saves only the changes you make to the structure and order. In other words, the text will look exactly the same in Acrobat Reader unless you choose Reflow in the Reader software.

To reflow a tagged PDF document, open it in Acrobat and click the Reflow tool on the toolbar. Alternatively, choose View, Reflow. Figure 23.3 shows a before-and-after example of a page that has been reflowed.

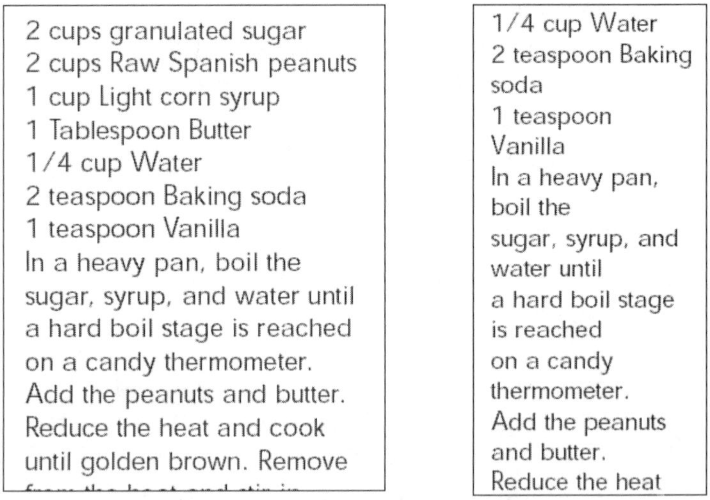

FIGURE 23.3

On the left, the original PDF document has set line breaks. On the right, the same PDF was reflowed so that the line breaks change based on the width of the Acrobat window.

2 cups granulated sugar
2 cups Raw Spanish peanuts
1 cup Light corn syrup
1 Tablespoon Butter
1/4 cup Water
2 teaspoon Baking soda
1 teaspoon Vanilla
In a heavy pan, boil the
sugar, syrup, and water until
a hard boil stage is reached
on a candy thermometer.
Add the peanuts and butter.
Reduce the heat and cook
until golden brown. Remove

1/4 cup Water
2 teaspoon Baking soda
1 teaspoon Vanilla
In a heavy pan, boil the
sugar, syrup, and water until
a hard boil stage is reached
on a candy thermometer.
Add the peanuts and butter.
Reduce the heat

Verifying Line Endings in a Reflowed PDF Document

You will want to make certain that words are properly divided when you reflow a tagged Adobe PDF document or make an Adobe PDF document accessible to users of screen-reading software. You can verify whether words are properly partitioned with word breaks, line breaks, and hyphenation. If you find that words aren't properly partitioned, you can edit your document by inserting special characters to control the line breaks.

Task: Verifying Line Endings

In this task, we will verify the line endings of a PDF file to confirm how it will look when reflowed.

1. Select the TouchUp Text tool.

2. Select a word or group of words where you want to confirm how the lines will flow.

3. Choose Tools, TouchUp, Text Breaks. A window appears, showing how the lines will break when the document is reflowed. Word breaks are indicated by three spaces, line breaks are indicated by a blank line, hard hyphens are the only hyphens that show.

4. If you are unhappy with the line breaks, modify them by inserting a special charac-ter where you want to force a break: Move the insertion point to that location and select Tools, Touch Up Text, Insert, Line Break (or one of the other line-break options).

After the document has been reflowed, you will see a check mark next to the View, Reflow menu command to let you know that this document has been reflowed.

Changing the Reflow Order in Tagged PDF Documents

After the document has been reflowed, you may discover that you want to change more than the line breaks. If the document reflowed in a sequence you do not like, you can use the TouchUp Order tool to change the order of reflowed items. For example, if you have a picture or a table in the middle of a text flow, you might want this item to be displayed following the text if it is reflowed.

Changing the reflow order is useful because the document otherwise might not flow in a logical manner when viewed in a screen reader.

Task: Changing the Reflow Order in a Document

If you test a document's reflow order using the Reflow command and are unhappy with the way it flows, you can change the sequence. For example, if the document goes from a headline to an unrelated story, you will want to change the sequence.

▼   1. To use the TouchUp Order tool, open a tagged PDF document. Be sure to maintain
        the standard page view before attempting to change the reflow order. You cannot
        change the reflow order while the PDF is already in a reflowed view on your
        screen.

     2. Choose the TouchUp Order tool from the toolbar. When you click the tool, boxes
        with sequence numbers appear around each item in the PDF file (see Figure 23.4).

     3. Click the items on the page in the order you want them to appear when reflowed.
        Continue clicking the items until you are satisfied with the reordering. You can
        start over if you make a mistake by selecting another tool in the toolbar and then
        returning to the TouchUp Order tool.

     4. When you have finished, switch to the Hand tool and reflow the document by
▲   clicking the Reflow icon to confirm your changes.

FIGURE 23.4

*Use the TouchUp
Order tool to reorder
items in a reflowed
document so that the
elements are presented
in a logical manner
when viewed in a dif-
ferent format.*

TouchUp Order tool

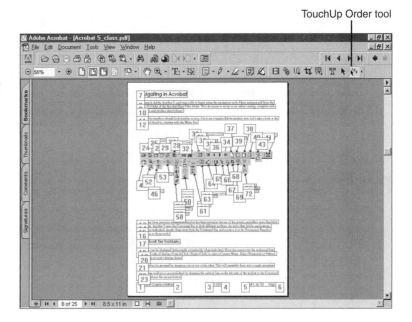

 To speed up the process of reordering, right-click (Ctrl+click for Macintosh
users) a sequence box and use the context menu to reorder by selection
options such as Make Last, Bring to Front, and so on.

Figure 23.5 shows the context menu that gives you great control over the
reordering of the sequence items.

FIGURE 23.5

The context menus pro-
vide a separate menu
of quick reordering
commands, which is
useful for changing the
sequence order of
reflowed, tagged PDF
documents.

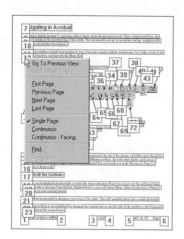

Converting Existing PDF Documents to Accessible PDF Documents

Because there are multitudes of applications from which a PDF can be created, not every PDF file can be made accessible during the creation process. Therefore, we need to discuss ways to make other PDF documents conform to the same accessibility standards. When converting a PDF to an accessible PDF, consider these points:

- Use the accessibility tools discussed in this hour.

- Edit the structure of the document, if necessary, using the Tags palette.

- Make use of the Accessibility Checker to verify and optimize your accessible files.

- If the native document (the one used to create the original PDF) is available, convert it to a PDF using Acrobat 5.0. Then use the Make Accessible plug-in (discussed later in this hour).

- If you don't have the original document, open the PDF in Acrobat 5.0 and use the Make Accessible plug-in to convert the document.

Using the Make Accessible Plug-In

The free make Accessible plug-in from Adobe converts untagged PDF documents to accessible (tagged) PDF documents. Note that this plug-in is for IBM-compatible users only.

We will be exploring the use of the Make Accessible plug-in on a single PDF file. To speed up the conversion process, consider using the batch processing feature of Acrobat to convert multiple PDF documents to accessible ones, all at the same time. For more on batch processing, see Hour 19, "Automating Acrobat with Batch Processing."

Task: Using the Make Accessible Plug-In to Convert a PDF

Let's begin by assuming that you have already downloaded the plug-in from Adobe's Web site at www.adobe.com/support/downloads/main.html and installed it. If you have not installed the plug-in, simply double-click the .exe file you downloaded and follow the instructions. As long as Acrobat 5.0 is already installed on your computer, the installer will locate it and quickly install the plug-in. After you have done this, you are ready to begin.

1. Launch Acrobat 5.0 and open the untagged document you want to convert.

2. Choose Document, Make Accessible. The plug-in makes the document accessible.

3. Always check the PDF for possible problems by using the Accessibility Checker.

Check your converted documents using the Accessibility Checker—and also view your documents in a screen reader before uploading them to the Web to ensure that things were converted in the proper order.

In addition, use the Tags palette to examine the structure of the PDF document. Both processes are described in the following sections.

Checking for Accessibility

Before you supply tagged PDF documents to users who require accessibility, there are a few things you can do to ensure that your document is accessible.

First, let's explore the preference settings that pertain to accessibility.

Task: Setting Your Preferences for Accessibility

With the untagged PDF open, this task explores the preference settings that can enhance the readability of the PDF for visually impaired persons.

1. Choose Edit, Preferences, General to open the Preferences dialog box. Select the Accessibility option from the pane at the left side of the dialog box to open the Accessibility sheet (see Figure 23.6).

FIGURE 23.6

The Accessibility sheet in the Preferences dialog box lets you more tightly control the appearance of the tagged PDF.

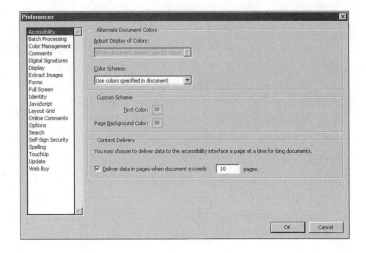

2. From the Color Scheme drop-down list, choose Custom Scheme. (Windows also supports a high-contrast viewing mode. If you have already set your monitor to that, you can choose Windows Colors instead here.)

3. In the Custom Scheme dialog box that opens, set the text color to the color of your choice (bright green is a good choice).

4. From the Adjust Display of Colors menu, select Always Overriding Document Colors.

5. Set the Page Background Color to a contrasting color, such as black.

6. Click OK.

Other Accessibility Preferences

Following is a list of the additional settings available to increase readability in your PDF documents:

- *Adjust Display of Colors:*

    When Document Doesn't Specify Colors—If the document does not specify a color scheme, Acrobat will alter the colors to match your color scheme.

    Always Override Document Colors—Acrobat will change the document colors to your chosen color scheme in every instance.

- *Color Scheme:*

    Use Colors Specified in Document—Acrobat will use the colors dictated by the creator of the document.

Use Custom Scheme—The colors you choose will take precedence in the document.

Use Windows Colors—System colors will be used in the document.

Note that when you choose a custom scheme, the text and page background color pop-up menu will be available for you to click on, to make a selection. Choose a preexisting color, or click Custom to create a custom color. (Macintosh users: There is no pop-up menu; instead, you click a color-swatch button for Text Color or Page Background Color and then choose a color from any of the Mac's built-in color palettes, including system colors.)

- *Content Delivery (IBM compatible only):*

    If the document being translated to a screen reader has a large number of pages, you can specify how you want to handle the pages. Set this field to 0, and the document will be transferred to the screen reader one page at a time. Disable the check box to transfer the entire document at once.

For more information on the preferences of Acrobat, refer Hour 20, "Setting Preferences and Properties."

Checking Accessibility

Just because a document has accessibility features applied, there is no guarantee that everything will work properly when the PDF is viewed in a screen reader. You can examine the accessibility of your PDF by using the Accessibility Checker; you can examine the structure of the PDF by using the Tags palette.

Task: Using the Accessibility Checker

The Accessibility Checker allows you to examine a document's accessibility and set options for better performance. Begin this task by opening the tagged PDF.

1. To access the Accessibility Checker, choose Tools, Accessibility Checker. The Accessibility Checker Options dialog box appears (see Figure 23.7).

2. If you want to save the results of the Accessibility Checker, enable the Create Logfile check box. You can then browse to choose the location in which you want to store the log file.

3. To add comments to the file (such as notes about certain problems), enable the Create Comments in Document check box. (These can be removed later, after problems have been fixed, by choosing Tools, Comments, Delete All.)

    The log file is a text file with the same root name as the PDF document and a .log extension.

FIGURE 23.7

The Accessibility Checker is used to check a PDF to ensure that it is properly created and that screen readers can read it logically.

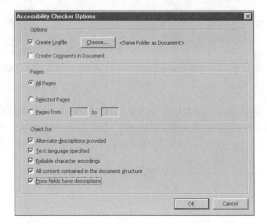

4. Specify the pages you want to check, or choose the All Pages option to check the entire document.

5. In the Check For section, select additional points for the Accessibility Checker to search for (such as descriptions for form fields) to make the translation to the screen reader more effective.

   - **Alternate Descriptions Provided**: Alternate tags help the screen reader describe the graphic that was originally intended to appear in the document. Alt tags are necessary in most instances, but not items such as decorative page borders that do not affect the content of the document directly. Getting an error on Alt tags does not necessarily indicate a problem.

   - **Reliable Character Encodings**: Choose this option to ensure that all characters include Unicode values. (Unicode is the universal format to which data from tagged PDFs is converted so that screen readers can decipher it and display it properly.)

   - **Text Language Specified**: At this time, it is not necessary to select this option. Currently, screen readers can read only one language.

   - **Form Fields Have Descriptions**: If the description of the form field was added, this option can help the screen reader interpret what was intended in the field. Without the description, the screen reader might not be able to decipher the form field correctly.

6. After you have set the options you want to use, click OK.

   Any problems that the Accessibility Checker finds are noted on the screen. If you chose to create a log file, you can open it to view more information on the problems found.

Editing the Logical Structure Tree Using the Tags Palette

You can use the Tags palette to examine the infrastructure of the PDF document and to make changes to it, if necessary. This process is performed only on tagged PDFs; you will receive an error message if you attempt to use it on an untagged PDF document.

Choose Window, Tags to display the Tags palette. For easier handling of this palette, drag it into the Navigation pane and select it there. (This action groups it with the other palettes, such as the Bookmarks and Comments palettes, as shown in Figure 23.8.

In the Tags palette, find the element you want to edit, such as an image with missing alternate text. Right-click that element and choose Element Properties from the context menu. Enter the alternate text you want to associate with the image and click OK.

Always test the PDF with a screen reader before posting it on the Web to ensure that proper readability has been established.

FIGURE 23.8

You can examine the logical structure tree by opening the tagged PDF and viewing the Tags palette.

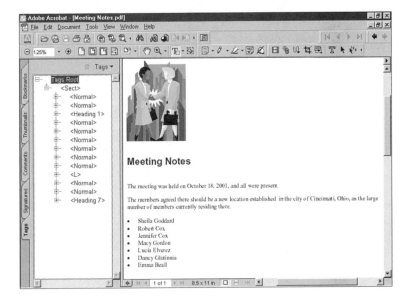

Summary

As we have learned in this hour, making PDF documents accessible for all persons is a requirement of the federal government so that the data contained in the documents can be viewed by everyone, regardless of their visual impairment.

We have learned which applications can be used to create tagged PDFs and how to create tagged PDFs from untagged documents. In addition, we have reviewed the changes we can make to a PDF document to increase its readability (such as preference settings) and learned how to view the logical structure tree using the Tags palette.

Acrobat's accessibility features give you greater control over the overall appearance of the document, as well as control over how the information contained within the document is translated to a screen reader.

23

Workshop

Now let's review what we have gained from this hour, beginning with a few questions on topics relating to accessibility. After the short multiple-choice session, you will find some hands-on exercises to reinforce the knowledge you have gained.

Q&A

Q In what format is the log file from the Accessibility Checker saved?

A The log file is saved as a text file at the location you chose in the Accessibility Checker Options dialog box. You can open the file as you would any text file: in Wordpad (for IBM-compatible computers), in Simple Text (for Macintosh computers), or in any text-editing program.

Q Can I create a tagged PDF document from a non-tagged PDF document?

A No. You must create the tagged PDF file from the native application, in which the original file was created.

Q How do I optimize a tagged PDF for accessibility?

A Tagged PDF documents created with Acrobat 5.0 are already optimized for accessibility.

Quiz

1. What is an advantage of a tagged PDF document?

  a. To add invisible coding that helps a screen reader translate the document.

  b. Tagged PDF documents appear larger onscreen for easier readability.

  c. Tagged PDF documents are translated to other languages.

2. Accessibility is

    a. The ability to find the documents easier online.

    b. The process of adding formatting and appearance features to allow visually impaired persons to read the documents on screen reader.

    c. A way to make the PDF files easier to open.

3. Setting custom color schemes is

    a. A way to make the documents look cool.

    b. An option on the Accessibility sheet of the Preferences dialog box, used to make the documents easier to read.

    c. A feature of the Accessibility Checker that provides a high contrast in the colors used onscreen.

Quiz Answers

1. **a**   Tagged PDFs have invisible coding, called tags, to help screen readers decipher the data.

2. **b**   Accessibility is the process of adding formatting and appearance features to increase readability for visually impaired persons.

3. **b**   Custom color schemes can increase readability and are set up in the preferences section.

Exercises

These exercises review what you have learned about creating and editing accessible PDFs.

1. Using Microsoft Office 2000 applications, practice creating tagged PDF documents and setting different color schemes for them.

2. Create a log file using the Accessibility Checker and examine the errors, if any, that it encountered.

3. Learn more about Section 508 and the Accessibility compliance by visiting `http://www.section508.gov`.

Hour **24**

Printing with Acrobat

PDF files might be called ePaper, but there are times when you need to have the real thing. For that, you will want to print your PDF files. Acrobat provides a host of options for printing your PDF files that can change the quality, size, and appearance of your document. Just because Acrobat files can be viewed on virtually every computer does not mean that they will print on every printer without a few glitches. But there are some troubleshooting tips that can help you overcome these obstacles. Even if you have a standard letter-size document and you're printing to a letter-size printer, there are still many things that are relevant for you to consider when printing a PDF file, all of which are covered in this hour.

In this hour, you'll learn the following:

- Using standard print settings
- Adjusting document sizes when printing
- Troubleshooting printing problems
- Understanding prepress settings
- Trapping and overprinting
- Using prepress plug-ins

Printing Annotations

Annotations and comments made on a PDF file can be enabled or disabled when printing. To print the annotations and comments with a PDF file, click the Print button in the toolbar or select File, Print and enable the Comments check box in the Print dialog box (see Figure 21.1). When this option is selected, annotations and comments made with any of Acrobat's tools appear on the printed document. These annotations often block out the text or other items on the page, or they might appear as small, dog-eared document icons in the middle of the page, both of which can be rather annoying. If you want to print your annotations, you might prefer to use the summarize annotations features, discussed in Hour 13, "Adding Comments and Annotations."

FIGURE 24.1

*The main Acrobat
Print window provides
many options.*

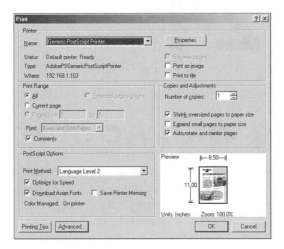

Printing Page Ranges and Nonconsecutive Pages

When you want to print several pages of the PDF that are not consecutive, you do not have to print each page individually. Instead, use the Thumbnails palette to select only the pages you want to print.

Task: Printing Nonconsecutive Pages

In this task, we will print non-adjacent pages.

1. Open a PDF document that contains multiple pages.
2. Open the Thumbnails palette.

3. If the document is too large for all the page icons to fit on the palette, open the Thumbnails palette; from the drop-down menu at the top of the palette, select Small Thumbnails.

4. Select the first page you want to print by clicking its icon on the Thumbnails palette.

5. Select the next pages you want to print by holding down the Ctrl key (Mac users press the Command key) while clicking the next pages' thumbnails (see Figure 24.2). It may be necessary to scroll within the Thumbnails palette to select additional pages.

6. If you want to select a contiguous group of pages, hold down the Shift key rather than the Ctrl/Command key and click the first and last pages' thumbnails to select all the pages in between those icons.

7. With the page thumbnails still selected, choose File, Print.

24

FIGURE 24.2
Thumbnails can be used to quickly select the pages of the PDF you want to print.

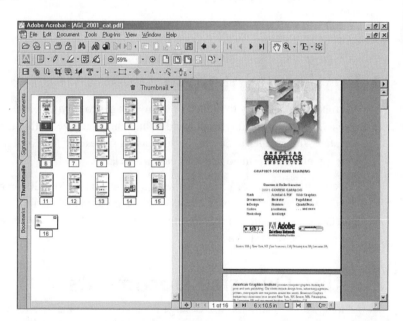

Printing a Portion of a Page

It is not necessary to print an entire page when you want to print only a small portion. Acrobat can print just a portion of a PDF page, which can be useful if you're working with large posters or other oversized documents.

Task: Printing a Section of a Page

In this task, we will print a portion of a page that we select with the Graphics Select tool.

1. Open a PDF document that contains a page of which you want to print only a portion.
2. Choose the Graphics Select tool from the toolbar, as shown in Figure 24.3.
3. Using the Graphics Select tool, draw a box around the portion of the page you want to print.
4. Select Print from the File menu.

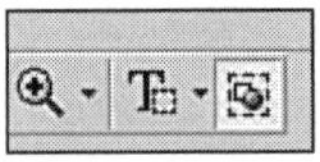

FIGURE 24.3

The Graphics Select tool, which is used for copying graphics, can also be used to define a region of a page for printing.

Adjusting Print Sizes

Acrobat makes it easy to reduce or enlarge pages to fit your printer. With oversized documents, you will probably want to do reduce the page size so that they fit onto a standard printer. With smaller documents—such as those designed for onscreen viewing—enlarging can make the printed versions easier to read.

Open any document or pages you want to print. In the Print dialog box, select the Shrink Oversized Pages to Paper Size option to make your large documents fit your printer. If the document is small and difficult to read, choose the Enlarge Small Pages to Paper Size option in the Print dialog box.

Printing Oversize Documents

Along with reducing the size of large documents, Acrobat version 5 adds a new option for printing oversize documents: tiling. Tiling prints a large document in multiple sections. You can then assemble the sections using tape or glue to create the completed page.

Task: Tiling an Oversized Document

In this task, we will print an oversized document in multiple pieces using tiling.

1. Open a PDF document that is too large to print on your printer.
2. Select Print from the File menu. The Print dialog box opens.

3. Click the Advanced button at the bottom of the Print dialog box.

4. Locate the Tiling section at the top of the Print Settings dialog box (see Figure 24.4). Click the Automatic radio button to enable that option.

5. In the Overlap box, type the amount you want each tile to overlap. This value is important because it allows you to find a good location to join each tile together; it allows you to make the seams between the tiles less visible. Try one-eighth of an inch to start, and increase this value if necessary.

6. The Tile Marks options produce marks on the printed pages that make it easier to join the tiles together. The Western Style produces marks that are commonly used in the North American and European printing industries. The Eastern Style option produces marks commonly used in the Asian printing industry. If you prefer to align each tile without these marks, choose None from the Tile Marks drop-down menu.

7. To have Acrobat print identifying information about the file and the tile being printed, enable the Emit Slug check box. Slugs are often used by commercial printers to help them identify the components of each job; they can also be useful for identification purposes if you find yourself tiling many documents.

Use the Scale option in the Print Settings dialog box to enlarge smaller documents. You can create posters from smaller documents using this feature and then use the tiling feature if desired.

FIGURE 24.4

Use the Print Settings dialog box to enable tiling and specify tiling options; you can also find an option for scaling documents to a specified percentage. Click the Advanced button in the Print dialog box to get to this window.

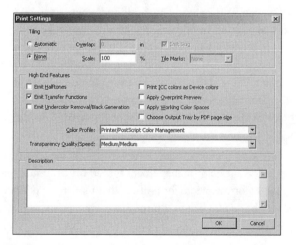

Prepress Options in Print Settings

The Print Settings dialog box, shown in Figure 24.4, also contains a host of options designed for graphic arts professionals such as commercial printers and service bureaus. These options are unnecessary for the average office user and typically should not be used unless you are involved in printing or graphic arts. These high-end features include the following prepress options:

- **Emit Halftones.** This option causes the PDF file to specify the halftone frequency (lines per inch) at which graphics will be printed, rather than using the default settings of the printer. With this option, you can build halftone frequencies into a graphic file using a program such as Photoshop or into an entire page using page layout software such as InDesign or PageMaker. Select this option only if you know the halftone resolution that was set for the document and are certain that it is appropriate for your printing needs.

- **Emit Transfer Functions.** Select this option if you want to include in the PDF file any transfer curves that were created to adjust for inconsistencies in a printer. The curves would have been saved into graphic files that are a part of the PDF.

- **Emit Undercolor Removal/Black Generation.** Undercolor Removal (UCR) and Gray Component Replacement (GCR) are used to help make images look better and avoid too much ink coverage in dark areas of graphics. UCR and GCR are also saved into graphic files that are a part of a PDF.

- **Print ICC Colors as Device Colors.** Select this option to disable ICC color management profiles from being sent to the printer when you print the PDF.

- **Apply Overprint Preview.** This option attempts to simulate what overprinted colors will look like when printed on a printing press. In some cases, colors will change dramatically when one color is printing on top of another color. This option can be used to create a color proof on a nontraditional color proofing device, such as a standard color laser printer. An overprinted page item is shown in Figures 24.5 and 24.6. This option can be used to preview *trapping*, a graphic arts process in which colors are intentionally overlapped to avoid a white gap between adjoining colors.

- **Apply Working Color Spaces.** In a very complicated way, this option is asking whether you want color management turned off or turned on. By enabling this option, the color management profiles that have been defined for your monitor and printer will be used when you print.

- **Color Profile.** Use this option to identify how your final printed piece will be produced if you are printing on an offset press. Select the printing type (such as sheet-fed or Web) and the paper type (coated or uncoated). Adobe's color management software will modify the color being printed to simulate the final printing press. If you do not want Acrobat to change the color when printing, you can disable color management by selecting the Same As Source option.

- **Transparency Quality/Speed.** PDF files that contain transparencies must have the transparency "flattened" while printing. The highest-quality transparency requires a long time when printing and may be too complex for some older printers. Setting this option for low quality and low speed works better for older printers, but causes all transparent objects to be converted to bitmap images, so they may appear to have jagged edges. Change this setting to eliminate problems with quality when printing or when pages containing transparencies will not print.

If you select a higher quality/speed setting, there is an increased probability of printing problems on older printers. If you select a lower quality, your page will take longer to print but will most likely work on most printers.

FIGURE 24.5

A document as it appears before the Apply Overprint Preview option is enabled.

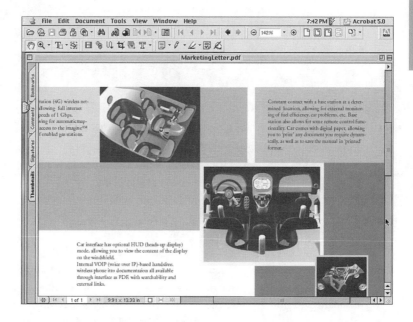

The overprint preview option is also available for onscreen viewing. Use it to see how colors will look when printed on top of each other. Access this command from the View menu (choose View, Overprint Preview). You can also simulate the overprint preview on a standard color printer by choosing options in the Print Settings dialog box, as described earlier in this hour.

FIGURE **24.6**
*The same document
shown in Figure 24.5,
after enabling the
Apply Overprint
Preview option.*

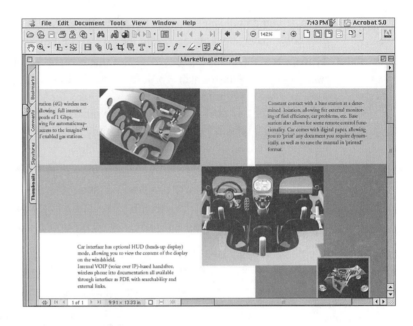

Trapping Key

Although Acrobat does not provide tools to apply trapping, you can note whether trapping has been applied to a PDF file. Do this by selecting File, Document Properties, Trapping Key. Select Yes if you have applied trapping to the file before it was converted to PDF; select No if trapping has not been applied.

Printing and Prepress Plug-ins

Printing and prepress plug-ins add functionality to Acrobat that is normally unavailable in the program. These plug-ins are not manufactured by Adobe Systems, but Adobe works with these companies to assist them in developing added features for Acrobat. It is typically safe to add these pieces of software into your Acrobat Plug-Ins folder. All these plug-ins can be purchased from the Power Xchange (www.thepowerxchange.com), a distributor of plug-ins for Acrobat and other publishing software. Some of my favorite plug-ins include the following:

- **PitStop.** This software plug-in lets you check for problems in your PDF file such as RGB images or missing fonts. It also provides more extensive graphic and text editing features. Check it out at www.enfocus.com.

- **Quite a Box of Tricks.** This plug-in provides assistance with eliminating RGB images along with options for scaling entire pages. Visit www.quite.com for more information.

- **Quite Imposing**. This Acrobat plug-in makes it easy to create digital impositions. It works only with PDF files, so it is not as complex and lacks features contained in other imposition software such as Preps. But it also costs thousands of dollars less than other imposition software. Go to www.quite.com for details.

- **PDFToolbox**. This plug-in includes a host of tools, such as PDF Inspektor, which looks for RGB images and missing fonts in your PDF files. Visit www.callas.de for more information.

- **pdfOutputPro.** This plug-in for Acrobat lets you print color separations directly from Acrobat. Visit www.callas.de for details.

24

Troubleshooting Printing Problems

When trouble arises as you're printing a PDF file, it is often because the page is too complicated to image. PDF is based on a very robust imaging and printing language known as PostScript. Although most printers used by professional graphic artists use the PostScript language, it is a less-common feature in general office printers.

If you repeatedly encounter errors when attempting to print a complex page, try the following: In the Print dialog box, select the Print as Image option. In Windows systems, this option is a check box; in the Mac OS, the option is a pull-down menu that offers two options: PostScript and Print as Image. Printing an entire page as an image takes longer to print, but it eliminates most printing problems.

Other problems can arise from pages that contain transparency. If you encounter problems on such a page, click the Advanced button in the Print dialog box and then choose Low/Low from the Transparency Quality/Speed drop-down menu.

Summary

After completing this hour, you should be able to print PDF files, regardless of their size. You should understand how to reduce or enlarge them to fit on the paper in your printer, and also how to take large PDF files and break them into multiple tiles that can then be reconstructed. You should also understand how to enable or disable the printing of annotations and comments. Finally, if you are a printer, you should understand the settings associated with how to enable or disable color management and halftone print settings.

Workshop

If you are sending or receiving files to be printed, you should understand the advantages of working with PDF files. We wrap up this final hour in the book by addressing some common questions about printing PDF files. The quiz confirms your understanding of the topics we've covered, and the additional exercises will give you some practice. As you wrap up your studies of Acrobat, don't forget to visit the companion Web site for this book at AcrobatIn24.com for updated information.

Q&A

Q Can I turn on certain annotations for printing but turn off others?

A Yes, but this is more of a function of the annotations filter that lets you show or hide annotations from individuals or certain types of annotations. Any annotations that are disabled using the filter manager will not print, even if annotations are set to print. These features are discussed in detail in Hour 13, "Adding Comments and Annotations."

Q Does my printer have to be a PostScript printer to be able to print a PDF file?

A No. Any printer can accept a PDF file, but some printers will print these documents better than others. PostScript printers tend to be better because they use a device-independent printing language. Even if you have problems printing, Adobe provides options to assist you, such as printing the PDF file as an image, which works on almost every printer but is often very slow.

Q Can I print from any version of Acrobat?

A As long as security features in the file do not prohibit printing, you can print from any version of Acrobat, including the free Reader.

Quiz

1. **If the color in your PDF looks very different on the printed product from a laser printer, what is one possible problem?**

    a. The printer is out of calibration.

    b. Color management is turned on in the Acrobat preferences.

    c. Emit Transfer Functions is selected in the Print Settings dialog box.

2. **Tiling describes what?**

    a. The jagged edges on a low-resolution graphic.

    b. Transparent sections of a file.

    c. Printing a large file in several smaller pieces.

3. **How can you print color separations from a PDF file for a commercial printer?**

    a. Select Color Setup from the Preferences dialog box.

    b. Install a plug-in from a third-party because Acrobat does not support this feature.

    c. Use Acrobat Distiller to convert all the pages to pages that can be separated.

Quiz Answers

1. **b** Color management can change the appearance of your PDF files. If you are not a graphic artist, you will probably want to disable this option in the Preferences dialog box. Choose Edit, Preferences, General; from the Settings drop-down list, choose Color Management Off.

2. **c** Tiling allows you to print very large documents on standard-size printer paper. This feature is accessed by clicking the Advanced button in the Print dialog box.

3. **b** Third-party software, such as that from Callas software, will allow you to print color separations directly from Acrobat. It is also possible to color separate PDF files using other prepress software such as Preps.

Exercises

Learn more about printing PDF files by trying the following exercises.

1. Open a PDF file that is oversized. Try printing it onto several tiles.

2. Open a long PDF file (one that contains many pages). Try printing several nonconsecutive pages. Also try printing only a section of a page.

24

INDEX

T

X

Y-Z

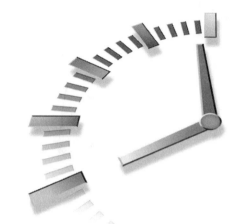